Windows Programmer's Guide to

Serial Communications

Windows Programmer's

Guide to

Serial

Communications

Timothy S. Monk

SAMS
PUBLISHING

A Division of Prentice Hall Computer Publishing
11711 North College, Carmel, Indiana 46032 USA

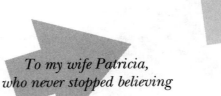

To my wife Patricia,
who never stopped believing

International Standard Book Number: 0-672-30030-3

Library of Congress Catalog Card Number: 92-61914

Trademarks

All terms mentioned in this book that are known to be trademarks or service marks have been appropriately capitalized. Sams Publishing cannot attest to the accuracy of this information. Use of a term in this book should not be regarded as affecting the validity of any trademark or service mark. Windows is a registered trademark of Microsoft Corporation.

Composed in New Baskerville and MCPdigital by
Prentice Hall Computer Publishing

Printed in the United States of America

Screen reproductions in this book were created by means of the program Collage Plus from Inner Media Inc., Hollis, NH.

Publisher
Richard K. Swadley

Acquisitions Manager
Jordan Gold

Acquisitions Editor
Joe Wikert

Development Editor
Ella Davis

Production Editors
Lynn Brown
Erik Dafforn

Copy Editor
Dean Miller

Editorial Coordinators
Rebecca S. Freeman
Bill Whitmer

Editorial Assistants
Rosemarie Graham
Lori Kelley

Technical Editor
Rik Logan

Cover Designer
Katherine Hanley

Director of Production and Manufacturing
Jeff Valler

Production Manager
Corinne Walls

Imprint Manager
Matthew Morrill

Book Designer
Michele Laseau

Production Analyst
Mary Beth Wakefield

Proofreading/Indexing Coordinator
Joelynn Gifford

Graphics Image Specialists
Jerry Ellis
Dennis Sheehan

Production
Debra Adams, Katy Bodenmiller,
Christine Cook, Terri Edwards,
Dennis Clay Hager,
Carla Hall-Batton,
R. Sean Medlock, Roger Morgan,
Juli Pavey, Angela Pozdol,
Linda Quigley, Michelle Self,
Susan M. Shepard, Greg Simsic,
Angie Trzepacz, Suzanne Tulley,
Alyssa Yesh

Indexer
Susan VandeWalle

About the Author

Timothy S. Monk is the President of The Software Mission, a custom software development and PC consulting firm. He has extensive experience in all areas of PC software development and communications.

Overview

Contents

Acknowledgments

A project such as this book is not possible without the help and understanding of many people. I would like to thank several people at Sams Publishing. First, Joe Wikert, for giving me the opportunity to write this book. My thanks also go to Ella Davis and Jordan Gold for seeing me through the writing and editing of this book. Special thanks to Lynn Brown of Brown Editorial Service for her editing and support. I also wish to thank everyone else at Sams Publishing who helped in the production of this book.

In addition, I want to thank Rik Logan of DigiBoard for his technical editing and help with the Microsoft C makefiles. My thanks also go to Peter Boswell for the use of his CRC routines and to Lauri Lentz of US Robotics for the use of the Courier HST Dual Standard modem.

Finally, my deepest thanks go to my wife, Patricia, who not only edited the draft of each chapter of this book, but understood when I needed quiet for writing.

Introduction

Microsoft Windows has been touted as the computing environment of the future. For the average user, Windows can be learned quickly, is easy to use, and is consistent across applications. Unfortunately, for the developer, Windows is anything but easy to program. It is a message-based system, a break from the traditional linear programming model. For the communications programmer, another problem is the lack of documentation for the Windows Communications Applications Programming Interface (API). The Microsoft Windows Software Development Kit (SDK) lists the communications functions but provides no real documentation on their usage. I hope that this book gives the developer the direction and documentation needed to program the Windows Communications API successfully.

When writing such a book, I must make some assumptions about you, the reader. The first assumption is that you are familiar with the basics of programming for Windows using either Microsoft C and the Windows SDK or Borland C++. I used the Borland C++ environment to develop the communications program in this book. The programs also compile under Microsoft C using the MAKEFILE.MSC files. These makefiles use special versions of the resource files included on the disk in the MSC subdirectories.

I also assume that you have some understanding of serial communications under MS-DOS. Programming experience with MS-DOS serial communications is not necessary, but you should understand the terms and principles involved.

Organization of This Book

Each chapter of this book covers a specific functional area. Chapter 1, "Serial Communications," covers the basics of serial communications from both hardware and MS-DOS standpoints. The program TSMTerm, developed throughout the remainder of the book, is introduced.

Chapter 2, "Windows Communications Basics," presents the basics of serial communications using the Windows API. You use the basics to develop high-level communications routines that encapsulate the Windows Communications API, giving a simpler API to use in programming.

Chapter 3, "Terminal Emulation," works ANSI terminal emulation into the communications program, creating the first working version of the program. Now that TSMTerm functions, Chapter 4, "Events, Errors, and Flow Control," adds event and error processing, as well as flow control, to both the TSM C Communications API and the TSMTerm program.

Chapter 5, "Message-Based Communications," looks at adding Windows 3.1 WM_COMMNOTIFY processing to the TSM Communications API and TSMTerm.

Chapter 6, "Modem Programming," takes a close look at programming modems. The US Robotics Dual Standard Courier modem is the standard used in the chapter. This is a popular modem on electronic bulletin boards throughout the country because of US Robotics' special prices for system operators.

File-transfer routines are covered in Chapter 7, "File Transfer." An XMODEM file-transfer routine for TSMTerm is developed in this chapter.

The book includes three appendixes. Appendix A, "Windows API Reference," contains a complete reference to the Windows Communications API routines. Appendix B, "TSM Communications API Reference," contains a complete reference to the TSM Communications API developed in this book. Finally, Appendix C, "ASCII Table," is devoted to ASCII character reference with some discussion about the ASCII characters used in serial communications.

What's on the Disk

In addition to the text portion of the book, a disk is included. This disk contains source code for each complete listing for all the chapters in the book. It also contains both Borland project files and makefiles for each program. The most important file on the disk is the README.TXT file. This file contains a complete description of both the files on the disk and the directory structure. It also contains the installation instructions.

Conventions Used in This Book

One way to make a book containing code easier to follow is establish a set of typeface conventions throughout the book. For this book, I use the following typeface conventions:

italics	used to introduce a new term
`monospace`	used for code listings
`bold monospace`	used for Windows function names, such as `CreateWindow()`
`italic monospace`	used to indicate variables and placeholders

Visual clues also can be useful. There are several special icons in this book:

> **Note:** This type of box and icon denotes an item of interest that you may not find in the documentation or that I have discovered.

Tip: This type of box and icon denotes a special suggestion for saving time and effort.

Caution: This type of box and icon flags a common problem to avoid or an action that can trigger damage to your data.

The Windows 3.1 icon highlights material specific to Windows 3.1.

Serial Communications

Serial communications is the process of converting an 8-bit byte to a stream of 8 single data bits traveling consecutively through a single wire. Sometimes a printer receives this serial data and re-creates the original 8-bit byte, printing a character. More often, a modem receives the serial data and converts it into a form that can be transmitted on a telephone line.

This chapter contains

- an overview of serial communications on the IBM PC, in terms of hardware and MS-DOS programming. This is intended as a brief refresher, not an all-encompassing discussion. The book *C Programmer's Guide to Serial Communications* by Joe Campbell (Howard W. Sams & Company, 1987) covers basic serial communications in more detail.

- a quick introduction to the communications program developed throughout the remainder of the book.

Serial Communications Hardware

Serial communications for the PC comes in two forms: stand-alone ports and ports built into internal modems. With either of these forms, the heart of the serial communications port is the Universal Asynchronous Receiver/Transmitter (UART). The original serial ports for the PC used the 8250 UART, and the AT introduced the 16450 UART. Newer serial ports use the 16550 UART. A stand-alone serial port communicates with other serial ports using the RS-232 standard. Each of these topics is discussed in the remainder of this section.

RS-232

The *RS-232* standard was developed by the Electronic Industries Association and is officially known as the *EIA interface standard RS232c*. It defines the electrical, control handshaking, transmission speed, signal rise time, and impedance parameters of the interface between Data Terminal Equipment

(DTE) and Data Communications Equipment (DCE). The RS232c standard does not specify the format or the content of the data being transferred, nor does it include any interface between DTE equipment. In the PC world, serial ports are considered DTE equipment, whereas modems are DCE equipment.

Although RS-232 specifies the electrical, signal rise time, and impedance parameters of the interface, a full coverage of these topics is beyond the scope of this book. However, the control handshaking and transmission speed are important to PC serial communications.

The RS-232 standard defines nine control lines used in the connection between DTE and DCE equipment. In a direct connection, these lines, shown in Figure 1.1, correspond one to one and are discussed in detail here. Be aware that data and control information only move in one direction on each control line.

Figure 1.1.
RS-232
DTE-to-DCE
connections.

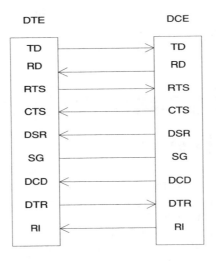

The DTE transmits data to the DCE on the Transmit Data (TD) line.

The DCE transmits data to the DTE on the Receive Data (RD) line.

The DTE requests permission to send information across the TD line on the Request to Send (RTS) control line. The DTE must leave this line high throughout the transmission sequence, because most modems hang up the phone line when RTS goes low.

The DCE responds to the RTS signal on the Clear to Send (CTS) control line. The DTE cannot transmit data until CTS is set to high.

The DCE shows that it is available to transmit on the Data Set Ready (DSR) control line. This line must be set high by the DCE before the DTE can set RTS.

The DTE and DCE share in common the Signal Ground (SG) control line.

The DTE indicates that it has detected a transmission-line carrier signal on the Data Carrier Detect (DCD) control line.

The DTE indicates to the DCE that it is ready to respond to signals and data from the DCE on the Data Terminal Ready (DTR) control line.

The DCE indicates to the DTE that the telephone is ringing on the Ring Indicator (RI) control line. This ring indicator can initiate a command to tell the modem to answer the line.

Each of these control lines has two states. They can be either high or low. The DTE and DCE can raise a control line high, a process also called "asserting the line," to indicate that this control is active. They can also drop the line to low to show that the control is inactive.

A typical sequence of control information in an RS-232 transmission might go like this:

1. The DTE raises DTR high to indicate that it is active and ready for transmission.

2. The DCE responds by raising the DSR line, indicating that it is also ready for communications.

3. The DTE asserts the RTS line to indicate that it is ready to start transmitting.

4. The DCE answers by raising the CTS line high, indicating that it is ready to receive the data.

5. Data can be transmitted on the TD and RD lines.

6. The DTE drops DTR low to disconnect.

8250/16450 UART

The 8250 UART is the standard serial port device for the IBM PC. The IBM PC/AT introduced the 16450 UART. These UARTs are compatible at both the hardware and software level. The discussion that follows is valid for both chips, although it refers to the 8250. The 8250 UART takes an 8-bit parallel

data byte and converts it to a stream of eight single bits, with start and stop bits added, a process illustrated in Figure 1.2. The UART also controls several status lines as defined by the RS-232 standard. These status lines were described previously.

Figure 1.2.
UART processing example.

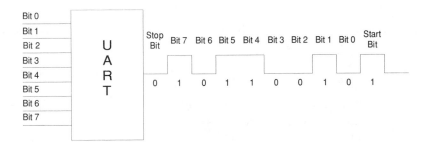

The programmer controls the 8250 UART through a series of I/O ports. Each port is specified as an offset from a base port address. This base port address is discussed in the COM Ports section. The ports used in programming the 8250 UART directly are discussed in the following paragraphs.

Port 0—Receive Buffer Register

The Receive Buffer Register reads the data from the 8250 after it has been received and assembled into a byte. An 8-bit byte is read from this register always, although the actual byte may contain as few as 5 bits. The extra bits are undefined and should be masked off by the software.

Port 0—Transmit Buffer Register

Writing to the Transmit Buffer Register breaks the byte into single bits transmitted on the TD line along with the appropriate start and stop bits, as well as a parity bit if necessary.

Note: The 8250's ports 0 and 1 are used for dual purposes. When bit 7 of the Line Control Register (port 3) is 0, ports 0 and 1 function as the Receive Buffer Register/Transmit Buffer Register and the Interrupt Enable Register, respectively. When bit 7 of the Line Control Register is set to 1, ports 0 and 1 function as the most significant byte (MSB) and the least significant byte (LSB) of the Baud Rate Divisor Latch.

Port 1—Interrupt Enable Register

The Interrupt Enable Register indicates which of the available interrupts should be generated by the 8250. Setting each of the lower 4 bits of this register to 1 enables the 8250 to generate an interrupt for the specified event. The definition of these bits is shown in Figure 1.3 and described in Table 1.1.

Bit 7	Bit 6	Bit 5	Bit 4	Bit 3	Bit 2	Bit 1	Bit 0
Unused (Always 0)	Unused (Always 0)	Unused (Always 0)	Unused (Always 0)	Modem Status Change	Error/ Break	Transmit Buffer Empty (TBE)	Received Data Ready (RxRDY)

Figure 1.3. Interrupt Enable Register.

Table 1.1. Interrupt Enable Register bits.

Bit	Name	Description
Bit 0	RxRDY	If this bit is set to 1, an interrupt is generated whenever a byte is ready to be read from the Receive Buffer Register.
Bit 1	TBE	If this bit is set to 1, an interrupt is generated each time the Transmit Buffer Register is ready to accept another character for transmission.
Bit 2	Error/Break	If this bit is set to 1, an interrupt is generated whenever the UART detects a parity error, overrun error, framing error, or break.
Bit 3	Modem Status	If this bit is set to 1, an interrupt is generated whenever one of the Modem Status inputs changes states.
Bits 4-7	Unused	These bits should always be set to 0.

Port 2—Interrupt Status Register

The Interrupt Status Register determines the reason an interrupt occurred. Bit 0 of this register indicates whether an interrupt is pending. This bit is 1 if no interrupt is pending and 0 if an interrupt is pending. When an interrupt is pending, bits 1 and 2 specify the actual interrupt that has occurred. This coding is shown in Table 1.2.

Table 1.2. Interrupt Status Register bits.

Bit 2	Bit 1	Bit 0	Priority	Interrupt
0	0	1	None	No interrupts pending
0	0	0	4	Modem Status change
0	1	0	3	Transmit Buffer empty (TBE)
1	0	0	2	Data received (RxRDY)
1	1	0	1	Error or break detected

Each pending interrupt has a priority associated with it. The priorities range from one to four, with one being the highest priority. While an interrupt is pending, all interrupts of an equal or lower priority are not reported. For example, a TBE interrupt does not occur when an RxRDY interrupt is pending.

Port 3—Line Control Register

The Line Control Register specifies the format of the data transmitted on the TD line and received on the RD line. Figure 1.4 shows the format of the Line Control Register and Table 1.3 discusses its bits.

Figure 1.4.
Line Control
Register.

Bit 7	Bit 6	Bit 5	Bit 4	Bit 3	Bit 2	Bit 1	Bit 0

| DLAB
0 = Normal
1 = Baud Rate
Divisor Latch | Break
Control
0 = off
1 = on | Parity
0 0 0 = None   0 0 1 = Odd
0 1 1 = Even   1 0 1 = Mark
1 1 1 = Space | Stop
Bits
0 = 1
1 = 2 (or 1.5) | Data Bits
0 0 = 5
0 1 = 6
1 0 = 7
1 1 = 8 |

Table 1.3. Line Control Register bits.

Bit	Name	Description
Bits 0–1	Data Bits	Specifies the number of data bits in the byte to be sent. Bit 1　Bit 0　Data Bits 0　　　0　　　5 0　　　1　　　6 1　　　0　　　7 1　　　1　　　8

Bit	Name	Description
Bit 2	Stop Bits	Specifies the number of stop bits to be appended to the byte being transmitted. A 0 is 1 stop bit whereas a 1 specifies 2 stop bits. If 5 data bits are transmitted, the 8250 automatically selects 1 1/2 stop bits.
Bits 3–5	Parity	These bits specify the parity to use when sending the data byte. The data sheets call these bits Parity Enable, Parity Select, and Stick Parity for bits 3, 4, and 5, respectively. The values for these bits are:

Bit 5	Bit 4	Bit 3	Parity
0	0	0	None
0	0	1	Odd
0	1	1	Even
1	0	1	Mark
1	1	1	Space

Bit	Name	Description
Bit 6	Break	This bit controls when a break condition is sent on the TD line. A break condition forces the TD line low. A 1 in this bit forces a break condition until 0 is written to this bit to terminate the break.
Bit 7	DLAB	The Divisor Latch Access Bit (DLAB) selects whether ports 0 and 1 are used as the Receive/Transmit Buffer Registers and the Interrupt Enable Register, or as the MSB and LSB of the Baud Rate Divisor Latch. If this bit is 0, ports 0 and 1 are the Receive/Transmit Buffer Registers and Interrupt Enable Register. If this bit is 1, ports 0 and 1 are the LSB and MSB of the Baud Rate Divisor Latch, respectively.

Port 4—Modem Control Register

The Modem Control Register controls the state of the RS-232 control lines, as shown in Figure 1.5. Each bit is discussed in Table 1.4. This register enables the programmer to set each RS-232 control line to a specific state. This is useful for modem initialization, flow control, and modem hang-up.

Figure 1.5.
Modem
Control
Register.

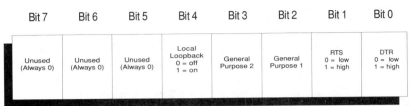

Bit 7	Bit 6	Bit 5	Bit 4	Bit 3	Bit 2	Bit 1	Bit 0
Unused (Always 0)	Unused (Always 0)	Unused (Always 0)	Local Loopback 0 = off 1 = on	General Purpose 2	General Purpose 1	RTS 0 = low 1 = high	DTR 0 = low 1 = high

Table 1.4. Modem Control Register bits.

Bit	Name	Description
Bit 0	DTR	Setting this bit to 1 causes the DTR line to go high. Clearing this bit to 0 causes the DTR line to go low.
Bit 1	RTS	Setting this bit to 1 causes the RTS line to go high. Clearing this bit to 0 causes the DTR line to go low.
Bit 2	GP01	General-purpose output bit is a user-definable output used by the hardware designer for various purposes.
Bit 3	GP02	This is the second general-purpose output bit. It is used by the internal Hayes Smartmodems to cause an unconditional reset.
Bit 4	LL	Setting this bit to 1 enables the local loop-back function of the 8250.
Bit 5-7	Unused	These bits should always be 0.

Port 5—Line Status Register

The Line Status Register provides the status of the data-transfer process. It includes indicators for Received Data Ready, all the errors that are detected by the 8250, and a break-received indicator. The error conditions reported in bits 1–4 generate an interrupt when bit 2 of the Interrupt Enable Register (port 1) is set. The Line Status Register also shows the status of the bytes being transmitted. The format of this register is shown in Figure 1.6 and discussed in Table 1.5.

Bit 7	Bit 6	Bit 5	Bit 4	Bit 3	Bit 2	Bit 1	Bit 0
Unused (Always 0)	Transmission Complete 0 = no 1 = yes	Transmit Buffer Empty 0 = full 1 = empty	Break 0 = no break 1 = break	Framing Error 0 = no error 1 = error	Parity Error 0 = no error 1 = error	Overrun Error 0 = no error 1 = error	RxRDY 0 = no data 1 = data received

Figure 1.6. Line Status Register.

Table 1.5. Line Status Register bits.

Bit	Name	Description
Bit 0	RxRDY	Set to 1 when a byte has been received by the 8250 and is ready to be read from the Receive Buffer Register. This bit is automatically reset when the byte has been read.
Bit 1	OE	Set when an overrun error occurs. An overrun exists when a new character has been received by the 8250 before the last character was read from the Receive Buffer Register. This bit is reset by reading this register.
Bit 2	PE	Set when a byte has been received with the incorrect parity as defined in the parity bits of the Line Control Register. This bit is reset by reading this register.
Bit 3	FE	Set when a framing error occurs. A framing error occurs when the data byte being received did not have a valid stop bit. This bit is reset by reading this register.
Bit 4	Break	Set when the 8250 has detected a break condition on the RD line. A break is any period of low line that lasts longer than a normal data character.
Bit 5	TBE	Set when the Transmit Buffer is empty and ready to receive another character.
Bit 6	TXE	Set when the Transmit Buffer is empty and the transmission of the last character written to the Transmit Buffer has been completed. This bit is used before terminating transmission to make sure that the last character is completely sent.
Bit 7	Unused	This bit should always be 0.

Port 6—Modem Status Register

The *Modem Status Register* provides the current state of the RS-232 control lines. It enables examination of the current state of the control lines and alerts any changes in the state of a control line since you last read this register. When one of the change bits is set by the 8250, an interrupt is generated if bit 3 of the Interrupt Enable Register is set to 1. Figure 1.7 shows the layout of the Modem Status Register and Table 1.6 explains the bits.

Figure 1.7.
Modem
Status
Register.

Bit 7	Bit 6	Bit 5	Bit 4	Bit 3	Bit 2	Bit 1	Bit 0
CD State 0 = off 1 = on	RI State 0 = off 1 = on	DSR State 0 = off 1 = on	CTS State 0 = off 1 = on	CD Changed 0 = no 1 = yes	RI Changed 0 = no 1 = yes	DSR Changed 0 = no 1 = yes	CTS Changed 0 = no 1 = yes

Table 1.6. Modem Status Register bits.

Bit	Name	Description
Bit 0	CCTS	Set to 1 when the CTS line has changed status since the last time this register was read. Reading this register resets the bit.
Bit 1	CDSR	Set to 1 when the DSR line has changed value since the last time this register was read. Reading this register resets the bit.
Bit 2	CRI	Set to 1 when the RI line changed from low to high since the last time this register was read. Reading this register resets the bit.
Bit 3	CDCD	Set to 1 when the CD line has changed status since the last time this register was read. Reading this register resets the bit.
Bit 4	CTS	This bit indicates the current state of the CTS line.
Bit 5	DSR	This bit indicates the current state of the DSR line.
Bit 6	RI	This bit indicates the current state of the RI line.
Bit 7	CD	This bit indicates the current state of the CD line.

Port 7—Scratch Pad

The Scratch Pad Register is not used by the 8250. It can be used as a general-purpose byte of memory, but you should be aware that early 8250s do not include this register.

Port 0—LSB Baud Rate Divisor Latch, and Port 1—MSB Baud Rate Divisor Latch

The *Baud Rate Divisor Latch* is accessed by setting bit 7, the DLAB, of the Line Control Register to 1. The LSB of this latch is accessed in port 0 and the MSB is accessed in port 1. This 2-byte register sets the transmit and receive baud rate of the UART. Table 1.7 lists the values to program into the latch to achieve the given baud rates. Note that these values assume a 1.8432-MHz clock rate.

Table 1.7. Baud Rate Divisor values.

Baud Rate	Latch Value
300	384
1200	96
2400	48
4800	24
9600	12
19.2K	6

For a more complete discussion of calculating these values, see either the 8250 data sheet or *C Programmer's Guide to Serial Communications* by Joe Campbell.

16550 UART

The 16550 UART was introduced with the PS/2. Most newer internal modems and serial port cards use the 16550 in place of the 8250 or 16450. The 16550 is software-compatible with the 8250, with some extensions. This section covers the differences from, and the extensions to, the 8250 that the 16550 embodies.

The most important enhancement is the 16550's 16-byte transmit and receive first-in, first-out (FIFO) queues. This allows 15 extra characters to be received by the UART before an overrun error occurs. For transmission, a communications program can now transmit 16 bytes at a time instead of just 1.

You program the 16550 through a series of ports similar to the 8250. All of the 8250 ports are duplicated on the 16550, with the following enhancements and additions.

Port 2—Interrupt Status Register/FIFO Control Register

On the 16550, port 2 accesses two separate registers. The Interrupt Status Register is a read-only register accessed when port 2 is read. The FIFO Control Register is a write-only register accessed when port 2 is written to. The Interrupt Status Register retains the same information as the 8250 version, but adds two bits of information regarding the FIFO status. Bits 6 and 7 are set to 0 when the 16550 is operating in 16450 mode and to 1 when they are operating in 16550 mode.

The FIFO Control Register (FCR) is accessed by writing to port 2 of the 16550. This register controls the transmit and receive FIFOs built into the 16550. With this register you can enable the FIFOs, clear the FIFOs, and set the FIFO interrupt-trigger level. The configuration of the FCR is shown in Figure 1.8 and discussed in Table 1.8.

Figure 1.8.
FIFO Control Register.

Bit 7	Bit 6	Bit 5	Bit 4	Bit 3	Bit 2	Bit 1	Bit 0
FIFO Trigger Level 00 = 01 10 = 08 01 = 04 11 = 14		Unused (Always 0)	Unused (Always 0)	Mode Change 0 = no change 1 = change	Transmit Clear 0 = no change 1 = clear	Receive Clear 0 = no change 1 = clear	FIFO Enable 0 = disable 1 = enable

Table 1.8. FIFO Control Register bits.

Bit	Name	Description
Bit 0	FIFO Enable	Setting this bit to 1 enables both the transmit and receive FIFOs. Clearing this bit to 0 disables the FIFOs. This bit should be set before the trigger level is established.
Bit 1	Receive Clear	Setting this bit to 1 clears the contents of the receive FIFO. The bit sets back to 0 automatically when the FIFO is cleared.
Bit 2	Transmit Clear	Setting this bit to 1 clears the transmit FIFO. The bit resets automatically when the FIFO is cleared.
Bit 3	Mode Change	Setting this bit to 1 changes RxRDY and TxRDY pins from mode "0" to mode "1."

Bit	Name	Description
Bits 4–5	Unused	Always set to 1.
Bits 6–7	FIFO Trigger Level	These bits define the number of bytes in the FIFO before an interrupt is generated. The levels defined are:

Bit 7	Bit 6	Trigger Level
0	0	01
0	1	04
1	0	08
1	1	14

Port 5—Line Status Register

The Line Status Register on the 16550 gives the same status information as the 8250 version. It also uses bit 7, unused by the 8250, for FIFO error indication. When bit 7 is set, there is at least one parity error, framing error, or break indication present in the FIFO. This bit is cleared when the LSR is read.

COM Ports

The serial ports of the PC are called *COM ports*. Each COM port is a separate serial port that you can use for RS-232 connections. With the IBM PC/AT you can define up to four COM ports, whereas with the IBM PS/2 you have eight COM ports definable. Each COM port is defined by two parameters. The first parameter of a COM port is its *base address*. The base address defines the address of the UART's port 0. Each UART port is then accessed as an offset of the base address.

The IBM PC standard defines the base address for COM ports 1 through 4. The PS/2 uses the same base address for COM ports 1 through 4 but also defines base addresses for COM port 5 through 8. Table 1.9 gives the standard COM port base addresses for both the PC and the PS/2 serial ports.

Table 1.9. IBM COM port base addresses.

Port	PC Base Address	PS/2 Base Address
COM1	03F8	03F8
COM2	02F8	02F8
COM3	03E8	3220
COM4	02E8	3228
COM5	n/a	4220
COM6	n/a	4228
COM7	n/a	5220
COM8	n/a	5228

The second parameter that defines a COM port is the *Interrupt Request (IRQ)* line used by the COM port. The IRQ lines are a set of special hardware interrupt lines handled specially by the PC. Each IRQ line is assigned a priority, IRQ0–IRQ7, which controls when an interrupt is handled. A lower-priority interrupt is not processed while a higher-priority interrupt is pending. The PC specification assigns a specific IRQ line to each of the COM ports. The IRQ assignments for the PC and the PS/2 are listed in Table 1.10.

Table 1.10. IBM COM Port IRQ Lines.

Port	PC IRQ	PS/2 IRQ
COM1	4	4
COM2	3	3
COM3	4	3
COM4	3	3
COM5	n/a	3
COM6	n/a	3
COM7	n/a	3
COM8	n/a	3

> **Caution:** Notice that on a PC, COM1 and COM3 share an IRQ line, as do COM2 and COM4. On the PS/2, COM2 through COM8 share the same IRQ line. Be careful that you do not have two active devices on the same IRQ line. Don't connect your mouse to COM1 and your modem to COM3 and expect them to work together. Putting two active devices on the same IRQ line causes either loss of characters or total communication failure, unless your hardware specifically enables IRQ sharing.

The PC's ROM BIOS keeps information about the serial ports in the BIOS data area at address 0x0040:0x0000. Each serial port is represented in the BIOS data by its base port address. The ROM BIOS also provides an interface to the serial ports, known as the INT 14h interface. This interface is very basic and does not enable interrupt-driven communications.

MS-DOS Serial Programming

Most serial communications programs for MS-DOS have bypassed the INT 14h interface because of its limitations, such as lack of interrupt support. MS-DOS communications programmers have learned to program the UART directly for speedier communications. This requires the following:

☐ Writing to the UART's ports to specify the communications parameters.

☐ Installing an interrupt driver to handle the interrupts generated by the 8250. Both transmission and reception can be interrupt-driven.

☐ Writing to the UART's Interrupt Enable Register to enable the interrupts you want to process.

☐ Writing to the UART's ports to set the control lines to the proper levels.

☐ Writing data to transmit to the UART and reading received data from the circular buffer maintained by the interrupt service routine.

The first step of this process, initializing the UART's communications parameters, can be accomplished through the code as shown here. This code initializes COM1 for 2400 baud, 8 data bits, no parity, and 1-stop-bit operation:

```
//
// serial port definitions
//
#define COM1_BASE        0x03F8
#define DLAB             0x00
#define LCR              0x03
#define LCR_8_DB         0x03
#define LCR_NO_PARITY    0x00
#define LCR_1_SB         0x00


//
// set up for 2400 baud operation by setting bit 7 of the
// Line Control Register, writing the baud divisor to ports 0
// and 1, and then setting the Line Control Register values
//
outportb( (COM1_BASE + LCR), 0x80 );
outport( (COM1_BASE + DLAB), 48 );


//
// set up for 8 data bits, no parity, and 1-stop-bit operation
//
outportb( (COM1_BASE + LCR), (LCR_8_DB | LCR_NO_PARITY |
                              LCR_1_STOP) );
```

Now that the UART is ready to communicate at the proper baud rate with the proper data-byte structure, you can install an interrupt handler that gives interrupt-driven reception. Because you are using COM1, you must trap IRQ4, which is interrupt 0x0c on both the PC and the PS/2. This code is shown here with the assumption that the interrupt handler is in the same code segment as the initialization routine:

```
//
// defines (note that anything already defined in a previous example
// is not redefined here)
//
#define IRQ4_INT    0x0C


//
// set up the interrupt 0C vector to point to the interrupt
// service routine
//
_dos_setvect( IRQ4_INT, int_0c_handler );
```

With the interrupt handler in place, you must set the Interrupt Enable Register for the interrupts that you want to process. In the example here, if you ignore errors and breaks, and only have interrupt-driven reception, setting the Interrupt Enable Register is simple. You also have to tell the PC that you want to receive interrupts from the UART. To do this, you program the 8259A Programmable Interrupt Controller (PIC). The PIC handles the IRQ lines and determines which ones generate an interrupt on the PC. Each IRQ is individually programmable for interrupt generation. In the example, the following code enables IRQ4 for COM1.

```
//
// defines
//
#define IER          0x01
#define IER_RXRDY    0x01
#define PIC_ ADDR    0x21
#define PIC_IRQ4     0x10


//
// variables
//
unsigned char cTempFlags;


//
// enable the RxRDY interrupt in the Interrupt Enable Register
//
cTempFlags = inportb( (COM1_BASE + IER) );
cTempFlags |= IER_RXRDY;
outportb( (COM1_BASE + IER), cTempFlags );


//
// enable the PIC to generate the IRQ4 interrupt
//
cTempFlags = inportb( PIC_ADDR );
cTempFlags &= (~PIC_IRQ4);
outportb( PIC_ADDR, cTempFlags );
```

The last thing you must do before you are ready to start communicating through the COM port is set the modem control lines. Specifically, you want to turn both DTR and RTS on. This is an overly simple view of the modem control lines, but it suffices for the example.

```
//
// defines
//
#define MCR         0x04
#define MCR_DTR     0x01
#define MCR_RTS     0x02
```

```
//
// turn on both the DTR and RTS lines
//
outportb( (COM1_BASE + MCR), (MCR_DTR | MCR_RTS) );
```

You now can communicate using the UART with interrupt-driven reception and polled transmission. The secret to interrupt-driven receives is the ring buffer. This buffer can be conceptualized as a circle, with two pointers, one indicating where you should add items to the buffer, and the other showing where you should remove items from the buffer. Figure 1.9 diagrams the concept of a ring buffer.

Figure 1.9.
Ring buffer.

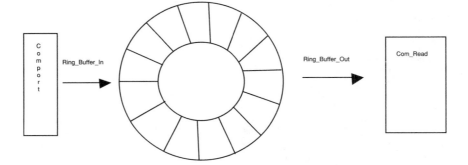

The interrupt service routine you installed for COM1 adds data to the ring buffer. The routine used by the application to "read" the COM port actually reads data from the ring buffer instead.

```
//
// defines
//
#define RING_BUFFER_SIZE    2048
#define ISR                 0x02
#define ISR_RXRDY           0x04
#define PIC_EOI             0x20
#define EOI_VALUE           0x20
//
// global variables
//
unsigned char ring_buffer[ RING_BUFFER_SIZE ];
int ring_buffer_in;
int ring_buffer_out;
```

```
//
// interrupt service routine for COM1 interrupt 0c
//
void interrupt far int_0c_handler( unsigned bp, unsigned di,
                                   unsigned si, unsigned ds,
                                   unsigned es, unsigned dx,
                                   unsigned cx, unsigned bx,
                                   unsigned ax )
{
   //
   // automatic variables
   //
   unsigned char cISR,
                 cData;

   //
   // allow higher priority interrupts again
   //
   enable();
   //
   // read the interrupt status register
   //
   cISR = inportb( (COM1_BASE + ISR );

   //
   // process only if this is an RxRDY interrupt
   //
   if ( (cISR & ISR_RXRDY) == cISR )
   {
      //
      // read the character from the receive buffer register
      //
      cData = inportb( (COM1_BASE + RBR) );

      //
      // add it to the ring buffer
      //
      ring_buffer[ ring_buffer_in ] = cData;
      ring_buffer_in++;
      if ( ring_buffer_in == RING_BUFFER_SIZE )
         ring_buffer_in = 0;
   }

   //
   // reenable interrupts by writing an EOI to the pic
   //
   outportb( PIC_ADDR_EOI, EOI_VALUE );
}
```

The Com_Read() function is used by the application to read a byte from the ring buffer.

```
//
// Com_Read--application to read data from the COM port,
// actually from the ring buffer
//
//  returns -1 if no character is available. Makes the
//  assumption that -1 is NOT a legal character.
//
unsigned char Com_Read()
{
   //
   // automatic variables
   //
   unsigned char cData;

   //
   // if both ring pointers are at the same character, the ring
   // buffer is empty--return -1.
   //
   if ( ring_buffer_out == ring_buffer_in )         return( -1 );

   //
   // read the data from the ring buffer and update the pointer
   //
   cData = ring_buffer[ ring_buffer_out ];
   ring_buffer_out++;
   if ( ring_buffer_out == RING_BUFFER_SIZE )
      ring_buffer_out = 0;

   //
   // return the character read
   //
   return( cData );
}
```

The last piece in the DOS communications programming puzzle is the routine to write data to the UART for transmission. This routine is a polled routine and does not return until the entire string has been written. Com_Write(), the following function code, ignores errors and timeouts to make the example simpler:

```
//
// Com_Write--write a zero-terminated string to the COM port.
// This routine assumes that zero is not a valid character to
```

```
// be transmitted.
//
void Com_Write( char *lpOutString )
{
   //
   // automatic variables
   //
   char *cCurrent = lpOutString;
   BOOL fDone = FALSE;

   //
   // loop until the fDone flag is set
   //
   while ( !fDone ) {
      //
      // see whether the transmit buffer is empty; if it is not,
      // just do the loop again.
      //
      if ( !(inportb( (COM1_BASE + LSR) ) & LSR_TBE) )
         continue;

      //
      // the transmit buffer is empty, so send the next character
      // if there are no more characters, then set fDone to TRUE
      //
      if ( *cCurrent )
         outportb( (COM1_BASE + TB), *cCurrent );
      else
         fDone = TRUE;

      //
      // increment the current character pointer
      //
      cCurrent++;
   }

   //
   // wait for both the Transmit Buffer and the Shift Registers to
   // be empty
   //
   while ( inportb( (COM1_BASE +_LSR) & LSR_TXE )
      ;
}
```

Now that you have examined the major sections of a MS-DOS communications program, the next section introduces TSMTerm, the Windows commu-

nications program that you'll see developed throughout the remaining chapters of this book.

TSMTerm: A Windows Communications Program

I have always believed that the best way to learn how to do something is just to do it. Therefore, over the course of this book, you will develop a general-purpose communications program. Following the development of this program should familiarize you with the concepts being presented. I strongly urge you to read the source code and compile the program to solidify the ideas.

In designing the program, I established several goals to guide the design process. The guidelines I established are:

☐ Modularity—designing a modular program enables you to work on specific sections of the program without affecting other parts.

☐ Extensibility—the design should enable you to extend the functionality of the program without reprogramming the existing code.

☐ Simplicity—the design should be simple because unnecessary complexity makes understanding, debugging, and maintenance more difficult.

☐ Standardization—the design should enable users to employ standard protocols such as XMODEM for file transfer and ANSI for terminal emulation.

These guidelines were used to develop the structure of TSMTerm, as shown in Figure 1.10. This modular design enables you to develop TSMTerm using dynamic link libraries (DLLs) to implement various standard protocols. These DLLs easily can be replaced with more advanced protocols as needed. The following paragraphs give a brief overview of each program module.

TSMTERM.EXE

This is the main executable file for TSMTerm. It contains all of the overhead, the main message loop, and the termination code. It uses the other modules TSMCOMM.DLL, MODEM.DLL, XMODEM.DLL, and ANSITERM.DLL to do most of the actual communications work.

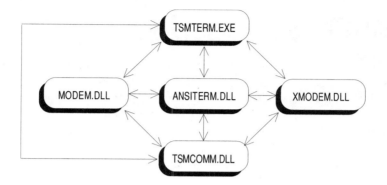

Figure 1.10.
TSMTerm
program
structure.

TSMCOMM.DLL

This dynamic link library provides high-level communications routines. These routines isolate the Windows Communications API from the application itself. This enables adaptation to new low-level communications APIs without affecting the application.

MODEM.DLL

This dynamic link library provides a series of routines that enables communication with any modem that uses the Hayes AT command set standard.

ANSITERM.DLL

This dynamic link library provides an ANSI terminal implementation. This implementation uses a standard set of functions that enable you to change the terminal emulation by loading a different library.

XMODEM.DLL

This dynamic link library provides both XMODEM file send and file receive functions. It implements both checksum and CRC error detection.

Summary

This chapter discussed the basics of serial communications hardware. It also covered the specifics of MS-DOS ports, I/O addresses, and interrupts. The chapter then discussed MS-DOS serial communications programming. The chapter concluded with an overview of TSMTerm, the communications program developed in this book.

Windows Communications Basics

The Windows Communications API insulates you from some of the gory details of serial communications programming. It provides routines you can use to open and close a communications port, change the settings of the port, and transmit and receive data through the port. Unfortunately, the Windows Communications API makes communications programming more complicated than it needs to be.

To make the Windows Communications API less cumbersome, you can develop your own API (the TSM Communications API) to encapsulate the Windows functions, making communications programming easier. In this chapter you

- are introduced to the Windows Communications API functions.

- explore communications programming using the Windows Communications API.

- begin developing your own communications API to encapsulate the Windows Communications API.

Windows Communications API

Windows provides 17 functions for communicating through the serial and parallel ports. The Windows Communications API also specifies two structures you use specifically for communications. These functions and data structures are fully referenced in Appendix A, "Windows API Reference." One of the biggest challenges facing the communications programmer is determining the order in which the Windows functions are called.

Every Windows communications program has a generalized flow similar to every other communications program. The program must open and initialize a communications port, transmit and receive data through that port, and then close the port. This basic program flow is shown in Figure 2.1. This section examines this flow in detail and shows how to use the Windows Communications API to accomplish these tasks.

Figure 2.1.
General
communica-
tions pro-
gram flow.

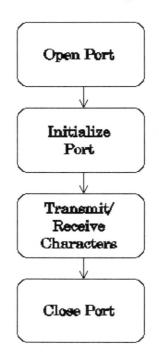

Opening and Initializing a Communications Port

The first task that every communications program must perform is to open a communications port, giving the program exclusive access to that port. The **OpenComm()** function returns an identification value for the port if successful. This identification value is used by the other communications routines (except **BuildCommDCB()**) to identify the port being used. Opening the port is a fairly simple process, as shown by this code segment:

```
//
// variables
//
int nComId;

//
// Open COM1
//
if ( (nComId = OpenComm("COM1", 2048, 2048)) < 0 )
    ProcessError();
```

Once the port is open, the next task in the communications program flow is the port initialization. The program uses two of the Windows Communications API functions, `BuildCommDCB()` and `SetCommState()`, for this operation. To initialize a port, you must know the value of the communications parameters. These parameters—baud rate, parity, and data and stop bits—can come from a couple of sources. First, you can use the settings the user has specified in the Ports applet of the Control Panel. You also can save and use your own configuration parameters and ignore the Control Panel settings. This chapter looks at both options.

The Windows Control Panel enables you to set the initial communications parameters for the serial ports. The Port applet enables you to set the baud, data bits, parity, stop bits, and flow control. The advanced options enable you to set the base address and IRQ for each serial port. These options are stored in the WIN.INI file. The [ports] section of this file contains an initialization string for COM1 through COM4. The format of this string is given in Figure 2.2.

BBBB,P,D,S,F

BBBB = Baud Rate
P = Parity
D = Data Bits
S = Stop Bits
F = Flow Control

Figure 2.2.
Port initialization string.

The following code retrieves this string from the WIN.INI file and massages it into the proper format for use by `BuildCommDCB()`.

```
//
// variables
//
char      szINISettings[ 15 ],
          szDCBSettings[ 25 ];
char far *lpszCurrent;
int       nComId,
          nCount;


//
// get the initialization string for COM1 from WIN.INI. Notice
// the necessary colon on the COM1 string. Also default to 2400
// baud, no parity, 8 data bits, 1 stop bit, and no flow control
// if COM1 is not present in WIN.INI.
```

```
//
GetProfileString( "ports", "COM1:", "2400,n,8,1",
                  szINISettings, sizeof( szINISettings ) );

//
// create the string that will be passed to the BuildCommDCB()
// function
//
lstrcpy( szDCBSettings, "COM1:" );
lstrcat( szDCBSettings, szINISettings );

//
// next truncate the flow control specification if it exists in
// the settings string
//
nCount = 0;
while ( lpszCurrent = fstrchr(szDCBSettings, ',') ) {
   if ( nCount == 3 )
      *lpszCurrent = '\0';
   else
      nCount++;
}
```

The other option is to read the communications parameters from either a proprietary configuration file or from a private .INI file. The latter is the preferred method. You should keep the communications parameters in a private .INI file as you develop the TSMTerm program.

Now that the program has an initialization string to use, it has to fill in a device control block (DCB) structure. Windows uses this structure as the standard method of defining the operating parameters of a communications port. The DCB structure is defined fully in Appendix A, "Windows API Reference." To fill in the fields of the DCB initially, you use the **BuildCommDCB()** function, as shown in the following code snippet.

```
//
// variables
//
DCB  dcb;
char szDCBSettings[ 25 ];
int  nError;

//
// initialize the DCB structure from the initialization string
// contained in szDCBSettings. It is assumed that the
// szDCBSettings string has been created elsewhere.
```

```
//
if ( (nError = BuildCommDCB( szDCBSettings, &dcb )) < 0 )
   ProcessError();
```

> **Caution:** It is important to note three things about **BuildCommDCB()**.
> First, it does not allocate any memory for the DCB. The program
> must have allocated this memory by either defining a structure
> variable or explicitly using either **GlobalAlloc()** or **LocalAlloc()**.
>
> The second important fact is that **BuildCommDCB()** does not modify the
> communications port itself. It only fills in the structure. The program
> must call **SetCommState()** to modify the port's settings.
>
> Lastly, **BuildCommDCB()** does not fill in the communications port id field
> of the DCB. It is up to the programmer to fill in this field before
> calling **SetCommState()**.

The program now has the two items needed to initialize the communications
parameters for the serial port it is using: a communications ID from **OpenComm()**
and an initialized DCB from **BuildCommDCB()**. The next step is to tell Windows
to change the serial port's parameters using the **SetCommState()** function.
The following code sets the communications parameters of the serial port
opened with **OpenComm()**:

```
//
// variables
//
DCB dcb;
int nComId;
int nError;

//
// copy the communications port ID to the DCB structure. This
// code assumes that both variables have been initialized
// earlier in the program.
//
dcb.Id = nComId;

//
// set the communications parameters for the port identified
// by dcb.Id
//
if ( (nError = SetCommState( &dcb )) < 0 )
   ProcessError();
```

At this point, the serial port is ready to use for transmitting and receiving characters.

Receiving Characters

The whole point of performing serial communications is to transmit and receive characters using the serial ports. The program has, up to this point, opened and initialized a serial port. Now this port can be used for transmitting and receiving characters. This sounds simple, but it is a complicated matter because of Windows' multitasking nature. Until Windows 3.1, all Windows communications programs had to poll the communications driver to see whether there were characters available. This polling took place during the message loop of the program.

Windows 3.1 introduced the `EnableCommNotification()` function. This function enables Windows to send a `WM_COMMNOTIFY` message when certain events take place. These events include reception of bytes in the input queue, the number of bytes in the output queue falling beneath a certain level, or an event occurring that was enabled using `SetCommEventMask()`.

First, let's look at receiving characters using the Windows 3.0 polling method. In this method you must modify your normal message-processing loop to allow for polling the communications port. The normal message loop is shown in the following code:

```
//
// variables
//
MSG msg;

//
// normal message loop
//
while( GetMessage( &msg, NULL, NULL, NULL ) ) {
   TranslateMessage( &msg );
   DispatchMessage( &msg ):
}
```

To poll for communications data successfully, the code must not go to "sleep" using `GetMessage()`; it must actively look to incoming data as well as allow other Windows applications to run. The program accomplishes this by calling `PeekMessage()`. If `PeekMessage()` indicates that there is a message to process, that message is processed. If not, the program polls the communications driver to see whether it has received any characters, as shown in this modified message-processing loop.

```
//
// variables
//
MSG      msg;
BOOL     fContinue;
HGLOBAL  hCommMem
LPSTR    lpCommMem;
int      nCommChars,
         nCommError,
         nCommId;
HWND     hWndComm;
COMSTAT  ComStat;

//
// modified message-processing loop
//
fContinue = TRUE;
while ( fContinue ) {
   //
   // check for a message in the queue
   //
   if ( PeekMessage( &msg, NULL, 0, 0, PM_REMOVE ) )
   {
      //
      // there is a message; is it a WM_QUIT message
      //
      if ( msg.message != WM_QUIT ) {
         //
         // it is a "normal" message, so process it
         //
         TranslateMessage( &msg );
         DispatchMessage( &msg );
      } else {
         //
         // process the WM_QUIT message
         //
         fContinue = FALSE;
      }
   } else {
      //
      // because there's no message, check
```

```
// whether there are characters from the serial port
//
GetCommError( nCommId, &ComStat );
if ( (nCommChars = ComStat.cbInQue) > 0 ) {
   //
   // allocate a global memory block for the characters
   //
   if ( (hCommMem = GlobalAlloc( GMEM_MOVEABLE,
                                 nCommChars ) ) ) {
      //
      // lock the memory in place
      //
      if ( !( lpCommMem = (LPSTR)GlobalLock(hCommMem) ) ) {
         ProcessError();
      } else {
         //
         // read the characters from the communications
         // port
         //
         nCommChars = ReadComm( nCommId, lpCommMem,
                                nCommChars );

         //
         // check for errors
         //
         if ( nCommChars < 0 ) {
            nCommChars = -nCommChars;
            nCommError = GetCommError( nCommId, NULL);

            //
            // clear the event mask
            //
            GetCommEventMask( nCommId, 0xFFFF );
         }

         //
         // send a message to the appropriate routine for
         // these characters to be processed
         //
         SendMessage( hWndComm, WM_COMM_CHARS, nCommChars,
                      (LONG)lpCommMem );

         //
         // unlock and free the memory
         //
```

```
            if ( GlobalUnlock( hCommMem ) )
                ProcessError();
            if ( GlobalFree( hCommMem ) )
                ProcessError();
        }
    }
  }
 }
}
```

This message-processing loop uses **PeekMessage()** to determine whether there are any messages in the queue for processing. If there is a message, the routine checks whether it is a WM_QUIT message. If it is, the fContinue flag is set to FALSE and the loop terminates. If the message is not WM_QUIT, it is processed like the normal message-processing loop. If there are no messages, the routine checks for characters in the received-character queue by calling **GetCommError()** to fill in the COMSTAT structure. The important field in the COMSTAT structure is the cbInQue field. This field's value is the number of characters received by COMM.DRV, waiting in the received-data queue. If this number is 0, the loop ends and the process starts again.

If there are characters to be received, several things happen. First, a global memory block is allocated to receive the data. This block is locked in memory, so it can be passed to the window function. The received characters are then read into this block of memory. Notice the error checks present at each step of this process. Once the data is in the global memory block, a special user-defined message is sent to the application's communications window. This message, WM_COMM_CHARS, is defined as an offset from WM_USER, and you must take care that the window does not define another message with the same value. When **SendMessage()** returns, the global memory block is freed and the message-processing loop continues. This message loop is still incomplete; it doesn't process modem control signals. Those issues are covered in Chapter 4, "Errors, Events, and Flow Control."

The polling method has several problems. First, every other Windows application must give up control promptly to enable it to continue polling. If the polling cannot continue quickly, characters are lost. Second, the same problem exists with your own message queue. If too many messages come at once, the communications polling is delayed and characters can be lost. Lastly, there is tremendous overhead throughout the message-polling process. Ultimately, this must slow down the program's response time.

To solve this problem, Windows 3.1 introduced a new function, `EnableCommNotification()`, and a new message, WM_COMMNOTIFY. With this function, Windows informs you when there are characters to read from the received-characters queue. Windows also can let you know when the transmit-characters queue is empty or when an event specified by `SetCommEventMask()` occurs. Therefore, you can use your normal message-processing loop, without the associated problems and overhead that polling caused. To use this option, you must enable the notification system, as shown in the following code:

```
//
// variables
//
int   nComId;
HWND hWndComm;


//
// Enable Windows to send the WM_COMMNOTIFY message, set it to
// send a received-data notification when one character
// is received and a transmit-queue notification
// when there are no characters in the buffer.
//
if ( !EnableCommNotification( nComId, hWndComm, 1, 0 ) )
   ProcessError();
```

Your window function processes the WM_COMMNOTIFY message as any other message. The code shown here processes this message:

```
//
// variables
//
WORD wNotify
//
// process the WM_COMMNOTIFY message
//
case WM_COMMNOTIFY:
   //
   // get the notification word for the parameter
   //
   wNotify = LOWORD (1Param);
   //
   // check for a CN_RECEIVE
   //
   if ( wNotify & CN_RECEIVE )
      Process Incoming Chars();
   //
      // check for a CN_TRANSMIT
      //
```

```
    if ( wNotify & CN_TRANSMIT )
    Process Transmit Empty();
    //
    // check for a CN_EVENT
    //
    if ( wNotify & CN_EVENT )
        Process CommEvent();
break;
```

Receiving characters is only half the picture, though; you still have to be able to transmit characters to the other side of the connection. The next section looks at transmitting characters.

Transmitting Characters

Now that your program can receive characters from the device it is communicating with, you can move on to how the program transmits characters. There are two options for transmitting characters:

☐ Polling the transmission status to complete transmission

☐ Interrupt transmission based on the new WM_COMMNOTIFY message

The polling transmission method has the disadvantage of tying up the system until the transmission is completed. The routine that follows starts by setting a temporary pointer to the start of the string and a counter for the number of characters that have been transmitted. It writes the characters to the serial port with the WriteComm() function. WriteComm() returns the number of characters transmitted or the negative of that value if an error occurs, so the routine checks whether the number of characters transmitted was negative. If it was, the routine processes the error and converts the value back to the positive number of characters transmitted. A real routine would have more extensive error checking at this point. The code then updates the current string pointer and the total number of characters transmitted. The loop terminates when all characters have been transmitted.

```
//
// variables
//
int   nComId,
char szTransString[128];
char *szCurrent;
int   nTransSize,
```

```
      nTotalSent;
      nCurrentSent;

//
// set the current pointer to the start of the string and set
// the starting value of nTotalSent
//
szCurrent = szTransString;
nTotalSent = 0;

//
// loop until all the characters have been sent
//
while ( nTotalSent < nTransSize ) {
   //
   // try to send all remaining characters
   //
   nCurrentSent = WriteComm( nComId, szCurrent,
                             ( nTransSize - nTotalSent ) );
   //
   // check whether an error occurred
   //
   if ( nCurrentSent < 0 ) {
      ProcessError();
      nCurrentSent = -nCurrentSent;
   }

   //
   // update the current string pointer and the total number
   // of characters sent
   //
   szCurrent += nCurrentSent;
   nTotalSent += nCurrentSent;
}
```

In some ways, it is incorrect to say that this routine actually *transmitted* any characters. It really wrote them to the transmission queue; it is COMM.DRV's job to transmit them through the serial port.

Message-driven transmission has several advantages. Control returns to the message-processing loop (Windows) between transmissions. This allows other applications and the incoming character stream to continue. This method can be duplicated in Windows 3.0, using timers in place of the WM_COMMNOTIFY message system of Windows 3.1.

The first step in using message-driven transmission is to declare some global variables and enable the WM_COMMNOTIFY message as shown here:

```
//
// global variables used throughout this example
//
int       nComId;
BOOL      fActiveTrans;
HANDLE    hTransHead,
          hTransTail;
LPSTR     lpTransHead,
          lpTransTail;
HWND      hWndComm;


//
// initialize the global variables
//
fActiveTrans = FALSE;
hTransHead = hTransTail = NULL;
//
// enable Windows to send the WM_COMMNOTIFY message when the
// transmission queue has fewer than 16 characters in it
//
if ( !EnableCommNotification( nComId, hWndComm, 1, 16 ) )
   ProcessError();
```

Transmitting characters follows this flow. First, the program writes characters as normal using **WriteComm()**. If not all characters are transmitted, the program calls a routine that stores the rest of the characters in a global block, part of a linked list of blocks to be transmitted. This code follows:

```
//
// structure defines
//
// transmission linked-list structure
//
typedef struct tagTRANSLIST {
   HANDLE   hNextBlock;
   int      nDataSize;
   char     cData;
} TRANSLIST;
typedef TRANSLIST FAR *LPTRANSLIST;


//
// variables
//
```

```
char   szTransBuff[128],
       *lpCurrent;
int    nTransSize,
       nCurrTrans;
HANDLE hTransHead,
       hTransTail;

//
// handle message-based transmission
//
if ( hTransHead ) {
   //
   // there is already data to be transmitted so just
   // add this data to the end of the linked list
   //
   AddTransmitBlock( szTransBuff, nTransSize );
} else {
   //
   // write the buffer to the output queue. If it succeeds,
   // we are done.
   //
   if ( (nCurrTrans = WriteComm( nComId, szTransBuff,
                                 nTransSize ) ) < 0 ) {
      //
      // not all the characters were transmitted, so add the
      // rest of the characters to the linked list
      //
      AddTransmitBlock( szTransBuff + nCurrTrans,
                        nTransSize - nCurrTrans );
   }
}


//
// AddTransmitBlock
//
// returns:
//    TRUE  - if block was added to the linked list
//    FALSE - if block was NOT added to the linked list
//
BOOL  AddTransmitBlock( LPSTR lpOutChars, int nCount )
{
   //
   // automatic variables
   //
```

```
int         nBlockSize;
HANDLE      hMemBlock;
LPTRANSLIST lpMemBlock;
LPTRANSLIST lpTransHead;
LPTRANSLIST lpTransTail;

//
// not all the characters were transmitted. Allocate a global
// memory block to hold the remaining characters and copy the
// characters to it.
//
nBlockSize = sizeof( TRANSLIST ) + nCount - 1;
hMemBlock = GlobalAlloc( GMEM_MOVEABLE, (DWORD)nBlockSize );
if ( !hMemBlock )
   return( FALSE );
lpMemBlock = (LPTRANSLIST)GlobalLock( hMemBlock );
if ( !lpMemBlock ) {
   GlobalFree( hMemBlock );
   return( FALSE );
}
lpMemBlock->hNextBlock = NULL;
lpMemBlock->nDataSize = nCount;
lstrcpy( &lpMemBlock->cData, lpOutChars );
GlobalUnlock( hMemBlock );

//
// link this memory block into the linked list
//
if ( hTransTail ) {
   lpTransTail = (LPTRANSLIST)GlobalLock( hTransTail );
   lpTransTail->hNextBlock = hMemBlock;
   GlobalUnlock( hTransTail );
   hTransTail = hMemBlock;
} else {
   hTransHead = hTransTail = hMemBlock;
}

//
// return a TRUE, indicating that everything worked
//
return( TRUE );
}
```

Next, the program must process the WM_COMMNOTIFY message in the window procedure for hWndComm. Part of this processing is illustrated here:

```
//
// process the WM_COMMNOTIFY message
//
case WM_COMMNOTIFY:
   //
   // process based on the type of COMMNOTIFY message
   //
   wNotify = LOWORD( lParam ) {
   if ( wNotify & CN_TRANSMIT ) {
      //
      // if there are no transmission blocks on the linked
      // list, ignore this message
      //
      if ( !hTransHead )
         break;


      //
      // there are blocks on the transmission queue.
      // Process the first one.
      //
      lpTransHead = GlobalLock( hTransHead );
      nTransSize = (INT)*(lpTransHead + sizeof( HANDLE ));
      nCurrTrans = WriteComm( nComId, lpTransHead +
                              sizeof( HANDLE ), sizeof( INT );
      if ( nCurrTrans != nTransSize ) {
         //
         // the complete block was not transferred.
         // Update the memory block.
         //
         ProcessError();
         if ( nCurrTrans < 0 )
            nCurrTrans = -nCurrTrans();
         lpCurrent = lpTransHead + sizeof( HANDLE ) +
                     sizeof( INT ) + nCurrTrans;
         lpStart = lpTransHead + sizeof( HANDLE ) +
                   sizeof( INT );
         memcpy( lpStart, lpCurrent,
                 (nTransSize - nCurrTrans ) );
         (INT)*(lpTransHead + sizeof( HANDLE ) ) = nTransSize
                                                   - nCurrTrans;
         GlobalUnlock( hTransHead );
         break;
      }
```

```
     //
     // the whole block was sent.
     // Remove it from the linked list.
     //
     hMemBlock = hTransHead;
     hTransHead = (HANDLE)*lpTransHead;
     GlobalUnlock( hMemBlock );
     GlobalFree( hMemBlock );
     break;
   }
   break;
```

This code sample demonstrates the processing that takes place for the WM_COMMNOTIFY message with a CN_TRANSMIT indication. First, the program checks whether it has any blocks in the linked list that need to be transmitted. If it does, WriteComm() writes them to the serial port. If the program does not write all the characters or receives an error indication, it must process the block, removing the data already sent. The program calculates the pointer position of the first character not sent and the number of characters not sent. Then the program copies these characters to the front of the buffer and updates the header. At this point, the program is finished processing this case. If the program transmitted the full block, it is removed from the head of the linked list, making the next block the new head. Finally, the program must release the memory the block was occupying.

So far, opening, initializing, and sending and receiving characters have been covered. The last step in the communications flow chart was closing the port so other programs can use it.

Closing the Communications Port

When the program is done communicating with the port, it must close the communications port so other applications can use it. The following code demonstrates how to close a port.

```
//
// variables
//
int     nComId,
BOOL    bContinue;
COMSTAT ComStat;

//
// wait for the transmission queue to be empty
//
```

```
bContinue = TRUE;
while ( bContinue ) {
   //
   // get the comstat structure
   //
   GetCommError( nComId, &ComStat );
   //
   // if the transmission queue is empty, quit from this loop
   //
   if ( !ComStat.cbOutQueue )
      bContinue = FALSE;
}


//
// close the communications port identified by nComId
//
if ( (nError = CloseComm( nComId ) ) < 0 )
   ProcessError();
```

Now that you have learned how to open and initialize a port, transmit and receive characters, and close the port, you can start developing the TSM Communications API in the next section.

TSM Communications API

Although Windows provides all the functions needed to communicate through the serial port, the functions are not very intuitive. There is a lot of repetitive code that has to be included each time a program wants to do something with the serial port. For this reason, this book develops an API that encapsulates the Windows Communications API, making serial communications easier to do.

The TSM Communications API breaks the communications routines into three areas:

- Setup routines
- Transmit/receive routines
- Miscellaneous routines

This section looks at the first pass of these routines.

Setup Routines

The setup routines enable your program to open, close, and set the parameters for a serial port. These routines use the appropriate Windows API routines to accomplish their goals. Like the Windows API, these routines use an identification value to indicate a specific port. This identification value is returned by TSMOpenComm(), and is the same value returned by **OpenComm()**. This ID value is passed to all other TSM Communications routines to indicate which port to work with.

> **Note:** There is one major limitation with the TSM Communications API developed in this book. Only one communications port can be open at a time. You can overcome this limitation by enhancing these routines to use a linked list for keeping more than one port open simultaneously.

The first routine discussed is TSMOpenComm(). This routine encapsulates several Windows API calls. It opens the port and sets the port's initial communication parameters. The arguments that this routine accepts are the port name, queue sizes for the serial port, and the initial settings. The following code fragment illustrates how you can use this routine:

```
//
// variables
//
WORD wBaudRate, wParity, wDataBits, wStopBits;
char szCommPort[5];
UINT uInQueueSize, uOutQueueSize;
int  nResult;

//
// this code assumes that the variables defined above have been
// initialized somewhere else in the code
//
nResult = TSMOpenComm( szCommPort, wBaudRate, wParity, wDataBits,
                       wStopBits, uInQueueSize, uOutQueueSize );
if ( nResult < 0 )
   ProcessError();
```

TSMOpenComm() first ensures that the program hasn't opened a port already using this routine. All TSM Communications routines make this check by testing the value of a global variable, hTSMCommInfo. This variable is initialized to

NULL and set when a port is opened. A non-NULL value indicates that a port is open already and TSMOpenComm() returns an error indication.

If the program is going to attempt to open the port, a block of memory for a TSMCOMMINFO structure is allocated and locked. Table 2.1 lists the fields of the structure (defined in tsmcomm.h).

Table 2.1. TSMCOMMINFO structure.

Field Name	Type	Description
ComString	char [6]	Communications port name, zero terminated.
ComId	int	Communications Port ID as returned by **OpenComm()**.
hDCB	HANDLE	Handle to the memory allocated for the Device Control Block of this communications port.

After allocating the TSMCOMMINFO structure, the program copies to the ComString field the device name that was passed. This field is not used currently, but it could enable multiple ports to be open concurrently. The program then allocates and locks memory for the DCB. The handle returned by **GlobalAlloc()** is stored in the hDCB field of the TSMCOMMINFO structure. The next section of the routine takes the passed parameters and converts them into a string that **BuildCommDCB()** can use. This string and the pointer to the DCB are passed to **BuildCommDCB()** to initialize the allocated DCB structure.

The program is now ready to open the communications port using **OpenComm()**. The value returned by **OpenComm()** is the communications port ID. It is stored in the TSMCOMMINFO structure. If the ID returned is greater than or equal to zero, the port has been opened successfully. The ID is saved in the DCB and the communications parameters of the port are set by calling **SetCommState()**, which returns a zero if it succeeds or an error code, which is less than zero, if it fails. If **SetCommState()** fails, the program closes the port, unlocks and frees both memory blocks, clears the hTSMCommInfo variable, and returns the error indication from **SetCommState()**.

If everything has worked so far, the program stores the ID in a temporary variable and unlocks the memory blocks. Finally, the ID, which could be an error indication from **OpenComm()**, is returned to the calling program. TSMOpenComm() is presented in Listing 2.1.

Listing 2.1. TCOPNCOM.C TSMOpenComm() routine.

```
//
// TSM Communications API DLL
//
// tcopncom.c
//
// open and initialize a communications port
//
// int FAR PASCAL _export TSMOpenComm( LPCSTR lpDevice,
//        WORD wBaudRate, WORD wParity, WORD wDataBits,
//        WORD wStopBits, UINT uInQueue, UINT uOutQueue )
//
// parameters:
//     LPCSTR lpDevice   - zero-terminated string giving COM port
//                         name to open
//     WORD   wBaudRate - baud rate to initialize the port to
//     WORD   wParity   - parity to initialize the port to
//     WORD   wDataBits - number of data bits to initialize the
//                        port to
//     WORD   wStopBits - number of stop bits to initialize the
//                        port to
//     UINT   uInQueue  - size of the receive queue for this port
//     UINT   uOutQueue - size of the transmit queue for this port
//
// returns:
//     ComId >= 0        if function was successful
//     error code < 0    if not successful
//
//
// system include files
//
#include <windows.h>
#ifdef __BORLANDC__
#pragma hdrstop
#endif


//
// local include files
//
#include "tsmcomm.h"
#include "tcglobal.h"


//
// TSMOpenComm
//
```

Listing 2.1. continued

```c
int FAR PASCAL _export TSMOpenComm( LPCSTR lpDevice,
                WORD wBaudRate, WORD wParity, WORD wDataBits,
                WORD wStopBits, UINT uInQueue, UINT uOutQueue )
{
   //
   // automatic variables
   //
   LPDCB lpDCB;
   char  szDeviceControl[20];
   int   nTemp;

   //
   // first, check whether a port is open already
   //
   if ( hTSMCommInfo )
      return( IE_OPEN );
   //
   // the port is not open, so allocate a TSMCOMMINFO structure
   //
   if ( !(hTSMCommInfo = GlobalAlloc( sizeof( TSMCOMMINFO ),
                           GMEM_MOVEABLE ¦ GMEM_ZEROINIT ) ) )
      //
      // allocation failed; return an error
      //
      return( IE_MEMORY );
   if ( !(lpTSMCommInfo = (LPTSMCOMMINFO)GlobalLock(hTSMCommInfo)
                                                    ) ) {
      //
      // lock failed; free the memory and return an error
      //
      GlobalFree( hTSMCommInfo );
      hTSMCommInfo = NULL;
      return( IE_MEMORY );
   }

   //
   // copy the port's string to the new structure
   //
   lstrcpy( lpTSMCommInfo->ComString, lpDevice );

   //
   // allocate a DCB for this port
   //
```

```
if ( !( lpTSMCommInfo->hDCB = GlobalAlloc( sizeof( DCB ),
                        GMEM_MOVEABLE | GMEM_ZEROINIT ) ) ) {
   //
   // allocation failed; free the memory and return an error
   //
   GlobalUnlock( hTSMCommInfo );
   GlobalFree( hTSMCommInfo );
   hTSMCommInfo = NULL;
   return( IE_MEMORY );
}
if ( !( lpDCB = (LPDCB)GlobalLock( lpTSMCommInfo->hDCB ) ) ) {
   //
   // lock failed; free the memory and return an error
   //
   GlobalFree( lpTSMCommInfo->hDCB );
   GlobalUnlock( hTSMCommInfo );
   GlobalFree( hTSMCommInfo );
   hTSMCommInfo = NULL;
   return( IE_MEMORY );
}

//
// build the device control string from the passed parameters
//
nTemp = lstrlen( lstrcpy( szDeviceControl, lpDevice ) );
if ( szDeviceControl[ nTemp - 1 ] != ':' )
   lstrcat( szDeviceControl, ":" );
switch( wBaudRate ) {
   case  CBR_110:
      lstrcat( szDeviceControl, "110," );
      break;

   case  CBR_300:
      lstrcat( szDeviceControl, "300," );
      break;
   case  CBR_600:
      lstrcat( szDeviceControl, "600," );
      break;

   case  CBR_1200:
      lstrcat( szDeviceControl, "1200," );
      break;

   case  CBR_2400:
```

continues

Listing 2.1. continued

```
              lstrcat( szDeviceControl, "2400," );
              break;

         case  CBR_4800:
              lstrcat( szDeviceControl, "4800," );
              break;

         case  CBR_9600:
              lstrcat( szDeviceControl, "9600," );
              break;

         case  CBR_14400:
              lstrcat( szDeviceControl, "14400," );
              break;

         case  CBR_19200:
              lstrcat( szDeviceControl, "19200," );
              break;

         case  CBR_38400:
              lstrcat( szDeviceControl, "38400," );
              break;
         case  CBR_56000:
              lstrcat( szDeviceControl, "56000," );
              break;

         case  CBR_128000:
              lstrcat( szDeviceControl, "128000," );
              break;

         case  CBR_256000:
              lstrcat( szDeviceControl, "256000," );
              break;

         default:
              lstrcat( szDeviceControl, "2400," );
              break;
    }
    switch ( wParity ) {
         case  NOPARITY:
              lstrcat( szDeviceControl, "n," );
              break;

         case  ODDPARITY:
```

```
        lstrcat( szDeviceControl, "o," );
        break;

    case  EVENPARITY:
        lstrcat( szDeviceControl, "e," );
        break;

    case  MARKPARITY:
        lstrcat( szDeviceControl, "m," );
        break;

    case  SPACEPARITY:
        lstrcat( szDeviceControl, "s," );
        break;

    default:
        lstrcat( szDeviceControl, "n," );
        break;
}
switch( wDataBits ) {
    case  FIVEDATABITS:
        lstrcat( szDeviceControl, "5," );
        break;

    case  SIXDATABITS:
        lstrcat( szDeviceControl, "6," );
        break;

    case  SEVENDATABITS:
        lstrcat( szDeviceControl, "7," );
        break;

    case  EIGHTDATABITS:
        lstrcat( szDeviceControl, "8," );
        break;

    default:
        lstrcat( szDeviceControl, "8," );
        break;
}
switch ( wStopBits ) {
    case  ONESTOPBIT:
        lstrcat( szDeviceControl, "1" );
        break;
```

continues

Listing 2.1. continued

```
  case  ONE5STOPBITS:
     lstrcat( szDeviceControl, "1.5" );
     break;

  case  TWOSTOPBITS:
     lstrcat( szDeviceControl, "2" );
     break;

  default:
     lstrcat( szDeviceControl, "1" );
     break;
}

//
// initialize the DCB
//
if (( nTemp = BuildCommDCB( szDeviceControl, lpDcB ))){
   Global Unlock ( lpTWMCommInfo->hDCB
   Global Free ( lpTSMCommInfo->hDCB );
   Global Unlock ( hTSMCommInfo );
   Global Free ( hTSMCommInfo );
   return ( nTemp );

//
// now put in the proper baud rate if the requested rate was greater
// than 1L9200
//
if (wBaudRate > CBR_19200 )
     lpDCB->BaudRate = wBaudRate;

//
// now open the communications port
//
lpTSMCommInfo->ComId = OpenComm( lpDevice, uInQueue,
                                    uOutQueue );

//
// if there's a good ComId, set the port parameters
//
if ( lpTSMCommInfo->ComId >= 0 ) {
   //
   // first copy the ID into the DCB
   //
   lpDCB->Id = lpTSMCommInfo->ComId;
```

```
//
// set the port's communications parameters
//
nTemp = SetCommState( lpDCB );
if ( nTemp < 0 ) {
   //
   // setting the COM port failed, so close the port,
   // release the memory, and indicate an error to the
   // caller
   //
   CloseComm( lpTSMCommInfo->ComId );
   GlobalUnlock( lpTSMCommInfo->hDCB );
   GlobalFree( lpTSMCommInfo->hDCB );
   GlobalUnlock( hTSMCommInfo );
   GlobalFree( hTSMCommInfo );
   hTSMCommInfo = NULL;
   return( nTemp );
   }
}


//
// save the ComId in a temporary variable so it can be
// returned
//
nTemp = lpTSMCommInfo->ComId;

//
// unlock the memory blocks that were locked
//
GlobalUnlock( lpTSMCommInfo->hDCB );
GlobalUnlock( hTSMCommInfo );

//
// return the ComId
//
return ( nTemp );
}
```

When a program is finished using a port it opened with TSMOpenComm(), the program must close the port with TSMCloseComm(). Before closing the port, this routine frees all the memory that was allocated when the port was opened. Listing 2.2 presents the TSMCloseComm() code.

Listing 2.2. TCCLSCOM.C `TSMCloseComm()` routine.

```
//
// TSM Communications API DLL
//
// tcclscom.c
//
// close the communications port
//
// int FAR PASCAL _export TSMCloseComm( int ComId )
//
// parameters:
//    int   ComId;    -   ID of the COM port to close
//
// returns:
//    0   if the close was successful
//   >0   if an error occurred
//


//
// system include files
//
#include <windows.h>
#ifdef __BORLANDC__
#pragma hdrstop
#endif

//
// local include files
//
#include "tsmcomm.h"
#include "tcglobal.h"

//
// TSMCloseComm
//
int FAR PASCAL _export TSMCloseComm( int ComId )
{
   //
   // automatic variables
   //
   int   nResult;

   //
   // if the TSMCOMMINFO handle is NULL, the ComId is not
   // open
```

```
    //
    if ( !hTSMCommInfo )
        return( IE_NOPEN );

    //
    // lock the TSMCOMMINFO structure
    //
    lpTSMCommInfo = (LPTSMCOMMINFO)GlobalLock( hTSMCommInfo );

    //
    // make sure that the ComIds are the same
    //
    if ( lpTSMCommInfo->ComId != ComId ) {
        GlobalUnlock( hTSMCommInfo );
        return( IE_NOPEN );
    }

    //
    // close this communications port
    //
    nResult = CloseComm( lpTSMCommInfo->ComId );

    //
    // release the memory
    //
    GlobalFree( lpTSMCommInfo->hDCB );
    GlobalUnlock( hTSMCommInfo );
    GlobalFree( hTSMCommInfo );
    hTSMCommInfo = NULL;
    //
    // return the result of the actual close
    //
    return( nResult );
}
```

The first action that TSMCloseComm() takes is to check the value of the variable TSMOpenComm() to ensure that a port is open. If no open port exists, the function returns an error. The routine then locks the TSMCommInfo block and compares the ComIds values. If they are not the same, an error is returned. Assuming that the port is the same, the routine calls **CloseComm()** to close the port, saving the return value. Memory allocated by TSMOpenComm() is freed and released, and the return value of **CloseComm()** is returned to the function that is called TSMCloseComm().

You have seen the TSM Communications routines that open and close a communications port, but you haven't seen how to change a port's parameters once it is open. The next routines added to the TSM Communications API enable you to examine and change the communication port's parameters. The eight routines are listed in Table 2.2.

Table 2.2 Examine/Modify parameters routines.

Routine	Description
TSMGetBaudRate()	Get the current baud-rate setting of the port. (File: TCGETBR.C)
TSMSetBaudRate()	Set a new baud rate for the communication port. (File: TCSETBR.C)
TSMGetParity()	Get the current parity setting of the port. (File: TCGETPAR.C)
TSMSetParity()	Set a new parity rate for the communications port. (File: TCSETPAR.C)
TSMGetDataBits()	Get the number of data bits the port is currently set for. (File: TCGETDB.C)
TSMSetDataBits()	Set the number of data bits expected by the port. (File: TCSETDB.C)
TSMGetStopBits()	Get the number of stop bits the port is currently set for. (File: TCGETSB.C)
TSMSetStopBits()	Set the number of stop bits expected by the communications port. (File: TCSETSB.C)

The Get/Set pairs of each of these routines parallel the other three sets of routines. The next section examines TSMGetParity() and TSMSetParity() as representative of all these routines.

Note: These routines are included on the disk that accompanies this book. The routines also are described in Appendix B, "TSM Communications API Reference."

The TSMGetParity() routine starts, as all TSM API routines do, by ensuring that a port is open and that the ComId of that open port is the same as the ID passed to the routine. The routine then locks the DCB in memory and calls **GetCommState()** to retrieve the current port settings. The parity setting is saved in a temporary variable and memory, locked earlier, is unlocked. Finally, the function returns the parity setting to the calling routine by using the TSMGetParity() routine, shown in Listing 2.3.

Listing 2.3. TCGETPAR.C `TSMGetParity()` routine

```
//
// TSM Communications API DLL
//
// tcgetpar.c
//
// get the current parity setting of a communications port
//
// WORD FAR PASCAL _export TSMGetParity( int nComId )
//
// parameters:
//     int nComId - ID of the COM port to retrieve the parity for
//
// returns:
//     >=0  current parity setting if successful
//             NOPARITY
//             EVENPARITY
//             ODDPARITY
//             SPACEPARITY
//             MARKPARITY
//     <0   if error occurred
//


//
// system include files
//
#include <windows.h>
#ifdef __BORLANDC__
#pragma hdrstop
#endif


//
// local include files
//
#include "tsmcomm.h"
#include "tcglobal.h"

//
```

continues

Listing 2.3. continued

```c
// TSMGetParity
//
WORD FAR PASCAL _export TSMGetParity( int nComId )
{
   //
   // automatic variables
   //
   LPDCB lpDCB;
   WORD  wParity;

   //
   // check to make sure that a COM port is open
   //
   if ( !hTSMCommInfo )
      return( IE_NOPEN );

   //
   // lock the CommInfo structure and check whether the ComIds
   // are the same
   //
   lpTSMCommInfo = (LPTSMCOMMINFO)GlobalLock( hTSMCommInfo );
   if ( lpTSMCommInfo->ComId != nComId ) {
      GlobalUnlock( hTSMCommInfo );
      return( (WORD)IE_NOPEN);
   }

   //
   // lock the DCB structure
   //
   lpDCB = (LPDCB)GlobalLock( lpTSMCommInfo->hDCB );
   //
   // get the current port settings
   //
   GetCommState( nComId, lpDCB );

   //
   // get the parity from the DCB
   //
   wParity = lpDCB->Parity;

   //
   // unlock both the DCB and the CommInfo structures
   //
   GlobalUnlock( lpTSMCommInfo->hDCB );
```

```
    GlobalUnlock( hTSMCommInfo );

    //
    // return the parity
    //
    return( wParity );
}
```

To change the parity of an open communications port, the program calls the TSMSetParity() routine. Like TSMGetParity(), the routine starts by ensuring that there's an open port and the ComIds are the same, returning an error if there is not. The routine then locks the DCB in memory and gets the current state of the port by calling **GetCommState()**. The routine modifies the parity setting in the DCB with the requested setting and sets the port's new parameters by calling **SetCommState()**. The return value is saved in a temporary variable and the memory, locked earlier, is unlocked. Finally, the function ends, returning the code saved in the temporary variable. TSMSetParity() is shown in Listing 2.4.

Listing 2.4. TCSETPAR.C TSMSetParity() routine.

```
//
// TSM Communications API DLL
//
// tcsetpar.c
//
// get the current stop bits of a communications port
//
// int FAR PASCAL _export TSMSetParity( int nComId, WORD wParity )
//
// parameters:
//    int    nComId  -   ID of the port to change the parity of
//    WORD   wParity -   new parity setting
//
// returns:
//    0     if successful
//    <0    if an error occurs
//

//
// system include files
//
```

continues

Listing 2.4. continued

```c
#include <windows.h>
#ifdef __BORLANDC__
#pragma hdrstop
#endif

//
// local include files
//
#include "tsmcomm.h"
#include "tcglobal.h"

//
// TSMSetParity
//
int FAR PASCAL _export TSMSetParity( int nComId, WORD wParity )
{
   //
   // automatic variables
   //
   LPDCB lpDCB;
   int   nResult;

   //
   // check to make sure that there is a COM port open
   //
   if ( !hTSMCommInfo )
      return( IE_NOPEN );

   //
   // lock the CommInfo structure and check whether the ComIds
   // are the same
   //
   lpTSMCommInfo = (LPTSMCOMMINFO)GlobalLock( hTSMCommInfo );
   if ( lpTSMCommInfo->ComId != nComId ) {
      GlobalUnlock( hTSMCommInfo );
      return( IE_NOPEN );
   }

   //
   // lock the DCB structure
   //
   lpDCB = (LPDCB)GlobalLock( lpTSMCommInfo->hDCB );

   //
```

```
    // get the current port settings
    //
    GetCommState( nComId, lpDCB );

    //
    // put the desired parity into the DCB
    //
    lpDCB->Parity = (BYTE)wParity;

    //
    // set the port to the new parameters
    //
    nResult = SetCommState( lpDCB );

    //
    // unlock both the DCB and the CommInfo structures
    //
    GlobalUnlock( lpTSMCommInfo->hDCB );
    GlobalUnlock( hTSMCommInfo );

    //
    // return the result
    //
    return( nResult );
}
```

The other Get/Set routines follow this same format.

You now can open and close a communications port and change its communications parameters. Next, you'll see ways to read from and write to a communications port.

Transmit/Receive Routines

As you learned earlier in this chapter, there are two different ways to send and receive characters in Windows. Polling works under both Windows 3.0 and Windows 3.1, and message-driven works only under Windows 3.1. This chapter uses polled communications in its TSM Communications API transmit and receive functions. Chapter 5, "Message-Based Communications," covers Windows 3.1 message-driven communications.

The first read/write routine covered is TSMEnablePolling(). This routine sets up the TSM API for polled communications. TSMEnablePolling() is presented in Listing 2.5.

Listing 2.5. TCENBPLL.C `TSMEnablePolling()` routine

```
//
// TSM Communications API DLL
//
// tcenbpll.c
//
// enable polling as the current method of communications
//
// int FAR PASCAL _export TSMEnablePolling( int nComId )
//
// parameters:
//    int nComId  -  ID of port to enable polling for
//
// returns:
//    0  if successful
//    <0 if an error occurred
//

//
// system include files
//
#include <windows.h>
#ifdef __BORLANDC__
#pragma hdrstop
#endif

//
// local include files
//
#include "tsmcomm.h"
#include "tcglobal.h"

//
// TSMEnablePolling
//
int FAR PASCAL _export TSMEnablePolling( int nComId )
{
   //
   // automatic variables
   //

   //
   // check to make sure that there is a COM port open
   //
   if ( !hTSMCommInfo )
      return( IE_NOPEN );
```

```
    //
    // lock the CommInfo structure and check whether the ComIds
    // are the same
    //
    lpTSMCommInfo = (LPTSMCOMMINFO)GlobalLock( hTSMCommInfo );
    if ( lpTSMCommInfo->ComId != nComId ) {
        GlobalUnlock( hTSMCommInfo );
        return( IE_NOPEN );
    }
    GlobalUnlock( hTSMCommInfo );

    //
    // set the polled mode flag to TRUE
    //
    bPolledComm = TRUE;

    //
    // return a successful indication
    //
    return( 0 );
}
```

This routine starts by ensuring that a port is open and the ComIds are the same. It returns an error indication if either test fails. It then unlocks the TSMCOMMINFO structure. Next, the polling is enabled by setting the global variable bPolledComm to TRUE. When this variable is TRUE, the TSM Communications routines use polling methods; when it is FALSE, the routines use message-based methods. Finally, both the transmit and receive queues are emptied using **FlushComm()**. The second parameter of **FlushComm()** indicates which queue to flush: 0 for the transmission queue and 1 for the reception queue. The routine returns a 0 to indicate that TSMEnablePolling() was successful. Now that polling communications methods are enabled, the program can receive characters.

The reception of characters in polled mode takes place in a modified message-processing loop. A sample of the message loop that can be used with the TSM Communications API polled mode is shown below.

```
//
// variables
//
MSG     msg;
BOOL    fContinue;
int     nComId;
HWND    hWndComm;
```

```
//
// modified message-processing loop
//
fContinue = TRUE;
while ( fContinue ) {
    //
    // check for a message in the queue
    //
    if ( PeekMessage( &msg, NULL, 0, 0, PM_REMOVE ) )
    {
        //
        // there is a message, so check whether it is a WM_QUIT
        // message
        //
        if ( msg.message != WM_QUIT ) {
            //
            // it is a "normal" message, so process it
            //
            TranslateMessage( &msg );
            DispatchMessage( &msg );
        } else {
            //
            // process the WM_QUIT message
            //
            fContinue = FALSE;
        }
    } else {
        //
        // no message, so call TSMReadComm() to
        // do polled mode communications receiving
        //
        TSMReadComm( nComId, hWndComm );
    }
}
```

The routine TSMReadComm() does all the processing for polled mode communications. It is called with the handle of the window that receives the characters in the WM_COMM_CHARS message. TSMReadComm() starts by ensuring that a port is open and the ComIds are the same. The function returns an error if either test fails. Next, the function checks for characters in the receive queue by calling **GetCommError()**, which fills in the COMSTAT structure. COMSTAT contains a field, cbInQue, the value of which equals the number of characters received. If this value is 0, the function returns without doing anything further.

If there are characters to be read, the routine first allocates a memory block large enough to hold all the characters. After locking the block, **ReadComm()**

reads the characters from the queue to the memory block. `ReadComm()` returns the number of characters it read. If an error occurs, the negative of the number of characters read is returned. The TSM routine checks for errors by testing whether the return value is less than zero. If it is, the function converts the value back to the number of characters read and clears the event mask using `GetCommEventMask()`. Next, the routine sends a WM_COMM_CHARS message to the window passed to it. The word parameter of the message contains the number of characters and the long parameter contains a far pointer to the characters. The application has to process this message.

It is imperative that the application use the characters during the message processing. TSMReadComm() assumes that it can free the memory block when `SendMessage()` returns. Once the memory block is unlocked and freed, the routine returns a 0 to indicate that the read process was successfully completed. Listing 2.6 contains TSMReadComm().

Listing 2.6. TCRDCOM.C `TSMReadComm()` routine.

```
//
// TSM Communications API DLL
//
// tcrdcom.c
//
// read characters from the communications port
//
// int FAR PASCAL _exportTSMReadComm( int nComId, HWND hWndComm )
//
// parameters:
//    int  nComId    -  ID of port to read from
//    HWND hWndComm   -  window to send any characters
//                       read to
//
// returns:
//    0  if successful
//    <0 if an error occurred
//


//
// system include files
//
#include <windows.h>
#ifdef __BORLANDC__
#pragma hdrstop
```

continues

Listing 2.6. continued

```
#endif

//
// local include files
//
#include "tsmcomm.h"
#include "tcglobal.h"

//
// TSMReadComm
//
int FAR PASCAL _export TSMReadComm( int nComId, HWND hWndComm )
{
   //
   // automatic variables
   //
   COMSTAT  CommStat;
   int      nCommChars,
            nResult = 0,
            nCommError;
   HANDLE   hCommMem;
   LPSTR    lpCommMem;

   //
   // check to make sure that there is a COM port open
   //
   if ( !hTSMCommInfo )
      return( IE_NOPEN );

   //
   // lock the CommInfo structure and check whether the ComIds
   // are the same
   //
   lpTSMCommInfo = (LPTSMCOMMINFO)GlobalLock( hTSMCommInfo );
   if ( lpTSMCommInfo->ComId != nComId ) {
      GlobalUnlock( hTSMCommInfo );
      return( IE_NOPEN );
   }
   GlobalUnlock( hTSMCommInfo );

   //
   // check whether there are any characters in the receive
   // queue
   //
```

```
GetCommError( nComId, &CommStat );
if ( (nCommChars = CommStat.cbInQue) > 0 ) {
   //
   // allocate a global memory block for the characters
   //
   if ( (hCommMem = GlobalAlloc( GMEM_MOVEABLE, nCommChars ) ) ) ) {
      //
      // lock the memory in place
      //
      lpCommMem = (LPSTR)GlobalLock( hCommMem );

      //
      // read the characters from the communications port
      //
      nCommChars = ReadComm( nComId, lpCommMem, nCommChars );

      //
      // check for errors
      //
      if ( nCommChars < 0 ) {
         //
         // change the number of characters back to the number
         // actually read
         //
         nCommChars = -nCommChars;
         nCommError = GetCommError( nComId, NULL );

         //
         // clear the event mask
         //
         GetCommEventMask( nComId, 0xFFFF );
      }

      //
      // send a message to the appropriate routine for
      // these characters to be processed
      //
      SendMessage( hWndComm, WM_COMM_CHARS, nCommChars,
                   (LONG)lpCommMem );

      //
      // unlock and free the memory
      //
      GlobalUnlock( hCommMem );
```

continues

Listing 2.6. continued

```
        GlobalFree( hCommMem );
    } else {
      //
      // the allocation failed so return an IE_MEMORY error
      //
      nResult = IE_MEMORY;
    }
  }


  //
  // return the result value
  //
  return( nResult );
}
```

TSMWriteComm() gives the capability to transmit characters through the communications port. This routine transmits characters with a polled method. Listing 2.7 contains TSMWriteComm().

Listing 2.7 TCWRTCOM.C TSMWriteComm() routine.

```
//
// TSM Communications API DLL
//
// tcwrtcom.c
//
// write characters to the communications port
//
// int FAR PASCAL _export TSMWriteComm( int nComId, int nCount,
//                                      LPCSTR lpOutChars )
//
// parameters:
//    int nComId        -   ID of COM port to write to
//    int nCount        -   number of characters to write
//    LPCSTR lpOutChars -   far pointer to the characters to be
//                          written
//
// returns:
//    0  if successful
//    <0 if an error occurred
//
```

```
//
// system include files
//
#include <windows.h>
#ifdef __BORLANDC__
#pragma hdrstop
#endif

//
// local include files
//
#include "tsmcomm.h"
#include "tcglobal.h"

//
// TSMWriteComm
//
int FAR PASCAL _export TSMWriteComm( int nComId, int nCount,
                                     LPCSTR lpOutChars )
{
   //
   // automatic variables
   //
   LPSTR szCurrent;
   int   nTotalSent,
         nCurrentSent;

   //
   // check to make sure that there is a COM port open
   //
   if ( !hTSMCommInfo )
      return( IE_NOPEN );

   //
   // lock the CommInfo structure and check whether the ComIds
   // are the same
   //
   lpTSMCommInfo = (LPTSMCOMMINFO)GlobalLock( hTSMCommInfo );
   if ( lpTSMCommInfo->ComId != nComId ) {
      GlobalUnlock( hTSMCommInfo );
      return( IE_NOPEN );
   }
   GlobalUnlock( hTSMCommInfo );
```

continues

Listing 2.7. continued

```
//
// set the current pointer to the start of the string and set
// the starting value of nTotalSent
//
szCurrent = (LPSTR)lpOutChars;
nTotalSent = 0;

//
// loop until all the characters have been sent
//
while ( nTotalSent < nCount ) {
   //
   // try to send all remaining characters
   //
   nCurrentSent = WriteComm( nComId, szCurrent,
                             ( nCount - nTotalSent ) );

   //
   // check whether an error occurred
   //
   if ( nCurrentSent < 0 )
      nCurrentSent = -nCurrentSent;

   //
   // update the current string pointer and the total number
   // of characters sent
   //
   szCurrent += nCurrentSent;
   nTotalSent += nCurrentSent;
}

//
// return that everything worked OK
//
return( 0 );
}
```

TSMWriteComm(), first, ensures that a port is open and the ComIds are the same. If not, the routine returns an IE_NOPEN error. The function then initializes two automatic variables essential to this routine. szCurrent keeps track of the next character to be sent and nTotalSent is the total number of characters that have been transmitted.

The routine then enters a loop that terminates when the total number of characters sent is equal to (or greater than) the number of characters to transmit. In this loop, `WriteComm()` transmits the characters. It is called with `szCurrent` as the pointer to the characters to transmit and the number of characters to be sent, minus the total already sent. `WriteComm()` returns the number of characters that it actually wrote or returns the negative of the number written if an error occurred. The routine is not doing any error checking right now; if an error occurs, the value is just negated to get the actual number of characters written.

The routine updates `szCurrent` and `nTotalSent` based on the number of characters that were written by this call to `WriteComm()`. The loop then goes back and continues until all characters have been transmitted. When the loop terminates, the function sends a 0 to the calling routine to indicate that the transmission was successful. Your program can transmit and receive characters now. The last set of routines the program needs are a couple of miscellaneous routines dealing with the specifics of dynamic link libraries.

Miscellaneous Routines

The TSM Communications API is contained in the dynamic link library TSMCOMM.DLL. As a DLL, several routines are necessary. This section covers those routines.

The first necessary DLL routine is `LibMain()`. This routine initializes the DLL—it is called automatically by Windows when the DLL is loaded. `LibMain()` initializes the global variables. `LibMain()` is presented in Listing 2.8.

Listing 2.8. TSMCOMM.C `LibMain()` routine.

```
//
// TSM Communications API DLL
//
// tsmcomm.c
//
// TSM Communications API DLL library initialization routine
//
// int CALLBACK LibMain( HINSTANCE hInst, WORD wDataSeg,
//                       WORD wHeapSize, LPSTR lpCmdLine )
//
// parameters:
```

continues

Listing 2.8. continued

```
//      HINSTANCE   hInst
//      WORD        wDataSeg
//      WORD        wHeapSize
//      LPSTR       lpCmdLine
//
// returns:
//      1    if initialization successful
//      0    if initialization failed
//


//
// system include files
//
#include <windows.h>
#ifdef __BORLANDC__
#pragma hdrstop
#endif


//
// local include files
//
#include "tsmcomm.h"
#define GLOBAL_DEF
#include "tcglobal.h"
#undef  GLOBAL_DEF


//
// LibMain
//
#ifdef __BORLANDC__
#pragma argsused
#endif
int CALLBACK LibMain( HINSTANCE hInst, WORD wDataSeg,
                      WORD wHeapSize, LPSTR lpCmdLine )
{
   //
   // initialize global variables
   //
   hTSMCommInfo  = NULL;        // indicate no open comm structures
   bPolledComm   = TRUE;        // indicate start in polled mode

   //
```

```
    // return that the initialization worked
    //
    return( 1 );
}
```

Along with `LibMain()`, every DLL must also contain a Windows Exit Procedure (WEP). TSMCOMM.DLL is no exception. Due to problems with Windows though, the WEP really can't do anything other than return a one. The WEP for TSMCOMM.DLL appears in Listing 2.9.

Listing 2.9. TCWEP.C `WEP()` routine.

```
//
// TSM Communications API DLL
//
// tcwep.c
//
// TSM Communications API DLL WEP function
//
// int CALLBACK WEP( int nExitType )
//
// parameters:
//    int    nExitType
//
// returns:
//    1    always
//


//
// system include files
//
#include <windows.h>
#ifdef _ _BORLANDC_ _
#pragma hdrstop
#endif


//
// WEP
//
#ifdef _ _BORLANDC_ _
#pragma argsused
#endif
```

continues

Listing 2.9. continued

```
int CALLBACK WEP( int nExitType )
{
    //
    // just return a 1
    //
    return( 1 );
}
```

Summary

This chapter covered ways to use the Windows Communications API to perform common communications programming tasks. It then started the development of the TSM Communications API. This API encapsulates the Windows API, making communications programming easier to do. Now you are ready to start developing a terminal program and look at terminal emulation.

Terminal
Emulation

S o far, this book has laid the groundwork for implementing a serial communications program. You have learned how to open and close communications ports, as well as the basics for character transmission and reception. Taking this basic information and the TSM Communications API, you are ready to start building a general-purpose communications program, starting with the most important component, the terminal emulation. In this chapter you

- Look at terminal emulations in general and ANSI terminal emulation specifically.

- Develop routines to implement an ANSI terminal emulation.

- Develop the initial version of TSMTerm, a general-purpose communications program.

Terminal Emulations

When most people think of communications programs, they actually think of the program's terminal emulation. This emulator is the interface most used in communications programs and is therefore one of the most important. If you have ever connected to a system that thought you had a different type of terminal than you really did, you know the problems that can result from an incorrect emulation. Unfortunately, in the days of mainframes, each terminal manufacturer developed its own control codes for working with its terminals (an attempt to lock users into a specific brand of terminal). Table 3.1 lists some common terminals and manufacturers.

Table 3.1. Terminals and their manufacturers.

Manufacturer	Terminals
Digital Equipment Corporation	VT-52, VT-100, VT-220
Televideo	900 Series
IBM	3270, 3101, 3161
ADDS	60, 90
WYSE	VT compatibles

Each of these popular terminals is emulated by many communications packages. Terminal emulations are designed to do two things:

- Emulate the screen of the terminal
- Emulate the keyboard of the terminal

Emulating the terminal's screen means correctly interpreting the control codes sent to the terminal to do things like move the cursor and change the screen colors. Emulating the keyboard means transmitting the correct codes for each key struck. There's a problem with either emulation—each terminal has it own control codes for both screen control and keyboard control.

The American National Standards Institute (ANSI) tried to bring the divergent terminal standards together with the X3.64 specification.

The ANSI Terminal

The ANSI X3.64 Standard Control Sequences for Video Terminal have been popularized by the IBM PC and the PC electronic bulletin board community. This standard is implemented for the PC in the ANSI.SYS driver that comes standard with MS-DOS. TSMTerm also implements the ANSI terminal specification.

ANSI codes consist of a sequence of ASCII characters. The first character of this sequence is always an ESC (0x1B). For this reason, these ANSI codes are referred to as ESC sequences. The second character of an ANSI ESC sequence is a [, known as the control sequence introducer. X3.64 defines other introducers, but TSMTerm does not implement them.

The sequence following the [introducer has a fairly fixed format of one or more parameters (possibly zero parameters), followed by a final character. Table 3.2 lists the codes that describe the ANSI ESC sequences. All numeric parameters must be given in decimal format.

Table 3.2. ANSI ESC sequence parameter codes.

Code	Description
ESC	ASCII ESC character (0x1B)
Pr	Numeric value that specifies a row value

Code	Description
Pc	Numeric value that specifies a column value
Pn	Numeric value used as a count
Ps	Series of numeric values separated by a semicolon (;)

For most ESC sequences, the parameters can be omitted. The descriptions of the implemented ANSI ESC sequences include the default values for omitted parameters. The implemented sequences are described in the following paragraphs. These ESC sequences start with the cursor movement sequences, then the display control sequences. Notice that this is not a complete implementation of the ANSI X3.64 standard. This implementation is consistent with the ANSI.SYS implementation and should suffice in most instances.

```
Cursor Position           ESC[Pr;PcH    Defaults: Pr=0  Pc=0
```

This ESC sequence moves the cursor to the row and column specified by `Pr` and `Pc`. The HOME position of the screen, the upper left corner, are coordinates 0,0.

```
Horizontal/Vertical Position  ESC[Pr;Pcf    Defaults: Pr=0  Pc=0
```

An alternate ESC sequence to the `Cursor Position` ESC sequence. This sequence also moves the cursor to the screen position specified by `Pr` and `Pc`.

```
Cursor Up                 ESC[PnA       Default: Pn=1
```

This sequence moves the cursor up by the specified number of lines. If the cursor is already on the top line of the screen, the sequence is ignored.

```
Cursor Down               ESC[PnB       Default: Pn=1
```

This sequence moves the cursor down by the specified number of lines. If the cursor is already on the bottom line of the screen, the sequence is ignored.

```
Cursor Forward            ESC[PnC       Default: Pn=1
```

This sequence moves the cursor forward (right) by the specified number of characters. It does not change the line of the cursor. If the cursor is in the rightmost column, the sequence is ignored.

```
Cursor Backward          ESC[PnD        Default: Pn=1
```

This sequence moves the cursor back (left) by the specified number of characters. It does not change the line of the cursor. If the cursor is in the leftmost column, the sequence is ignored.

```
Save Cursor Position     ESC[s
```

This sequence stores the current cursor position. This position is used for the Restore Cursor Position sequence.

```
Restore Cursor Position  ESC[u
```

This sequence moves the cursor back to the location it was in when the last Save Cursor Position sequence occurred.

```
Erase Display            ESC[2J
```

This sequence erases the entire screen and places the cursor in the HOME position.

```
Erase Line               ESC[K
```

This sequence erases the screen from the current cursor position to the end of the screen. The current cursor position is included in the erase. The cursor position does not change.

```
Set Graphics Rendition   ESC[Psm
```

This sequence changes the color of the screen. Ps is a series of values that represents the color modifications to make. Table 3.3 lists the allowable values of Ps. Any changes that are made remain effective until the next Set Graphics Rendition control sequence.

Table 3.3. Set Graphics Rendition Ps values.

Value	Description
0	All attributes off (normal white on black text)
1	Bold On
4	Underscore On
5	Blink On
7	Reverse On
8	Concealed On
30	Black Foreground

Value	Description
31	Red Foreground
32	Green Foreground
33	Yellow Foreground
34	Blue Foreground
35	Magenta Foreground
36	Cyan Foreground
37	White Foreground
40	Black Background
41	Red Background
42	Green Background
43	Yellow Background
44	Blue Background
45	Magenta Background
46	Cyan Background
47	White Background

```
Select Mode                 ESC[=Psh
```

This sequence changes the screen width or type. This implementation only changes the screen width and height. Table 3.4 lists the allowable values of Ps. Once a mode has been selected, it remains active until the next Select Mode or Reset Mode sequence.

Table 3.4. Select Mode Ps values.

Value	Description
0	40×25 monochrome text
1	40×25 color text
2	80×25 monochrome text
3	80×25 color text

continues

Table 3.4. continued

Value	Description
4	320 × 200 color graphics
5	320 × 200 monochrome graphics
6	640 × 200 monochrome graphics
7	Enable line wrapping
13	320 × 200 color graphics
14	640 × 200 16-color graphics
15	640 × 350 monochrome graphics
16	640 × 350 16-color graphics
17	640 × 480 monochrome graphics
18	640 × 480 16-color graphics
19	320 × 200 256-color graphics

Reset Mode   ESC[=Psl

This sequence resets the screen width or type. This implementation only changes the screen width and height. Table 3.5 lists the allowable values of Ps. Once a mode has been selected, it remains active until the next Select Mode or Reset Mode sequence. The only difference between this sequence and the Select Mode sequence is that code 7 disables line-wrap mode in this sequence.

Table 3.5. Reset Mode Ps values.

Value	Description
0	40 × 25 monochrome text
1	40 × 25 color text
2	80 × 25 monochrome text
3	80 × 25 color text
4	320 × 200 color graphics
5	320 × 200 monochrome graphics

Value	Description
6	640 × 200 monochrome graphics
7	Disable line wrapping
13	320 × 200 color graphics
14	640 × 200 16-color graphics
15	640 × 350 monochrome graphics
16	640 × 350 16-color graphics
17	640 × 480 monochrome graphics
18	640 × 480 16-color graphics
19	320 × 200 256-color graphics

Tip: The X3.64 specification starts with the screen in normal mode, with text on a black background. It also initializes with line wrapping disabled.

Now that you have seen the codes that the terminal emulation of the ANSI X3.64 specification recognizes, you can start the implementation. Most of the time, terminal emulations are best coded as finite state machines (FSM). The concepts of an FSM are discussed in the next section.

Finite State Machines

A finite state machine describes a process consisting of states and inputs. Each state responds to a given input in a fixed manner and either stays in the same state or moves to a new state. Figure 3.1 shows a representation of a section of an FSM. This FSM starts in state X. When it receives input, it moves to state J when the input is A, state K when the input is B, and so on. Each of the other states—J, K, and L—then accepts input, moving on to other states based on that input.

Whenever the finite state machine in the example is in State X and receives input A, it must move to state J. For your ANSI terminal emulation, there is a state, CHAR_RECEIVE_STATE, and whenever an ESC character is received while the emulation is in CHAR_RECEIVE_STATE, the machine must move to ESCAPE_RCVD_STATE. Your ANSI terminal emulation has only three states:

- CHAR_RECEIVE_STATE—normal character reception, waiting for an ESC character and displaying the other characters.

- ESCAPE_RCVD_STATE—expects to receive the [character as the next character.

- PARAM_RECEIVE_STATE—receives the ESC sequence parameters until a final character is found.

Each of these states handles the characters it processes differently. The next discussion describes processing for each of these states.

Figure 3.1.
Finite state machine representation.

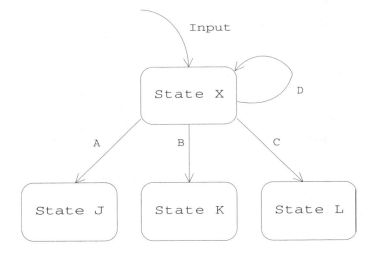

ANSITERM.DLL

The ANSI terminal emulation resides in the file ANSITERM.DLL. This dynamic link library (DLL) contains the entry points for the terminal emulation interface. Table 3.6 lists the entry points and a quick description of each of the entry points. Each of these routines is covered in detail in the following sections. The remaining miscellaneous routines of ANSITERM.DLL are discussed also.

Table 3.6. ANSITERM.DLL entry points.

Entry Point	Description
TE_Initialize()	Initialize the terminal emulation system.
TE_Terminate()	Terminate the terminal emulation system.
TE_ProcessSize()	Process the WM_SIZE message.
TE_ProcessFocus()	Process the WM_SETFOCUS and WM_KILLFOCUS messages.
TE_ProcessPaint()	Process the WM_PAINT message.
TE_ProcessChars()	Display characters to the screen.

DLL-Specific Routines

ANSITERM.DLL, like TSMCOMM.DLL, must include two routines, LibMain() and WEP(). Unlike its counterpart in TSMCOMM.DLL, LibMain() in ANSITERM.DLL does not initialize the system. It only allocates memory for the global variables. Listings 3.1 and 3.2 present these routines.

Listing 3.1. ANSITERM.C LibMain() routine.

```
//
// ANSI Terminal Emulation DLL
//
// ansiterm.dll
//
// ANSI Terminal Emulation DLL library initialization routine
//
// int CALLBACK LibMain( HINSTANCE hInst, WORD wDataSeg,
//                       WORD wHeapSize, LPSTR lpCmdLine )
//
// parameters:
//    HINSTANCE    hInst
//    WORD         wDataSeg
//    WORD         wHeapSize
//    LPSTR        lpCmdLine
//
// returns:
//    1    if initialization succeeded
//    0    if initialization failed
```

continues

Listing 3.1. continued

```
//

//
// system include files
//
#include <windows.h>
#ifdef __BORLANDC__
#pragma hdrstop
#endif

//
// local include files
//
#include "ansiterm.h"
#define GLOBAL_DEF
#include "atglobal.h"
#undef  GLOBAL_DEF

//
// LibMain
//
#ifdef __BORLANDC__
#pragma argsused
#endif
int CALLBACK LibMain( HINSTANCE hInst, WORD wDataSeg,
                      WORD wHeapSize, LPSTR lpCmdLine )
{
   //
   // return that the initialization worked
   //
   return( 1 );
}
```

Listing 3.2. ATWEP.C WEP() routine.

```
//
// ANSI Terminal Emulation DLL
//
// atwep.c
//
// ANSI Terminal Emulation DLL WEP function
```

```
//
// int CALLBACK WEP( int nExitType )
//
// parameters:
//     int   nExitType
//
// returns:
//     1   always
//

//
// system include files
//
#include <windows.h>
#ifdef __BORLANDC__
#pragma hdrstop
#endif

//
// WEP
//
#ifdef __BORLANDC__
#pragma argsused
#endif
int CALLBACK WEP( int nExitType )
{
    //
    // just return a 1
    //
    return( 1 );
}
```

Initialization Routines

The terminal emulation contained in ANSITERM.DLL is initialized with a call to TE_Initialize(). TE_Initialize() starts by initializing the screen colors. The ANSI terminal specification calls for starting colors of white text on a black background. Next, the height and width of a character are determined after a call to the function TE_GetDC().

TE_GetDC() is a generalized routine that gets a device context (DC) for the screen. The function also changes the characteristics of that DC to those necessary for terminal emulation. The routine

Selects the SYSTEM_FIXED_FONT as the font for displaying the terminal.

Sets the color for displaying text.

Sets the color for the text background and whether the background should be opaque.

Caution: These settings must be set every time your program gets a device context because they are lost when your program releases the DC.

Listing 3.3 presents TE_GetDC().

Listing 3.3. ATUTILS.C, containing various ANSITERM utility routines.

```
//
// ANSI Terminal Emulation DLL
//
// atutils.c
//
// various utility functions
//

//
// system include files
//
#include <windows.h>
#ifdef __BORLANDC__
#pragma hdrstop
#endif

//
// local include files
//
#include "ansiterm.h"
#include "atglobal.h"

//
// HDC TE_GetDC( HWND hWnd )
//
// parameters:
//     HWND  hWnd  handle to the window that needs a device context
```

```
//
// returns:
//     HDC    handle to a device context for this window
//
HDC    TE_GetDC( HWND hWnd )
{
    //
    // automatic variables
    //
    HDC    hDC;

    //
    // get the device context for the client area
    //
    hDC = GetDC( hWnd );

    //
    // set the display parameters for this DC
    //
    TE_SetupDC( hDC );

    //
    // return the device context handle
    //
    return( hDC );
}

//
// void TE_SetupDC( HDC hDC )
//
// parameters:
//     HDC    hDC    handle to the CD to set up
//
// returns:
//     nothing
//
void TE_SetupDC( HDC hDC )
{
    //
    // select a fixed font for this context
    //
    SelectObject( hDC, GetStockObject( OEM_FIXED_FONT ) );

    //
    // set up the default color of white text on a black
```

continues

Listing 3.3. continued

```
      // background
      //
      SetTextColor( hDC, dwTextColor );
      SetBkColor( hDC, dwBkGndColor );
      SetBkMode( hDC, OPAQUE );
}


//
// void TE_RemoveBufferChars( void )
//
// parameters:
//    none
//
// returns:
//    nothing
//
void TE_RemoveBufferChars( void )
{
   //
   // automatic variables
   //
   BOOL   bContinue = TRUE;

   //
   // loop until done
   //
   while ( bContinue ) {
      //
      // see whether the head and tail are the same
      //
      if ( nBufferHead == nBufferTail ) {
         bContinue = FALSE;
         continue;
      }

      //
      // see whether the head points to a line feed
      //
      if ( szCharBuffer[ nBufferHead ] == 0xA )
         bContinue = FALSE;

      //
      // update the buffer head pointer
      //
```

```
        nBufferHead++;
        if ( nBufferHead == CHAR_BUFFER_SIZE )
            nBufferHead = 0;
    }
}
```

Once `TE_Initialize()` has a DC, it calls **`GetTextMetrics()`** to fill the TEXTMETRIC structure. This structure contains the fields needed to save the height and width of a character. Then the variables that control the screen display are initialized. The cursor is placed in the HOME position, the saved cursor position is initialized to HOME, and line wrapping is disabled. ANSITERM.DLL saves the characters it has processed so that it can redraw the screen when it needs to. This character buffer is initialized next. Finally, `TE_Initialize()` sets the FSM. The starting state is CHAR_RECEIVE_STATE and the current parameter is 0. Listing 3.4 presents `TE_Initialize()` in its entirety.

Listing 3.4. ATINIT.C `TE_Initialize()` routine.

```
//
// ANSI Terminal Emulation DLL
//
// atinit.c
//
// initialize the terminal emulation system
//
// BOOL FAR PASCAL _export TE_Initialize( HWND hWnd )
//
// parameters:
//    HWND   hWnd  handle to the terminal display window
//
// returns:
//    TRUE  if successful
//    FALSE if an error occurred
//


//
// system include files
//
#include <windows.h>
#ifdef __BORLANDC__
#pragma hdrstop
#endif
```

continues

Listing 3.4. continued

```c
//
// local include files
//
#include "ansiterm.h"
#include "atglobal.h"

//
// TE_Initialize
//
BOOL FAR PASCAL _export TE_Initialize( HWND hWnd )
{
   //
   // automatic variables
   //
   HDC        hDC;
   TEXTMETRIC  TextMetric;

   //
   // set the default colors (white text on black background)
   //
   dwTextColor  = COLOR_WHITE;
   dwBkGndColor = COLOR_BLACK;
   hBkBrush = CreateSolidBrush( COLOR_BLACK );
   if ( hBkBrush )
      SetClassWord( hWnd, GCW_HBRBACKGROUND, (WORD)hBkBrush );

   //
   // get and save the text metrics
   //
   hDC = TE_GetDC( hWnd );
   GetTextMetrics( hDC, &TextMetric );
   ReleaseDC( hWnd, hDC );
   nXChar = TextMetric.tmAveCharWidth;
   nYChar = TextMetric.tmHeight + TextMetric.tmExternalLeading;

   //
   // set the current screen locations
   //
   nCurrCol = nCurrRow = 0;

   //
   // initialize the saved screen locations
   //
   nSaveCol = nSaveRow = 0;
```

```
    //
    // initialize the line wrapping setting to FALSE
    //
    bLineWrap = FALSE;

    //
    // initialize the character buffer
    //
    nBufferHead = nBufferTail = 0;
    bBufferChars = TRUE;

    //
    // initialize the finite state machine
    //
    nFSMState = CHAR_RECEIVE_STATE;
    nFSMCurrParam = 0;

    //
    // indicate that the function succeeded
    //
    return( TRUE );
}
```

WM_SIZE Processing

One important piece of information that the terminal emulation needs is the size of the client area of the window. This value determines how many rows and columns of characters fit on the screen. Windows sends this information in the WM_SIZE message, and your terminal emulation gets this message when the program calls TE_ProcessSize(). This routine is shown in Listing 3.5.

Listing 3.5. ATPRCSZ.C TE_ProcessSize() routine.

```
//
// ANSI Terminal Emulation DLL
//
// atprcsz.c
//
// process window size changes
//
// void FAR PASCAL _export TE_ProcessSize( HWND hWnd,
```

continues

Listing 3.5. continued

```
//                                       LONG lSize )
//
// parameters:
//      HWND hWnd       handle of the window being sized
//      LONG lSize      size of the client area with the width being
//                      in the low word and the height in the high
//                      word
//
// returns:
//      nothing
//


//
// system include files
//
#include <windows.h>
#ifdef __BORLANDC__
#pragma hdrstop
#endif

//
// local include files
//
#include "ansiterm.h"
#include "atglobal.h"

//
// TE_ProcessSize
//
void FAR PASCAL _export TE_ProcessSize( HWND hWnd, LONG lSize )
{
    //
    // save the number of rows and columns in the client area
    //
    nRows = HIWORD( lSize ) /  nYChar;
    nCols = LOWORD( lSize ) /  nXChar;

    //
    // change the current location back to 0, 0
    //
    nCurrRow = nCurrCol = 0;

    //
    // invalidate the client area, so it is redrawn
```

```
    //
    InvalidateRect( hWnd, NULL, TRUE );

    //
    // return to the calling procedure
    //
    return;
}
```

`TE_ProcessSize()` calculates the number of columns in the client area by dividing the width of the client area by the width of a character. The number of rows is calculated using the height of the client area and a character. Next, the cursor is moved back to the HOME position and the entire client area is invalidated to force a repaint. The cursor is discussed next.

Focus Processing

The terminal screen cursor, called a *caret* by Windows, is a system-wide resource. Only one caret can exist in Windows at a time. For this reason, it makes sense to create a caret for the screen when your program receives the focus and to destroy that caret when the program loses the focus. `TE_ProcessFocus()` does this. The parameter `bFocus` indicates whether the program is receiving or losing the focus. `TE_ProcessFocus()` starts by checking `bFocus`. If the routine is gaining the focus, it creates a caret, positions it to the current screen location, and shows it. Conversely, if the routine is losing the focus, it hides the caret and then destroys it. Listing 3.6 presents `TE_ProcessFocus()`.

> **Tip:** The caret should be hidden before any drawing takes place on the screen. If the caret isn't hidden, the screen can become corrupted. The caret is shown again after drawing is complete.

Listing 3.6. ATPRCFCS.C `TE_ProcessFocus()` routine.

```
//
// ANSI Terminal Emulation DLL
//
// atprcfcs.c
//
```

continues

Listing 3.6. continued

```
// process focus changes
//
// void FAR PASCAL _export TE_ProcessFocus( HWND hWnd,
//                                          BOOL bFocus )
//
// parameters:
//    HWND hWnd    the handle of the window that got the focus
//    BOOL bFocus  this is TRUE if the function is receiving the
//                 focus and FALSE if it is losing it
//
// returns:
//    nothing
//


//
// system include files
//
#include <windows.h>
#ifdef __BORLANDC__
#pragma hdrstop
#endif

//
// local include files
//
#include "ansiterm.h"
#include "atglobal.h"

//
// TE_ProcessFocus
//
void FAR PASCAL _export TE_ProcessFocus( HWND hWnd, BOOL bFocus )
{
    //
    // decide whether the program gaining or losing the focus
    //
    if ( bFocus ) {
        //
        // gaining the focus: create, position, and display
        // the caret
        //
        CreateCaret( hWnd, NULL, nXChar, nYChar );
        SetCaretPos( nCurrCol * nXChar, nCurrRow * nYChar );
        ShowCaret( hWnd );
```

```
    } else {
      //
      // losing the focus: hide and destroy the caret
      //
      HideCaret( hWnd );
      DestroyCaret();
    }
    //
    // return to the calling procedure
    //
    return;
}
```

Processing Characters

The main part of the ANSI terminal emulation is the TE_ProcessChars() routine. This routine implements your program's finite state machine. The routine also stores the characters in a buffer, allowing the screen to be repainted during a WM_PAINT message. Listing 3.7 presents TE_ProcessChars().

Listing 3.7. ATPRCCHR.C TE_ProcessChars() routine.

```
//
// ANSI Terminal Emulation DLL
//
// atprcchr.c
//
// process characters for the display
//
// BOOL FAR PASCAL _export TE_ProcessChars( HWND hWnd,
//                                          LPCSTR szChars,
//                                          int nNumChars )
//
// parameters:
//    HWND      hWnd        handle of the window to display the
//                          characters in
//    LPCSTR    szChars     far pointer to the characters to
/                           process
//    int       nNumChars   number of characters to process
//
// returns:
//    TRUE  if successful
//    FALSE if an error occurred
```

continues

Listing 3.7. continued

```
//

//
// system include files
//
#include <windows.h>
#ifdef __BORLANDC__
#pragma hdrstop
#endif
#include <string.h>
#include <ctype.h>

//
// local include files
//
#include "ansiterm.h"
#include "atglobal.h"

//
// local function prototypes
//
void CharReceiveState( HWND hWnd, char cChar );
void EscapeRcvdState( HWND hWnd, char cChar );
void ParamReceiveState( HWND hWnd, char cChar );
void DisplayChar( HWND hWnd, char cChar );

//
// TE_ProcessChars
//
BOOL FAR PASCAL _export TE_ProcessChars( HWND hWnd,
                                         LPCSTR szChars,
                                         int nNumChars )
{
   //
   // automatic variables
   //
   int   i;
   BOOL  bSucceed = TRUE;
   LPSTR lpCurrChar;

   //
   // loop through each character received
   //
   for ( i = 0, lpCurrChar = (LPSTR)szChars; i < nNumChars;
```

```
                                    i++, lpCurrChar++ ) {
        //
        // add the character to the buffer if the program is
        // currently buffering characters
        //
        if ( bBufferChars ) {
           szCharBuffer[ nBufferTail ] = *lpCurrChar;
           nBufferTail++;
           if ( nBufferTail == CHAR_BUFFER_SIZE )
              nBufferTail = 0;
        }

        //
        //
        // process the characters based on the state
        //
        switch( nFSMState ) {
           case CHAR_RECEIVE_STATE:
              CharReceiveState( hWnd, *lpCurrChar );
              break;

           case ESCAPE_RCVD_STATE:
              EscapeRcvdState( hWnd, *lpCurrChar );
              break;

           case PARAM_RECEIVE_STATE:
              ParamReceiveState( hWnd, *lpCurrChar );
              break;

           default:
              nFSMState = CHAR_RECEIVE_STATE;
              break;
        }
     }

     //
     // return the succeed flag
     //
     return( bSucceed );
}

//
// CharReceiveState( HWND hWnd,  char cChar )
//
// parameters:
```

continues

Listing 3.7. continued

```
//    HWND      hWnd  handle of the window to display the
//                    characters in
//    char      cChar character to process
//
// returns:
//    nothing
//
void CharReceiveState( HWND hWnd, char cChar )
{
   //
   // process based on the character
   //
   switch( cChar ) {
      case VK_ESCAPE:
         //
         // ESCAPE, move to a new state
         //
         nFSMState = ESCAPE_RCVD_STATE;
         break;

      default:
         //
         // display the rest of the characters
         //
         DisplayChar( hWnd, cChar );
         break;
   }
}


//
// void EscapeRcvdState( HWND hWnd, char cChar )
//
// parameters:
//    HWND      hWnd  handle of the window to display the
//                    characters in
//    char      cChar character to process
//
// returns:
//    nothing
//
#pragma argsused
void EscapeRcvdState( HWND hWnd, char cChar )
{
   //
```

```
      // process based on the character
      //
      switch( cChar ) {
         case '[':
            //
            // correct character was received, so move to the next
            // state and initialize the parameter stack
            //
            nFSMState = PARAM_RECEIVE_STATE;
            nFSMCurrParam = 0;
            nFSMParams[ nFSMCurrParam ] = -1;
            break;

         default:
            //
            // an error occurred, so just go back to original state
            //
            nFSMState = CHAR_RECEIVE_STATE;
            break;
      }
}


//
// void ParamReceiveState( HWND hWnd, char cChar )
//
// parameters:
//    HWND     hWnd   handle of the window to display the
//                    characters in
//    char     cChar  character to process
//
// returns:
//    nothing
//
#pragma argsused
void ParamReceiveState( HWND hWnd, char cChar )
{
   //
   // automatic variables
   //
   int      i, nTemp, nTemp2;
   DWORD    dwTemp;
   HBRUSH   hBrush;

   //
   // process based on the character
```

continues

Listing 3.7. continued

```
//
switch( cChar ) {
   case 'H':
      //
      // cursor position
      //
      if ( nFSMParams[ 0 ] == -1 )
         nCurrRow = 0;
      else
          nCurrRow = nFSMParams[ 0 ];
      if ( nFSMParams[ 1 ] == -1 )
         nCurrCol = 0;
      else
         nCurrCol = nFSMParams[ 1 ];
      nFSMState = CHAR_RECEIVE_STATE;
      break;

   case 'f':
      //
      // horizontal/vertical position
      //
      if ( nFSMParams[ 0 ] == -1 )
         nCurrRow = 0;
      else
          nCurrRow = nFSMParams[ 0 ];
      if ( nFSMParams[ 1 ] == -1 )
         nCurrCol = 0;
      else
         nCurrCol = nFSMParams[ 1 ];
      nFSMState = CHAR_RECEIVE_STATE;
      break;

   case 'A':
      //
      // cursor up
      //
      if ( nFSMParams[ 0 ] == -1 )
         nTemp = 1;
      else
         nTemp = nFSMParams[ 0 ];
      nCurrRow -= nTemp;
      if ( nCurrRow < 0 )
```

```
        nCurrRow = 0;
    nFSMState = CHAR_RECEIVE_STATE;
    break;

case 'B':
    //
    // cursor down
    //
    if ( nFSMParams[ 0 ] == -1 )
        nTemp = 1;
    else
        nTemp = nFSMParams[ 0 ];
    nCurrRow += nTemp;
    if ( nCurrRow > ( nRows - 2 ) )
        nCurrRow = nRows - 2;
    nFSMState = CHAR_RECEIVE_STATE;
    break;

case 'C':
    //
    // cursor forward
    //
    if ( nFSMParams[ 0 ] == -1 )
        nTemp = 1;
    else
        nTemp = nFSMParams[ 0 ];
    nCurrCol += nTemp;
    if ( nCurrCol >= ( nCols - 1 )  )
        nCurrCol = nCols - 2;
    nFSMState = CHAR_RECEIVE_STATE;
    break;

case 'D':
    //
    // cursor backward
    //
    if ( nFSMParams[ 0 ] == -1 )
        nTemp = 1;
    else
        nTemp = nFSMParams[ 0 ];
    nCurrCol -= nTemp;
    if ( nCurrCol < 0 )
        nCurrCol = 0;
    nFSMState = CHAR_RECEIVE_STATE;
    break;
```

continues

Listing 3.7. continued

```
case 's':
   //
   // save cursor position
   //
   nSaveCol = nCurrCol;
   nSaveRow = nCurrRow;
   nFSMState = CHAR_RECEIVE_STATE;
   break;

case 'u':
   //
   // restore cursor position
   //
   nCurrCol = nSaveCol;
   nCurrRow = nSaveRow;
   nFSMState = CHAR_RECEIVE_STATE;
   break;

case 'J':
   //
   // erase display
   //
   if ( nFSMParams[ 0 ] == 2 ) {
      nCurrRow = nCurrCol = 0;
      InvalidateRect( hWnd, NULL, TRUE );
   }
   nFSMState = CHAR_RECEIVE_STATE;
   break;

case 'K':
   //
   // erase line
   //
   nTemp = nCurrCol;
   nTemp2 = nCurrRow;
   for ( i = nCurrCol; i < nCols - 1; i++ )
      DisplayChar( hWnd, ' ' );
   nCurrRow = nTemp2;
   nCurrCol = nTemp;
   nFSMState = CHAR_RECEIVE_STATE;
   break;

case 'm':
   //
```

```
// set graphics rendition
//
// loop through the parameters
//
for ( i = 0; i <= nFSMCurrParam; i++ ) {
   //
   // if it's an unused parameter the
   // break from the loop
   if ( nFSMParams[ i ] == -1 )
      break;

   //
   // process based on the parameter
   //
   switch( nFSMParams[i] ) {
      case 0:
         //
         // all attributes off
         //
         dwTextColor = COLOR_WHITE;
         dwBkGndColor = COLOR_BLACK;
         hBrush = CreateSolidBrush( dwBkGndColor );
         if ( hBrush ) {
            SetClassWord( hWnd, GCW_HBRBACKGROUND,
                                             (WORD)hBrush );
            if ( hBkBrush )
               DeleteObject( hBkBrush );
            hBkBrush = hBrush;
         }
         break;

      case 1:
         //
         // bold on
         //
         dwTextColor = COLOR_WHITE;
         dwBkGndColor = COLOR_BLACK;
         hBrush = CreateSolidBrush( dwBkGndColor );
         if ( hBrush ) {
            SetClassWord( hWnd, GCW_HBRBACKGROUND,
                                             (WORD)hBrush );
            if ( hBkBrush )
               DeleteObject( hBkBrush );
            hBkBrush = hBrush;
         }
```

continues

107

Listing 3.7. continued

```
                break;

            case 4:
                //
                // underscore on
                //
                dwTextColor = COLOR_WHITE;
                dwBkGndColor = COLOR_BLACK;
                hBrush = CreateSolidBrush( dwBkGndColor );
                if ( hBrush ) {
                    SetClassWord( hWnd, GCW_HBRBACKGROUND,
                                                    (WORD)hBrush );
                    if ( hBkBrush )
                        DeleteObject( hBkBrush );
                    hBkBrush = hBrush;
                }
                break;

            case 5:
                //
                // blink on
                //
                dwTextColor = COLOR_WHITE;
                dwBkGndColor = COLOR_BLACK;
                hBrush = CreateSolidBrush( dwBkGndColor );
                if ( hBrush ) {
                    SetClassWord( hWnd, GCW_HBRBACKGROUND,
                                                    (WORD)hBrush );
                    if ( hBkBrush )
                        DeleteObject( hBkBrush );
                    hBkBrush = hBrush;
                }
                break;

            case 7:
                //
                // reverse on
                //
                dwTemp = dwTextColor;
                dwTextColor = dwBkGndColor;
                dwBkGndColor = dwTemp;
                hBrush = CreateSolidBrush( dwBkGndColor );
                if ( hBrush ) {
                    SetClassWord( hWnd, GCW_HBRBACKGROUND,
```

```
                                        (WORD)hBrush );
        if ( hBkBrush )
            DeleteObject( hBkBrush );
        hBkBrush = hBrush;
    }
    break;

case 8:
    //
    // concealed on
    //
    dwTextColor = dwBkGndColor;
    break;

case 30:
    //
    // black foreground
    //
    dwTextColor = COLOR_BLACK;
    break;

case 31:
    //
    // red foreground
    //
    dwTextColor = COLOR_RED;
    break;

case 32:
    //
    // green foreground
    //
    dwTextColor = COLOR_GREEN;
    break;

case 33:
    //
    // yellow foreground
    //
    dwTextColor = COLOR_YELLOW;
    break;

case 34:
    //
    // blue foreground
```

continues

Listing 3.7. continued

```
                            //
                            dwTextColor = COLOR_BLUE;
                            break;

                    case 35:
                            //
                            // magenta foreground
                            //
                            dwTextColor = COLOR_MAGENTA;
                            break;

                    case 36:
                            //
                            // cyan foreground
                            //
                            dwTextColor = COLOR_CYAN;
                            break;

                    case 37:
                            //
                            // white foreground
                            //
                            dwTextColor = COLOR_WHITE;
                            break;

                    case 40:
                            //
                            // black background
                            //
                            dwBkGndColor = COLOR_BLACK;
                            hBrush = CreateSolidBrush( dwBkGndColor );
                            if ( hBrush ) {
                                SetClassWord( hWnd, GCW_HBRBACKGROUND,
                                                            (WORD)hBrush );
                                if ( hBkBrush )
                                    DeleteObject( hBkBrush );
                                hBkBrush = hBrush;
                            }
                            break;

                    case 41:
                            //
                            // red background
                            //
```

```
        dwBkGndColor = COLOR_RED;
        hBrush = CreateSolidBrush( dwBkGndColor );
        if ( hBrush ) {
            SetClassWord( hWnd, GCW_HBRBACKGROUND,
                                            (WORD)hBrush );
            if ( hBkBrush )
                DeleteObject( hBkBrush );
            hBkBrush = hBrush;
        }
        break;

    case 42:
        //
        // green background
        //
        dwBkGndColor = COLOR_GREEN;
        hBrush = CreateSolidBrush( dwBkGndColor );
        if ( hBrush ) {
            SetClassWord( hWnd, GCW_HBRBACKGROUND,
                                            (WORD)hBrush );
            if ( hBkBrush )
                DeleteObject( hBkBrush );
            hBkBrush = hBrush;
        }
        break;

    case 43:
        //
        // yellow background
        //
        dwBkGndColor = COLOR_YELLOW;
        hBrush = CreateSolidBrush( dwBkGndColor );
        if ( hBrush ) {
            SetClassWord( hWnd, GCW_HBRBACKGROUND,
                                            (WORD)hBrush );
            if ( hBkBrush )
                DeleteObject( hBkBrush );
            hBkBrush = hBrush;
        }
        break;

    case 44:
        //
        //  Blue Background
        //
        dwBkGndColor = COLOR_BLUE;
```

continues

111

Listing 3.7. continued

```
        hBrush = CreateSolidBrush( dwBkGndColor );
        if ( hBrush ) {
           SetClassWord( hWnd, GCW_HBRBACKGROUND,
                                        (WORD)hBrush );

           if ( hBkBrush )
              DeleteObject( hBkBrush );
           hBkBrush = hBrush;
        }
        break;

     case 45:
        //
        // magenta background
        //
        dwBkGndColor = COLOR_MAGENTA;
        hBrush = CreateSolidBrush( dwBkGndColor );
        if ( hBrush ) {
           SetClassWord( hWnd, GCW_HBRBACKGROUND,
                                        (WORD)hBrush );

           if ( hBkBrush )
              DeleteObject( hBkBrush );
           hBkBrush = hBrush;
        }
        break;

     case 46:
        //
        // cyan background
        //
        dwBkGndColor = COLOR_CYAN;
        hBrush = CreateSolidBrush( dwBkGndColor );
        if ( hBrush ) {
           SetClassWord( hWnd, GCW_HBRBACKGROUND,
                                        (WORD)hBrush );

           if ( hBkBrush )
              DeleteObject( hBkBrush );
           hBkBrush = hBrush;
        }
        break;

     case 47:
        //
        // white background
        //
```

```
                dwBkGndColor = COLOR_WHITE;
                hBrush = CreateSolidBrush( dwBkGndColor );
                if ( hBrush ) {
                    SetClassWord( hWnd, GCW_HBRBACKGROUND,
                                                (WORD)hBrush );
                    if ( hBkBrush )
                        DeleteObject( hBkBrush );
                    hBkBrush = hBrush;
                }
                break;

            default:
                break;
        }
    }

    //
    // reset the current state
    //
    nFSMState = CHAR_RECEIVE_STATE;
    break;

case 'h':
    //
    // select mode
    //
    // loop through the parameters
    //
    for ( i = 0; i <= nFSMCurrParam; i++ ) {
        //
        // if there's an unused parameter
        // break from the loop
        if ( nFSMParams[ i ] == -1 )
            break;

        //
        // process based on the parameter
        //
        switch( nFSMParams[i] ) {
            case 0:
                //
                // 40 x 25 monochrome text
                //
            case 1:
                //
```

continues

Listing 3.7. continued

```
        // 40 x 25 color text
        //
        MoveWindow( hWnd, 0, 0,  40 * nXChar,
                    25 * nYChar, TRUE );
        break;

    case 2:
        //
        // 80 x 25 monochrome text
        //
    case 3:
        //
        // 80 x 25 color text
        //
        MoveWindow( hWnd, 0, 0,  80 * nXChar,
                    25 * nYChar, TRUE );
        break;

    case 4:
        //
        // 320 x 200 color graphics
        //
    case 5:
        //
        // 320 x 200 monochrome graphics
        //
    case 13:
        //
        // 320 x 200 color graphics
        //
    case 19:
        //
        // 320 x 200 256-color graphics
        //
        MoveWindow( hWnd, 0, 0,  320, 200, TRUE );
        break;

    case 6:
        //
        // 640 x 200 monochrome graphics
        //
    case 14:
        //
        // 640 x 200 16-color graphics
```

```
            //
            MoveWindow( hWnd, 0, 0,  640, 200, TRUE );
            break;

        case 7:
            //
            // enable line wrapping
            //
            bLineWrap = TRUE;
            break;

        case 15:
            //
            // 640 x 350 monochrome graphics
            //
        case 16:
            //
            // 640 x 350 16-color graphics
            //
            MoveWindow( hWnd, 0, 0,  640, 350, TRUE );
            break;

        case 17:
            //
            // 640 x 480 monochrome graphics
            //
        case 18:
            //
            // 640 x 480 16-color graphics
            //
            MoveWindow( hWnd, 0, 0,  640, 350, TRUE );
            break;

        default:
            break;
        }
    }

    //
    // reset the current state
    //
    nFSMState = CHAR_RECEIVE_STATE;
    break;
case 'l':
    //
```

continues

Listing 3.7. continued

```
// reset mode
//
// loop through the parameters
//
for ( i = 0; i <= nFSMCurrParam; i++ ) {
   //
   // if there's an unused parameter
   // break from the loop
   if ( nFSMParams[ i ] == -1 )
      break;

   //
   // process based on the parameter
   //
   switch( nFSMParams[i] ) {
      case 0:
         //
         // 40 x 25 monochrome text
         //
      case 1:
         //
         // 40 x 25 color text
         //
         MoveWindow( hWnd, 0, 0,  40 * nXChar,
                     25 * nYChar, TRUE );
         break;

      case 2:
         //
         // 80 x 25 monochrome text
         //
      case 3:
         //
         // 80 x 25 color text
         //
         MoveWindow( hWnd, 0, 0,  80 * nXChar,
                     25 * nYChar, TRUE );
         break;

      case 4:
         //
         // 320 x 200 color graphics
         //
      case 5:
```

```
    //
    // 320 x 200 monochrome graphics
    //
case 13:
    //
    // 320 x 200 color graphics
    //
case 19:
    //
    // 320 x 200 256-color graphics
    //
    MoveWindow( hWnd, 0, 0,  320, 200, TRUE );
    break;

case 6:
    //
    // 640 x 200 monochrome graphics
    //
case 14:
    //
    // 640 x 200 16-color graphics
    //
    MoveWindow( hWnd, 0, 0,  640, 200, TRUE );
    break;

case 7:
    //
    // disable line wrapping
    //
    bLineWrap = FALSE;
    break;

case 15:
    //
    // 640 x 350 monochrome graphics
    //
case 16:
    //
    // 640 x 350 16-color graphics
    //
    MoveWindow( hWnd, 0, 0,  640, 350, TRUE );
    break;

case 17:
    //
```

continues

Listing 3.7. continued

```
                          // 640 x 480 monochrome graphics
                          //
                      case 18:
                          //
                          // 640 x 480 16-color graphics
                          //
                          MoveWindow( hWnd, 0, 0,  640, 350, TRUE );
                          break;

                      default:
                          break;
                  }
              }

              //
              // reset the current state
              //
              nFSMState = CHAR_RECEIVE_STATE;
              break;

          case ';':
              //
              // go on to the next parameter
              //
              nFSMCurrParam++;
              nFSMParams[ nFSMCurrParam ] = -1;
              break;

          default:
              //
              // make sure the character is a digit
              //
              if ( isascii( cChar ) ) {
                  if ( isdigit( cChar ) ) {
                      //
                      // it is, so add it to the current parameter
                      //
                      if ( nFSMParams[ nFSMCurrParam ] == -1 )
                          nFSMParams[ nFSMCurrParam ] = 0;
                      else
                          nFSMParams[ nFSMCurrParam ] *= 10;
                      nFSMParams[ nFSMCurrParam ] += (cChar - '0');
                  } else {
                      //
```

```
                    // an error occurred, so go back to the original
                    // state
                    //
                    nFSMState = CHAR_RECEIVE_STATE;
                }
            } else {
                //
                // an error occurred, so go back to the original state
                //
                nFSMState = CHAR_RECEIVE_STATE;
            }
            break;
    }
}

//
// void DisplayChar( HWND hWnd, char cChar )
//
// parameters:
//    HWND     hWnd  handle of the window to display the characters in
//    char     cChar character to display
//
// returns:
//    nothing
//
void DisplayChar( HWND hWnd, char cChar )
{
    //
    // automatic variables
    //
    HDC    hDC;

    //
    // get a device context for the client area
    //
    hDC = TE_GetDC( hWnd );

    //
    // hide the caret
    //
    HideCaret( hWnd );

    //
    // process each character
    //
```

continues

Listing 3.7. continued

```
switch ( cChar ) {
    case VK_RETURN:
        //
        // process a carriage return
        //
        nCurrCol = 0;
        break;

    case 0xA:
        //
        // process a new line
        //
        nCurrRow++;
        if ( nCurrRow == ( nRows - 1 ) ) {
            TE_RemoveBufferChars();
            ScrollWindow( hWnd, 0, -nYChar, NULL, NULL );
            ValidateRect( hWnd, NULL );
            UpdateWindow( hWnd );
            nCurrRow = nRows - 2;
        }
        break;

    case VK_BACK:
        //
        // process a backspace
        //
        if ( nCurrCol )
            nCurrCol--;
        break;

    default:
        //
        // process the "normal" characters - display it on the
        // window
        //
        TextOut( hDC, nCurrCol * nXChar, nCurrRow * nYChar,
                (LPSTR)&cChar, 1 );

        //
        // increment the column and see whether it is at the end
        // of a line
        //
        nCurrCol++;
```

```
          if ( nCurrCol == ( nCols - 1 ) ) {
            //
            // end of a line
            // check to see if line wrap is on
            //
            if ( bLineWrap ) {
              //
              // line wrapping is on; move to the next line
              //
              nCurrCol = 0;
              nCurrRow++;

              //
              // does program need to scroll the window?
              //
              if ( nCurrRow == ( nRows - 1 ) ) {
                TE_RemoveBufferChars();
                ScrollWindow( hWnd, 0, -nYChar, NULL, NULL );
                ValidateRect( hWnd, NULL );
                UpdateWindow( hWnd );
                nCurrRow = nRows - 2;
              }
            } else {
              //
              // line wrapping is off; just reset the column
              //
              nCurrCol--;
            }
          }
          break;
    }

    //
    // update the caret position and show it
    //
    SetCaretPos( nCurrCol * nXChar, nCurrRow * nYChar );
    ShowCaret( hWnd );

    //
    // release the device context
    //
    ReleaseDC( hWnd, hDC );
}
```

TE_ProcessChars() starts by setting a for loop to process each character individually. The loop adds the character to the character buffer if the buffer flag is set. This is a circular buffer, used to repaint the screen during a WM_PAINT message. Characters are added to the tail of the buffer, and then the tail is moved forward by one character. When the tail pointer reaches the end of the buffer, it is reset to the first character of the buffer. Then, the character is processed based on the current state of the FSM. Each state is discussed in the following paragraphs. Finally, TE_ProcessChars() goes back and processes the next character. When all characters have been processed, the routine returns to the calling procedure.

When the FSM is in CHAR_RECEIVE_STATE, each character (the input for this state) is processed by the routine CharReceiveState(). This procedure, included in Listing 3.7, processes most of the characters the TE_ProcessChars() receives. CharReceiveState() does one of two things: finds an ESC character and changes to ESCAPE_RCVD_STATE, or passes the character on to DisplayChar(). This is done in a switch statement.

The switch statement makes implementing a finite state machine simple. Each specific input to the FSM is a case of a switch statement. Adding processing for different inputs is easy.

DisplayChar() writes the character to the screen. This routine, contained in Listing 3.7, starts by getting a device context. It then hides the caret, which must be done before you write to the screen. The routine then uses a switch statement to process special characters, such as Return, Line Feed, and Backspace. For the Line Feed, the screen must be checked to see whether it needs to be scrolled to accommodate the new line. If it does, the routine calls TE_RemoveBufferChars() to remove the characters that will be scrolled off the screen from the character buffer. The function then scrolls the window using **ScrollWindow()**. Finally, the function validates the client area to keep it from being erased, updates the screen, and resets the current row.

Most characters are processed through the default case. In this case, the function puts the character on the screen. It starts by calling **TextOut()** to display the character. The location to display the character is found by multiplying the current row by the height of a character and the current column by the width of a character. The routine then increments the current column. If the cursor is past the end of the line, the routine checks the line-wrap variable. If line wrapping is not enabled (and the default state is disabled), the program resets the current column to the last screen column. If line wrap is enabled, the program increments the current line as if a Line Feed character had been sent, then moves the cursor back to the leftmost column. Once again, the program checks for screen scrolling. `DisplayChar()` completes by moving the caret to the new position and showing it.

`TE_RemoveBufferChars()` was presented in Listing 3.3. It moves the head pointer of the character buffer past the characters that are about to be scrolled off the screen. It increments the head pointer until either the buffer is empty or the character being removed is a newline.

When the FSM is in `ESCAPE_RCVD_STATE`, the routine `EscapeRcvdState()` processes the character received by `If_ProcessChars()`. This state is unusual for the FSM, because it only receives one character as input. If this character is the `[`, the state is changed to `PARAM_RECEIVE_STATE`, and two global variables are initialized for storing the ANSI sequence parameters, as described in the next paragraph. If the character is not `[`, an error has occurred, and the FSM is reset to `CHAR_RECEIVE_STATE`. When an error occurs during an ANSI ESC sequence, the characters in the sequence are ignored. `EscapeRcvdState()` was presented in Listing 3.7.

The most complicated and important state of the ANSI terminal FSM is `PARAM_RECEIVE_STATE`. As you recall, each ESC sequence can have zero or more numeric parameters after the `ESC[` and before the final character. Your program must be able to tell if these parameters are present and preserve their values for use when it finds the final character. The routine `ParamReceiveState()`, shown previously in Listing 3.7, processes the input for this state. ANSITERM.DLL defines two global variables used for storing the parameters. They are `nFSMParams`, an array of integers used to hold the parameter values, and `nFSMCurrParam`, used to indicate the current parameter. When a new parameter is expected, either by changing from `ESCAPE_RCVD_STATE` or processing a semicolon, the current parameter variable is incremented or set to 0, and the value of the current parameter is set to -1. All valid parameters are positive values. When a character is processed, if it is a digit, the value of the current parameter is checked; if the value is -1, it is reset to 0; and if the value is anything else, the value is multiplied by 10. Then the new digit is added to the value. This is the `default` case processing for the `ParamReceiveState()` switch statement. If the `default` case is taken, and the character is not a digit, an error has occurred, and the FSM returns to `CHAR_RECEIVE_STATE`.

Each case of the `ParamReceiveState()` switch statement (other than the default and the semicolon cases) looks for a final character of the ANSI ESC sequences that the emulation recognizes. Table 3.7 describes the processing that takes place for each of these final characters. All final characters cause the FSM to return to `CHAR_RECEIVE_STATE`.

Table 3.7. Final character processing.

Character	Command	Action
H	Cursor Position	Changes the current column and row to those specified by the first two parameters, or their defaults.
f	Horizontal/Vertical Pos	Changes the current column and row to those specified by the first two parameters, or their defaults.
A	Cursor Up	Decreases the current row by the specified number of lines. The cursor stops at the top of the screen.
B	Cursor Down	Increases the current row by the specified number of lines. The cursor stops at the bottom of the screen.
C	Cursor Forward	Increases the current column by the specified number of characters, stopping at the right edge of the screen.
D	Cursor Backward	Decreases the current column by the specified number of characters, stopping at the leftmost screen position.
s	Save Cursor Position	Stores the current row and column in the saved cursor position global variables.
u	Restore Cursor Position	Changes the current row and column to those stored in the saved cursor position global variables.
J	Erase Screen	Sets the current row and column back to the HOME position and invalidates the entire client area.
K	Erase Line	Displays space characters from the current cursor position to the end of the line. Keeps the current row and column the same.

Character	Command	Action
m	Set Graphics Rendition	Loops through the parameters, quitting if it finds an invalid one. For each parameter, sets the text color and the background color as appropriate. If the background color is changed, changes the class background brush also.
h	Select Mode	Changes the size of the window using **MoveWindow()**. Case 7 is an exception, setting the enable line-wrap flag to TRUE.
l	Reset Mode	Changes the size of the window using **MoveWindow()**. Case 7 is an exception, setting the enable line-wrap flag to FALSE.

WM_PAINT Processing

By storing the characters processed by TE_ProcessChars() in a special buffer, the program is able to redraw the screen when it receives WM_PAINT messages. TE_ProcessPaint() handles this processing and is shown in Listing 3.8. This routine starts by calling **BeginPaint()** (as all WM_PAINT processing routines must). **BeginPaint()** returns a device context handle used to set the device context. Once this handle is returned, the current row and column are reset to the HOME position.

Listing 3.8. ATPRCPNT.C TE_ProcessPaint() routine.

```
//
// ANSI Terminal Emulation DLL
//
// atprcpnt.c
//
// process the WM_PAINT command
//
// BOOL FAR PASCAL _export TE_ProcessPaint( HWND hWnd )
//
// parameters:
//     HWND  hWnd  handle of window being painted
//
// returns:
```

continues

Listing 3.8. continued

```c
//      TRUE   if successful
//      FALSE if not successful
//

//
// system include files
//
#include <windows.h>
#ifdef __BORLANDC__
#pragma hdrstop
#endif

//
// local include files
//
#include "ansiterm.h"
#include "atglobal.h"

//
// TE_ProcessPaint
//
BOOL FAR PASCAL _export TE_ProcessPaint( HWND hWnd )
{
    //
    // automatic variables
    //
    HDC          hDC;
    PAINTSTRUCT  PaintStruct;
    int          nChars;

    //
    // start the paint process
    //
    hDC = BeginPaint( hWnd, &PaintStruct );

    //
    // set up the device context
    //
    TE_SetupDC( hDC );

    //
    // set the current location back to the HOME position
    //
    nCurrCol = nCurrRow = 0;
```

```
    //
    // calculate the number of characters to process
    //
    nChars = nBufferTail - nBufferHead;
    if ( nChars < 0 )
       nChars += CHAR_BUFFER_SIZE;

    //
    // process the buffer characters
    //
    if ( nChars > 0 ) {
       bBufferChars = FALSE;
       TE_ProcessChars( hWnd, &szCharBuffer[ nBufferHead ], nChars );
       bBufferChars = TRUE;
    }

    //
    // complete the paint process
    //
    EndPaint( hWnd, &PaintStruct );

    //
    // return that the paint worked fine
    //
    return( TRUE );
}
```

TE_ProcessPaint() then calculates the number of characters in the buffer by subtracting the head from the tail. If the result is negative, the program adds the size of the buffer to that value to get the number of characters in the buffer. Then TE_ProcessChars() is called to redisplay the characters on the screen. Once the screen has been repainted, **EndPaint()** is called to complete the paint process.

Terminating the Emulation

The last entry point for the ANSI terminal emulation is TE_Terminate(). This routine is used to complete the terminal emulation. The only processing this routine performs is destroying the background brush if one was created by the emulation.

> **Caution:** Brushes are an hDI object. hDI objects are not automatically
> deleted by Windows when an application terminates. Therefore, it is
> important to make sure all hDI objects are destroyed before the
> program terminates.

Listing 3.9 presents this routine.

Listing 3.9. ATTERM.C `TE_Terminate()` routine.

```
//
// ANSI Terminal Emulation DLL
//
// atterm.c
//
// terminate the terminal emulation system
//
// BOOL FAR PASCAL _export TE_Terminate( HWND hWnd )
//
// parameters:
//    HWND  hWnd  handle of terminating window
//
// returns:
//    TRUE  if successful
//    FALSE if an error occurred
//


//
// system include files
//
#include <windows.h>
#ifdef __BORLANDC__
#pragma hdrstop
#endif

//
// local include files
//
#include "ansiterm.h"
#include "atglobal.h"
```

```
//
// TE_Terminate
//
BOOL FAR PASCAL _export TE_Terminate( HWND hWnd )
{
    //
    // automatic variables
    //

    //
    // delete the brush if it exists
    //
    if ( hBkBrush ) {
        SetClassWord( hWnd, GCW_HBRBACKGROUND,
                        (WORD)GetStockObject( WHITE_BRUSH ) );
        DeleteObject( hBkBrush );
        hBkBrush = NULL;
    }

    //
    // for now, just indicate that the function failed
    //
    return( FALSE );
}
```

ANSITERM.DLL provides a simple emulation of the ANSI X3.64 specification, but it is useless without a program to use it. The next section looks at the first version of your terminal program.

TSMTERM.EXE

TSMTERM.EXE is a general-purpose terminal program that you develop throughout the remainder of this book. Figure 3.2 shows the main TSMTERM screen. This application uses all the normal Windows niceties, including a caption bar, a system menu, minimize and maximize buttons, a resizing border, and an application menu. TSMTERM.EXE is composed of several distinct parts. Each of these parts is discussed in detail next.

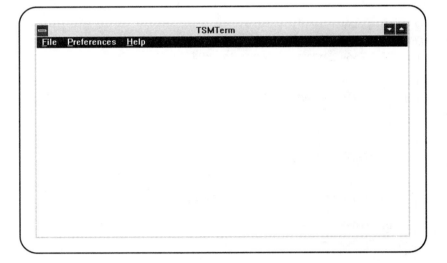

Figure 3.2.
TSMTerm
application
window.

Startup Routines

The main routine of every Windows program is WinMain(). TSMTerm is no exception, with WinMain() residing in TSMTERM.C. TSMTERM.C is presented in Listing 3.10. This routine starts by saving the instance handle in a global variable and loading the application name from the string table. It then checks for any previous instances of TSMTerm and displays an error message box and terminates if there are any errors. The Windows version is checked also, and an error message is displayed if the version is lower than 3.0.

Listing 3.10. TSMTERM.C WinMain() routine.

```
//
// TSM Terminal Program
//
// tsmterm.c
//
// main entry point for TSM Terminal
//
// int PASCAL WinMain( HANDLE hInstance, HANDLE hPrevInstance,
//                     LPSTR lpCmdLine, int nCmdShow )
//
// parameters:
//    HANDLE   hInstance       instance handle for this instance of TSMTERM
//    HANDLE   hPrevInstance   instance handle of a previous instance
```

```
//      LPSTR    lpCmdLine        far pointer to the command line
//      int      nCmdShow         initial show window command
//
// returns:
//      0      if successful
//      NULL   if an error occurs
//

//
// system include files
//
#include <windows.h>
#ifdef __BORLANDC__
#pragma hdrstop
#endif

//
// local include files
//
#include "..\tsmcomm\tsmcomm.h"
#include "tsmterm.h"
#define GLOBAL_DEF
#include "ttglobal.h"
#undef  GLOBAL_DEF
#include "ttstring.h"

//
// WinMain
//
#ifdef __BORLANDC__
#pragma argsused
#endif
int PASCAL WinMain( HANDLE hInstance, HANDLE hPrevInstance,
                    LPSTR lpCmdLine, int nCmdShow )
{
   //
   // automatic variables
   //
   WNDCLASS WndClass;
   BOOL     fContinue;
   MSG      msg;
   int      nResult;

   //
   // save the instance handle in a global variable
```

continues

Listing 3.10. continued

```
//
hInst = hInstance;

//
// load the application name to a global variable
//
LoadString( hInst, IDS_TSMTERM, szTSMTerm,
            sizeof( szTSMTerm ) );

//
// check whether another instance already exists and
// terminate if it does
//
if ( hPrevInstance ) {
    //
    // get the error message string
    //
    LoadString( hInst, IDS_1INSTANCE, szTemp1,
                sizeof( szTemp1 ) );

    //
    // display a message box containing the error message
    //
    MessageBox( NULL, szTemp1, szTSMTerm,
                MB_ICONSTOP ¦ MB_OK );

    //
    // return a value indicating the program did not start
    //
    return( NULL );
}

//
// check that Windows is version 3.0 or above
//
if ( LOWORD( LOBYTE( GetVersion() ) ) ) < 3 ) {
    //
    // get the error message string
    //
    LoadString( hInst, IDS_WRONGVERSION, szTemp1,
                sizeof( szTemp1 ) );

    //
    // display the error message
```

```
        //
        MessageBox( NULL, szTemp1, szTSMTerm,
                    MB_ICONSTOP | MB_OK );

        //
        // return a value indicating the program did not start
        //
        return( NULL );
    }

    //
    // register the Window class
    //
    WndClass.style          =   CS_HREDRAW | CS_VREDRAW;
    WndClass.lpfnWndProc    =   TSMTermWndProc;
    WndClass.cbClsExtra     =   0;
    WndClass.cbWndExtra     =   0;
    WndClass.hInstance      =   hInst;
    WndClass.hIcon          =   LoadIcon( hInst, szTSMTerm );
    WndClass.hCursor        =   LoadCursor( NULL, IDC_ARROW );
    WndClass.hbrBackground  =   (HBRUSH)(COLOR_WINDOW + 1);
    WndClass.lpszMenuName   =   szTSMTerm;
    WndClass.lpszClassName  =   szTSMTerm;
    if ( !RegisterClass( &WndClass ) ) {
        //
        // the class did not register correctly, so display an error
        // and exit the program
        //
        LoadString( hInst, IDS_REGCLASSERR, szTemp1,
                    sizeof( szTemp1 ) );
        MessageBox( NULL, szTemp1, szTSMTerm, MB_OK );
        return( NULL );
    }

    //
    // create a window based on the class just registered
    //
    hWndTerm = CreateWindow( szTSMTerm, szTSMTerm,
                             WS_OVERLAPPEDWINDOW, CW_USEDEFAULT,
                             CW_USEDEFAULT, CW_USEDEFAULT,
                             CW_USEDEFAULT, HWND_DESKTOP,
                             NULL, hInst, NULL );
    if ( !hWndTerm ) {
        //
        // the window was not created correctly. Display an error
```

continues

Listing 3.10. continued

```
            // message if it did not fail because of a communications
            // failure.
            //
            if ( !bCommFailedErr ) {
                LoadString( hInst, IDS_CREATEWINERR, szTemp1,
                            sizeof( szTemp1 ) );
                MessageBox( NULL, szTemp1, szTSMTerm, MB_OK );
            }

            //
            // exit the program
            //
            return( NULL );
        }

    //
    // load the keyboard accelerators
    //
    hAccelerators = LoadAccelerators( hInst, szTSMTerm );

    //
    // show the window based on the nCmdShow parameter
    //
    ShowWindow( hWndTerm, nCmdShow );
    UpdateWindow( hWndTerm );

    //
    // message-processing loop
    //
    fContinue = TRUE;
    while ( fContinue ) {
        //
        // check for a message in the queue
        //
        if ( PeekMessage( &msg, NULL, 0, 0, PM_REMOVE ) ) {
            //
            // there's a message; check whether if it is a WM_QUIT
            // message
            //
            if ( msg.message != WM_QUIT ) {
                //
                // it is a "normal" message, so process it
                //
                if ( !TranslateAccelerator( hWndTerm, hAccelerators,
```

```
                                         &msg ) ) {
                TranslateMessage( &msg );
                DispatchMessage( &msg );
            }
        } else {
            //
            // process the WM_QUIT message
            //
            fContinue = FALSE;
            nResult = msg.wParam;
        }
    } else {
        //
        // no message; call TSMReadComm() to
        // do polled-mode communications receiving
        //
        TSMReadComm( nComId, hWndTerm );
    }
}


//
// return the result from the WM_QUIT message
//
return( nResult );
}
```

Next, the program registers the window class, indicating the following:

- The window should be redrawn when it is resized either horizontally or vertically.

- The function TSMTermWndProc() is the window procedure for this class.

- The icon called TSMTerm is used for this class, and the standard arrow is used for the mouse cursor.

- The menu named TSMTerm is used for this class.

- The class name is TSMTerm.

If this class does not register correctly, a message box is displayed and the program terminates. Once the class is registered, the program creates a window based on this class. This is a standard overlapped window, created at the default location with the default size. Again, if the creation of this window fails, an error message box is displayed and the program terminates.

Loading the keyboard accelerators is the next step in WinMain(). This is followed by **ShowWindow()** and **UpdateWindow()**, which display the application window for the first time. This window is shown in Figure 3.2. The program then enters a message-processing loop like the one discussed in Chapter 2, "Windows Communications Basics," with the exception of the accelerator handling. Once the message-processing loop exits, the program terminates with the exit code from the WM_QUIT message. Several of the functions called from WinMain() cause messages to be sent to the application's window. These messages are processed by the window procedure.

The Window Procedure

TSMTerm's window procedure is called TSMTermWndProc(). This procedure processes the messages that Windows sends to the window. These messages come from function calls, user input, and by select messages sent within SendMessage(). TSMTermWndProc() also implements a TTY terminal emulation that is used if an external terminal emulation can't be found. Each of the major messages that the window procedure handles is discussed in the following sections. Listing 3.11 presents the complete windows procedure. Each Windows message sent to TSMTermWndProc() must be processed, either by this routine or by **DefWindowProc()**. TSMTermWndProc() keeps a variable, fCallDef, that marks whether the routine should call **DefWindowProc()** or return the result.

Listing 3.11. TTWINDOW.C TSMTermWndProc() routine.

```
//
// TSM Terminal Program
//
// ttwindow.c
//
// TSM Terminal program main window procedure
//
// LRESULT CALLBACK _export TSMTermWindowProc( HWND hWnd, UINT msg,
//                                 WPARAM wParam,
//                                 LPARAM lParam )
//
// parameters:
//    HWND    hWnd     window handle of the window this message
//                     is for
//    UINT    msg      actual Windows message
//    WPARAM  wParam   word parameter of the message
```

```
//      LPARAM    lParam     long parameter of the message
//
// returns:
//      LRESULT   the result of each specific message
//


//
// system include files
//
#include <windows.h>
#ifdef __BORLANDC__
#pragma hdrstop
#endif
#include <string.h>

//
// local include files
//
#include "..\tsmcomm\tsmcomm.h"
#include "tsmterm.h"
#include "ttglobal.h"
#include "ttstring.h"
#include "ttmenu.h"
#include "tttrmemu.h"

//
// local function prototypes
//
void TTYWriteScreen( HWND hWnd, LPSTR lpOutString );
void StartTerminalEmulation( HWND hWnd );
void StopTerminalEmulation( HWND hWnd );

//
// local "global" variables
//
int     nRows, nCols, nCurrRow, nCurrCol;
int     nXChar, nYChar;

//
// TSMTermWindowProc
//
LRESULT CALLBACK _export TSMTermWndProc( HWND hWnd, UINT msg,
                                         WPARAM wParam,
                                         LPARAM lParam )
{
```

continues

Listing 3.11. continued

```
//
// automatic variables
//
TEXTMETRIC   TextMetric;
PAINTSTRUCT  PaintStruct;
HDC          hDC;
BOOL         fCallDef      = FALSE;
LONG         lResult       = 0;
HMENU        hMenu, hPeferences;
BOOL         bChecked;
char         szValue[32];
RECT         ClientRect;

//
// process the message based on the message type
//
switch( msg ) {
   case WM_CREATE:
      //
      // get the text metrics
      //
      hDC = GetDC( hWnd );
      SelectObject( hDC,
                    GetStockObject( OEM_FIXED_FONT ) );
      GetTextMetrics( hDC, &TextMetric );
      ReleaseDC( hWnd, hDC );
      nXChar = TextMetric.tmAveCharWidth;
      nYChar = TextMetric.tmHeight +
               TextMetric.tmExternalLeading;

      //
      // try to open the communications port
      //
      if ( !OpenTermPort() ) {
         //
         // opening the port failed. Display a message and
         // quit the program.
         //
         LoadString( hInst, IDS_COMOPENERR, szTemp1,
                     sizeof( szTemp1 ) );
         wsprintf( szTemp2, szTemp1, nComId );
         if ( MessageBox( hWnd, szTemp2, szTSMTerm,
                          MB_ICONSTOP ¦ MB_YESNO ) == IDYES ) {
            //
```

```
                   // the user wants to run the settings dialog
                   //
                   if ( SendMessage( hWnd, WM_COMMAND,
                               IDM_PREFERENCES_SETTINGS, 0L ) == 1 ) {
                       //
                       // it still failed, so indicate that
                       //
                       bCommFailedErr = TRUE;
                       lResult = -1;
                       break;
                   }
             } else {
                 //
                 // indicate that the open failed
                 //
                 bCommFailedErr = TRUE;
                 lResult = -1;
                 break;
             }
       }
       bCommFailedErr = FALSE;

       //
       // get the duplex value from the .INI file
       //
       LoadString( hInst, IDS_INI_FILE_NAME, szTemp1,
                   sizeof( szTemp1 ) );
       LoadString( hInst, IDS_INI_SECTION_NAME, szTemp2,
                   sizeof( szTemp2 ) );
       GetPrivateProfileString( szTemp2, "Duplex", "TRUE",
                                szValue, sizeof( szValue ),
                                szTemp1 );
       if ( !lstrcmp( szValue, "TRUE" ) )
          bFullDuplex = TRUE;
       else if ( !lstrcmp( szValue, "FALSE" ) )
          bFullDuplex = FALSE;
       else
          bFullDuplex = TRUE;

       //
       // check (or don't check) the Full Duplex menu item
       //
       hMenu = GetMenu( hWnd );
       hPeferences = GetSubMenu( hMenu, 1 );
       CheckMenuItem( hPeferences, IDM_PREFERENCES_DUPLEX,
```

continues

Listing 3.11. continued

```
                        MF_BYCOMMAND ¦ ( bFullDuplex ?
                        MF_CHECKED : MF_UNCHECKED ) );

    //
    // enable polled communications
    //
    TSMEnablePolling( nComId );

    //
    // get the terminal emulation setting from the .INI file
    //
    LoadString( hInst, IDS_INI_FILE_NAME, szTemp1,
                sizeof( szTemp1 ) );
    LoadString( hInst, IDS_INI_SECTION_NAME, szTemp2,
                sizeof( szTemp2 ) );
    nTermEmu = GetPrivateProfileInt( szTemp2,
                        "Terminal Emulation", 1, szTemp1 );

    //
    // initialize the terminal emulation (if there is one)
    //
    StartTerminalEmulation( hWnd );
    break;

case WM_SIZE:
    //
    // is it external terminal emulation?
    //
    if ( !bTerminalEmulation ) {
        //
        // use the internal TTY emulation
        //
        // save the number of rows and columns in the client
        // area
        //
        nRows = HIWORD( lParam ) /  nYChar;
        nCols = LOWORD( lParam ) /  nXChar;

        //
        // change the current location back to 0,0
        //
        nCurrRow = nCurrCol = 0;
```

```
            //
            // invalidate the client area so it can be redrawn
            //
            InvalidateRect( hWnd, NULL, TRUE );
        } else {
            //
            // call the terminal emulation process size routine
            //
            if ( lpfnTE_ProcessSize )
                lpfnTE_ProcessSize( hWnd, lParam );
        }
        break;

    case WM_SETFOCUS:
        //
        // receiving the focus
        //
        if ( !bTerminalEmulation ) {
            //
            // use internal TTY emulation
            //
            CreateCaret( hWnd, NULL, nXChar, nYChar );
            SetCaretPos( nCurrCol * nXChar, nCurrRow * nYChar );
            ShowCaret( hWnd );
        } else {
            //
            // use the external emulation
            //
            if ( lpfnTE_ProcessFocus )
                lpfnTE_ProcessFocus( hWnd, TRUE );
        }
        break;

    case WM_KILLFOCUS:
        //
        // losing the focus
        //
        if ( !bTerminalEmulation ) {
            //
            // use internal TTY emulation
            //
            HideCaret( hWnd );
            DestroyCaret();
        } else {
            //
```

continues

Listing 3.11. continued

```
                // use the external emulation
                //
                if ( lpfnTE_ProcessFocus )
                    lpfnTE_ProcessFocus( hWnd, FALSE );
            }
            break;

        case WM_COMMAND:
            //
            // process the command based on the menu item
            //
            switch( wParam ) {
                case IDM_EXIT:
                    //
                    // the user selected EXIT from the File menu.
                    // Send a WM_CLOSE message to the window.
                    //
                    SendMessage( hWnd, WM_CLOSE, 0, 0L );
                    break;

                case IDM_PREFERENCES_SETTINGS:
                    LoadString( hInst, IDS_SETTINGS_DIALOG, szTemp1,
                                sizeof( szTemp1 ) );
                    if ( DialogBox( hInst, szTemp1, hWnd,
                                    SettingDialogProc ) ) {
                        //
                        // close the open port
                        //
                        TSMCloseComm( nComId );

                        //
                        // open the port with the new settings
                        //
                        if ( !OpenTermPort() ) {
                            //
                            // the reopen failed, so issue an error
                            // message
                            //
                            LoadString( hInst, IDS_BAD_SETTINGS,
                                        szTemp1, sizeof( szTemp1 ) );
                            wsprintf( szTemp2, szTemp1, nComId );
                            if ( MessageBox( hWnd, szTemp2, szTSMTerm,
                                    MB_ICONSTOP | MB_YESNO ) == IDNO ) {
                                //
```

```
                    // send a close message to terminate the
                    // application
                    //
                    SendMessage( hWnd, WM_CLOSE, 0, 0L );

                    //
                    // indicate that the resetting failed
                    //
                    lResult = 1;
                    break;
                } else {
                    //
                    // the user wants to rerun the Settings
                    // dialog box
                    //
                    if ( SendMessage( hWnd, WM_COMMAND,
                        IDM_PREFERENCES_SETTINGS, 0L ) == 1 ) {
                        //
                        // it still failed, so close the
                        // application
                        //
                        SendMessage( hWnd, WM_CLOSE, 0, 0L );

                        //
                        // indicate that the resetting failed
                        //
                        lResult = 1;
                        break;
                    }
                }
            }
        }
        break;

    case IDM_PREFERENCES_TE:
        //
        // run the terminal emulation selection dialog
        //
        LoadString( hInst, IDS_TE_DIALOG, szTemp1,
                    sizeof( szTemp1 ) );
        if ( DialogBox( hInst, szTemp1, hWnd,
                        TermEmuDialogProc ) ) {
            //
            // if the user selected OK, stop the old
            // terminal emulation
```

continues

Listing 3.11. continued

```
            //
            StopTerminalEmulation( hWnd );

            //
            // then start the new terminal emulation
            //
            StartTerminalEmulation( hWnd );

            //
            // send a fake WM_SIZE to the window
            //
            GetClientRect( hWnd, &ClientRect );
            SendMessage( hWnd, WM_SIZE, SIZE_RESTORED,
                        MAKELONG( ClientRect.right,
                                    ClientRect.bottom ) );
        }
        break;

    case IDM_PREFERENCES_DUPLEX:
        //
        // either check or uncheck the menu item
        //
        hMenu = GetMenu( hWnd );
        hPeferences = GetSubMenu( hMenu, 1 );
        bChecked = GetMenuState( hPeferences,
                    IDM_PREFERENCES_DUPLEX, MF_BYCOMMAND );
        CheckMenuItem( hPeferences, IDM_PREFERENCES_DUPLEX,
                        MF_BYCOMMAND ¦
                        ( bChecked == MF_CHECKED ?
                        MF_UNCHECKED : MF_CHECKED ) );

        //
        // set the global duplex flag
        //
        bFullDuplex = ( bChecked == MF_CHECKED ?
                        FALSE : TRUE );

        //
        // save the value in the .INI file
        //
        LoadString( hInst, IDS_INI_FILE_NAME, szTemp1,
                    sizeof( szTemp1 ) );
        LoadString( hInst, IDS_INI_SECTION_NAME, szTemp2,
                    sizeof( szTemp2 ) );
```

```
                    lstrcpy( szValue, (bFullDuplex ? "TRUE" :
                            "FALSE" ) );
                    WritePrivateProfileString( szTemp2, "Duplex",
                                               szValue, szTemp1 );
                    break;

            case IDM_HELP_INDEX:
                LoadString( hInst, IDS_HELP_TSMTERM, szTemp1,
                            sizeof( szTemp1 ) );
                WinHelp( hWnd, szTemp1, HELP_CONTENTS, 0L );
                break;

            case IDM_HELP_USINGHELP:
                LoadString( hInst, IDS_HELP_USINGHELP_FILE,
                            szTemp1, sizeof( szTemp1 ) );
                WinHelp( hWnd, szTemp1, HELP_HELPONHELP, 0L );
                break;

            case IDM_HELP_ABOUT:
                LoadString( hInst, IDS_ABOUT_DIALOG, szTemp1,
                            sizeof( szTemp1 ) );
                DialogBox( hInst, szTemp1, hWnd,
                           AboutDialogProc );
                break;

            default:
                fCallDef = TRUE;
                break;
        }
        break;

    case WM_CHAR:
        //
        // process keystrokes
        //
        switch( wParam ) {
            default:
                //
                // normal keys are sent to the serial port
                //
                TSMWriteComm( nComId, 1, (LPCSTR)&wParam );

                //
                // and written to the screen if not in full-duplex
                // mode
                //
```

Listing 3.11. continued

```
                     if ( !bFullDuplex ) {
                        //
                        // check for an external terminal emulation
                        //
                        szTemp1[0] = (char)wParam;
                        szTemp1[1] = '\0';
                        if ( !bTerminalEmulation ) {
                           //
                           // use the internal TTY emulation
                           //
                           TTYWriteScreen( hWnd, szTemp1 );
                        } else {
                           //
                           // use the external emulation
                           //
                           lpfnTE_ProcessChars( hWnd, szTemp1, 1 );
                        }
                     }
                     break;
               }
               break;

         case WM_COMM_CHARS:
            //
            // check for an external terminal emulation
            //
            if ( !bTerminalEmulation ) {
               //
               // use the internal TTY emulation
               //
               _fstrncpy( szTemp1, (LPSTR)lParam, wParam );
               szTemp1[wParam] = '\0';
               TTYWriteScreen( hWnd, szTemp1 );
            } else {
               //
               // use the external emulation
               //
               lpfnTE_ProcessChars( hWnd, (LPCSTR)lParam, wParam );
            }
            break;

         case WM_ERASEBKGND:
            //
```

```
    // process only for the internal emulation
    //
    if ( !bTerminalEmulation ) {
        //
        // change the current location back to 0, 0
        //
        nCurrRow = nCurrCol = 0;
    }

    //
    // call the default routine
    //
    fCallDef = TRUE;
    break;

case WM_PAINT:
    //
    // process this only if you're using an external
    // emulation
    //
    if ( bTerminalEmulation ) {
        //
        // call the process paint function
        //
        if ( lpfnTE_ProcessPaint )
            lpfnTE_ProcessPaint( hWnd );
        else
            fCallDef = TRUE;
    } else {
        //
        // call the default routine if you're using
        // internal emulation
        //
        fCallDef = TRUE;
    }
    break;

case WM_CLOSE:
    //
    // send a message to help to close it
    //
    WinHelp( hWnd, NULL, HELP_QUIT, 0L );

    //
    // terminate the terminal emulation
    //
```

Listing 3.11. continued

```
                if ( bTerminalEmulation ) {
                    //
                    // stop the terminal emulation
                    //
                    StopTerminalEmulation( hWnd );
                }

                //
                // close the communications port
                //
                if ( nComId >= 0 )
                    TSMCloseComm( nComId );

                //
                // destroy the terminal window
                //
                DestroyWindow( hWnd );

                //
                // post a quit message to terminate the program
                //
                PostQuitMessage( 0 );
                break;

            default:
                //
                // call the default routine
                //
                fCallDef = TRUE;
                break;
        }

        //
        // call the default window procedure or return lResult
        //
        if ( fCallDef )
            return( DefWindowProc( hWnd, msg, wParam, lParam ) );
        else
            return( lResult );
    }
```

```
//
// TTYWriteScreen
//
void TTYWriteScreen( HWND hWnd, LPSTR lpOutString )
{
    //
    // automatic variables
    //
    int    i;
    HDC    hDC;
    LPSTR lpCurrChar;

    //
    // get a device context for the client area
    //
    hDC = GetDC( hWnd );
    SelectObject( hDC, GetStockObject( OEM_FIXED_FONT ) );

    //
    // hide the caret
    //
    HideCaret( hWnd );

    //
    // loop through the character string
    //
    for ( lpCurrChar = lpOutString; *lpCurrChar; lpCurrChar++ ) {
        //
        // process each character
        //
        switch ( *lpCurrChar ) {
            case VK_RETURN:
                //
                // process a carriage return
                //
                nCurrCol = 0;
                break;

            case 0xA:
                //
                // process a new line
                //
                nCurrRow++;
                if ( nCurrRow == ( nRows - 1 ) ) {
                    ValidateRect( hWnd, NULL );
```

continues

Listing 3.11. continued

```
            ScrollWindow( hWnd, 0, -nYChar, NULL, NULL );
            UpdateWindow( hWnd );
            nCurrRow = nRows - 2;
        }
        break;

    default:
        //
        // process the "normal" characters
        //
        TextOut( hDC, nCurrCol * nXChar, nCurrRow * nYChar,
                lpCurrChar, 1 );
        nCurrCol++;
        if ( nCurrCol == ( nCols - 1 ) ) {
            //
            // move to the next line
            //
            nCurrCol = 0;
            nCurrRow++;

            //
            // check whether window needs to be scrolled
            //
            if ( nCurrRow == ( nRows - 1 ) ) {
                ScrollWindow( hWnd, 0, -nYChar, NULL, NULL );
                nCurrRow = nRows - 2;
            }
        }
        break;
    }
}

//
// update the caret position and show it
//
SetCaretPos( nCurrCol * nXChar, nCurrRow * nYChar );
ShowCaret( hWnd );

//
// release the device context
//
ReleaseDC( hWnd, hDC );
}
```

```
//
// StartTerminalEmulation
//
void   StartTerminalEmulation( HWND hWnd )
{
   //
   // automatic variables
   //
   UINT   uOldError;

   //
   // get the current emulation name from the string table
   //
   switch( nTermEmu ) {
      case TTY_EMU:
         szTemp1[0] = '\0';
         break;

      case ANSI_EMU:
         LoadString( hInst, IDS_ANSI_EMU_DLL, szTemp1,
                     sizeof( szTemp1 ) );
         break;
      default:
         szTemp1[0] = '\0';
         break;
   }

   //
   // if the emulation is TTY, set the emulation flag and quit
   //
   if ( szTemp1[0] == '\0' ) {
      bTerminalEmulation = FALSE;
      nTermEmu = TTY_EMU;
      return;
   }

   //
   // load the terminal emulation library
   //
   uOldError = SetErrorMode( SEM_NOOPENFILEERRORBOX );
   hInstTE = LoadLibrary( "ANSITERM.DLL" );
   SetErrorMode( uOldError );
   if ( hInstTE > HINSTANCE_ERROR ) {
      //
      // the library was loaded, so get the address of the
```

continues

Listing 3.11. continued

```
// initialization routine
//
if ( !(lpfnTE_Initialize = GetProcAddress( hInstTE,
                                    "TE_Initialize" ) ) ) {
   //
   // no address was gotten, so free the library and set the
   // terminal emulation flag
   //
   FreeLibrary( hInstTE );
   bTerminalEmulation = FALSE;
   nTermEmu = TTY_EMU;
} else {
   //
   // call the initialization routine
   //
   if ( !lpfnTE_Initialize( hWnd ) ) {
      //
      // the initialization failed, so free the library and
      // set the terminal emulation flag
      //
      FreeLibrary( hInstTE );
      bTerminalEmulation = FALSE;
      nTermEmu = TTY_EMU;
   } else {
      //
      // the initialization worked, so load the addresses of
      // the remaining terminal emulation functions
      //
      lpfnTE_ProcessChars      =  GetProcAddress(
                              hInstTE, "TE_ProcessChars" );
      lpfnTE_ProcessPaint      =  GetProcAddress(
                              hInstTE, "TE_ProcessPaint" );
      lpfnTE_ProcessSize       =  GetProcAddress(
                              hInstTE, "TE_ProcessSize" );
      lpfnTE_ProcessFocus      =  GetProcAddress(
                              hInstTE, "TE_ProcessFocus" );
      lpfnTE_Terminate         =  GetProcAddress(
                              hInstTE, "TE_Terminate" );
      //
      // set the terminal emulation flag to TRUE
      //
      bTerminalEmulation = TRUE;
   }
```

```
        }
    } else {
        //
        // the library was not loaded, so set the terminal emulation
        // flag to FALSE
        //
        bTerminalEmulation = FALSE;
        nTermEmu = TTY_EMU;
    }
}


//
// StopTerminalEmulation
//
void StopTerminalEmulation( HWND hWnd )
{
    //
    // if you're using an external emulation, call the
    // terminate routine
    //
    if ( bTerminalEmulation )
        if ( lpfnTE_Terminate )
            lpfnTE_Terminate( hWnd );

    //
    // reset the terminal emulation flag
    //
    bTerminalEmulation = FALSE;

    //
    // free the terminal emulation library
    //
    if ( hInstTE )
        FreeLibrary( hInstTE );
}
```

Processing the WM_CREATE Message

The WM_CREATE message is sent to the window procedure when `CreateWindow()` is called. WM_CREATE handles most of the initialization for TSMTerm. This processing was shown in Listing 3.11. The WM_CREATE processing starts by getting and

saving the character width and height for the internal TTY emulation. Next, the program tries to open the communications port by calling OpenTermPort(). This routine opens the serial communications port using the parameters stored in the private .INI file named TSMTERM.INI. This routine, shown in Listing 3.12, reads the parameters from the .INI file and converts them to the values needed for the TSMOpenComm() call.

Listing 3.12. TTOPNPRT.C OpenTermPort() routine.

```
//
// TSM Terminal Program
//
// ttopnprt.c
//
// open communications port using .INI file settings
//
// BOOL OpenTermPort( void )
//
// parameters:
//    None
//
// returns:
//    TRUE  if successful
//    FALSE if an error occurred
//


//
// system include files
//
#include <windows.h>
#pragma hdrstop

//
// local include files
//
#include "..\tsmcomm\tsmcomm.h"
#include "tsmterm.h"
#include "ttglobal.h"
#include "ttstring.h"

//
// OpenTermPort
//
BOOL OpenTermPort( void )
{
```

```
//
// automatic variables
//
char szCommPort[6], szTempParity[2], szItemName[10];
int nTempDataBits, nTempStopBits;
UINT uTempBaudRate;
WORD wBaudRate, wParity, wDataBits, wStopBits;

//
// load the filename and section name
//
LoadString( hInst, IDS_INI_FILE_NAME, szTemp1,
            sizeof( szTemp1 ) );
LoadString( hInst, IDS_INI_SECTION_NAME, szTemp2,
            sizeof( szTemp2 ) );

//
// initialize the automatic variables
//
LoadString( hInst, IDS_INI_COM_PORT, szItemName,
            sizeof( szItemName ) );
GetPrivateProfileString( szTemp2, szItemName, "COM1",
                szCommPort, sizeof( szCommPort ), szTemp1 );
LoadString( hInst, IDS_INI_PARITY, szItemName,
            sizeof( szItemName ) );
GetPrivateProfileString( szTemp2, szItemName, "N",
              szTempParity, sizeof( szTempParity ), szTemp1 );
LoadString( hInst, IDS_INI_BAUD_RATE, szItemName,
            sizeof( szItemName ) );
nTempBaudRate = GetPrivateProfileInt( szTemp2, szItemName,
                                  2400, szTemp1 );
LoadString( hInst, IDS_INI_DATA_BITS, szItemName,
            sizeof( szItemName ) );
nTempDataBits = GetPrivateProfileInt( szTemp2, szItemName,
                                   8, szTemp1 );
LoadString( hInst, IDS_INI_STOP_BITS, szItemName,
            sizeof( szItemName ) );
nTempStopBits = GetPrivateProfileInt( szTemp2, szItemName, 1,
                                  szTemp1 );

//
// set up the baud rate's word value
//
wBaudRate= (WORD)uTempBaudRate;
```

continues

155

Listing 3.12. continued

```
//
// set up the parity's word value
//
switch( szTempParity[0] ) {
  case 'N':
     wParity = NOPARITY;
     break;

  case 'E':
     wParity = EVENPARITY;
     break;

  case 'O':
     wParity = ODDPARITY;
     break;

  case 'M':
     wParity = MARKPARITY;
     break;

  case 'S':
     wParity = SPACEPARITY;
     break;

  default:
     wParity = NOPARITY;
     break;
}

//
// set up the data bits' word value
//
switch ( nTempDataBits ) {
  case 7:
     wDataBits = SEVENDATABITS;
     break;

  case 8:
     wDataBits = EIGHTDATABITS;
     break;
```

```
    default:
        wDataBits = EIGHTDATABITS;
        break;
}

//
// set up the stop bit's word value
//
switch ( nTempStopBits ) {
    case 1:
        wStopBits = ONESTOPBIT;
        break;

    case 2:
        wStopBits = ONE5STOPBITS;
        break;

    case 3:
        wStopBits = TWOSTOPBITS;
        break;

    default:
        wStopBits = ONESTOPBIT;
        break;
}

//
// attempt to open the communications port
//
nComId = TSMOpenComm( szCommPort, wBaudRate, wParity,
                      wDataBits, wStopBits, 4096, 4096 );

//
// return to the calling program
//
if ( nComId >= 0 )
    return TRUE;
else
    return FALSE;
}
```

If the serial port does not open correctly, the user gets the option of running the Communication Settings dialog box (discussed later) or terminating the program. Next, the WM_CREATE processing sets the duplex flag. When the

full-duplex flag is set, TSMTerm expects the remote system to echo characters back to the program. When the flag is not set, the program automatically puts the character on the screen. The initial value of the full-duplex flag comes from the TSMTERM.INI file. Then the program enables polled communications and reads the terminal emulation setting from TSMTERM.INI.

After the program has the terminal emulation setting, it calls StartTerminalEmulation() to begin the terminal emulation. This routine, shown in Listing 3.11, begins by loading the library name from the string table or forcing it to NULL. The program then checks for a NULL name; if the name is NULL, the program uses the internal TTY emulation. The global variable bTerminalEmulation is TRUE if the program is using an external emulation and FALSE if it is using the internal emulation.

When using an external emulation, the program tries to load the DLL. The routine does not call any of the routines in the DLL explicitly. This means that the program can use different terminal emulations just by loading a different DLL. Each emulation must have the same function names and expect the same parameters though. If the library loaded correctly, the program gets the procedure address for TE_Initialize(), calling it to start the terminal emulation. The program then gets the procedure address for the rest of the defined entry points to the terminal emulation library. These pointers are used throughout the program to access the terminal emulation functions.

Processing the WM_SIZE Message

The WM_SIZE message is sent to the window every time the size of the window is changed. The message also is sent once at startup, so the program knows how big the initial window is. TSMTermWndProc() processing for WM_SIZE differs by terminal emulation. With TTY emulation, the number of rows and columns on the screen is calculated. The current row and column are then set back to 0, and the entire client area is invalidated. However, with external emulation, the external routine TE_ProcessSize() is called to do any processing.

Processing the Focus Messages

The processing for WM_SETFOCUS and WM_KILLFOCUS are closely related. For external emulations, they both call TE_ProcessFocus() with the parameters set accordingly. Using the TTY emulation, the WM_SETFOCUS creates, places, and shows the caret, whereas WM_KILLFOCUS hides and destroys the caret. This processing was shown in Listing 3.11.

Processing the WM_COMMAND Message

The WM_COMMAND message is used only for the application menu in TSMTerm. The application menu has three submenus. Each of these submenus has menu items that cause the WM_COMMAND message to be sent to the window. The word parameter of the WM_COMMAND message contains an identification value that specifies which control caused the message to be sent. The WM_COMMAND processing is a switch statement based on that identification value. Each of the drop-down menus is covered in turn next.

File Menu

The only menu item available on the File menu is Exit, as seen in Figure 3.3. Clicking Exit sends the IDM_EXIT command to the window procedure. When processing this command, TSMTermWndProc() sends a WM_CLOSE command to itself. The WM_CLOSE command is covered in a later section.

Preferences Menu

The Preferences menu contains three items—Settings, Terminal Emulation..., and Full Duplex, as shown in Figure 3.4. When Settings is selected, an IDM_PREFERENCES_SETTINGS command is sent. This command displays the Communication Settings dialog box, shown in Figure 3.5. In this box, the user selects the communications parameters used by TSMTerm. The dialog window processing is done in the source file, TTSETTNG.C. It is straightforward and therefore is not listed here. When you are processing the IDM_PREFERENCES_SETTINGS command, if the dialog box returns a TRUE value, the currently open serial port is closed, and the new settings are used to open another port. If this process fails, the user gets the option of running the Communication Settings dialog box again. If the process fails again, the application terminates.

Figure 3.3.
File menu.

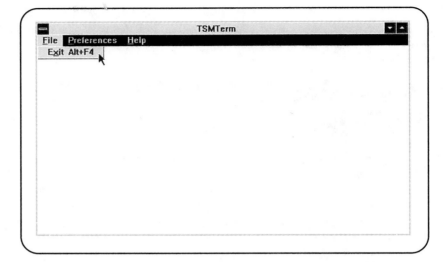

Figure 3.4.
Preferences
menu.

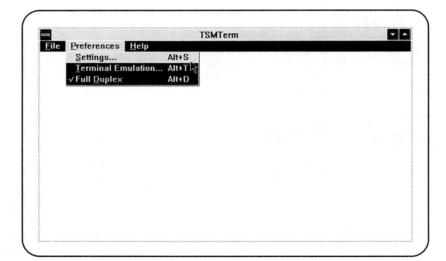

160

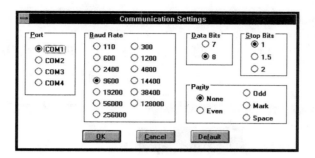

Figure 3.5. Communication Settings dialog box.

Clicking the **T**erminal Emulation menu item brings up the Terminal Emulation dialog box, shown in Figure 3.6. This dialog-box processing is done in the file TTTRMEMU.C. Once again, the dialog-box processing is straightforward and is not listed here. If a user selects either TTY or ANSI terminal emulation in the dialog box, the current emulation is stopped and the new one is started. This code is shown in Listing 3.11. Finally a WM_SIZE command is sent for the new terminal emulation.

Figure 3.6. Terminal Emulation dialog box.

The last menu item on the **P**references menu is the Full **D**uplex selection. This menu item works as a toggle switch rather than presenting a dialog box. The menu item has a check mark next to it when it is active and no check mark when it is inactive. When full-duplex mode is active, TSMTerm expects the remote system to send all characters to be displayed to it; without full-duplex mode, TSMTerm automatically displays the characters the user types. During processing, the program first checks or unchecks the menu item, then updates the global variable and the TSMTERM.INI file.

Help Menu

The final application menu item is the **H**elp menu, shown in Figure 3.7. The menu enables access to help about TSMTerm. The menu also has an item

that displays the About box for this application. Selecting either of the first two help choices sends an IDM_HELP_INDEX or IDM_HELP_USINGHELP to the window procedure. These two commands load a help file using **WinHelp()**.

Figure 3.7.
Help menu.

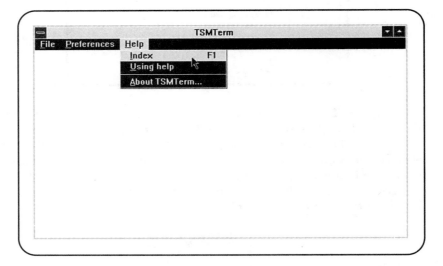

The final item on the **H**elp menu is **A**bout TSMTerm.... Clicking this menu item sends an IDM_HELP_ABOUT command. This command starts the About TsmTerm dialog box. The box is shown in Figure 3.8, and its processing is shown in Listing 3.13.

Figure 3.8.
About
TSMTerm
dialog box.

Listing 3.13. TTABOUT.C AboutDialogProc() routine.

```
//
// TSM Terminal Program
//
// ttabout.c
//
// TSM Terminal About dialog procedure
```

```
//
// BOOL FAR PASCAL _export AboutDialogProc( HWND hDlg, UINT wMsg,
//                                          WPARAM wParam,
//                                          LPARAM lParam )
//
// parameters:
//     HWND      hDlg       handle to the dialog window
//     UINT      wMsg       window message being sent
//     WPARAM    wParam     word parameter of the message
//     LPARAM    lParam     long parameter of the message
//
// returns:
//     TRUE   if the message has been processed
//     FALSE  if the message is not processed
//

//
// system includes
//
#include <windows.h>
#ifdef __BORLANDC__
#pragma hdrstop
#endif
#include <stdlib.h>

//
// local includes
//
#include "tsmterm.h"
#include "ttglobal.h"
#include "ttabout.h"
#include "ttver.h"

//
// AboutDialogProc
//
#ifdef __BORLANDC__
#pragma argsused
#endif
BOOL CALLBACK _export AboutDialogProc( HWND hDlg, UINT wMsg,
                                       WPARAM wParam,
                                       LPARAM lParam )
{
   //
   // automatic variables
```

continues

Listing 3.13. continued

```
//
BOOL  bProcessed = TRUE;

//
// process based on the message type
//
switch( wMsg )
{
   case WM_INITDIALOG:
      //
      // update the version number field
      //
      SetWindowText( GetDlgItem( hDlg, ABOUT_VERSION ),
                     TSM_VERSION_TEXT );
      break;

   case WM_COMMAND:
      switch( wParam )
      {
         case IDOK:
            //
            // exit indicating that the comm port
            // needs to be reset
            //
            EndDialog( hDlg, TRUE );
            break;

         default:
            bProcessed = FALSE;
            break;
      }
      break;

   default:
      bProcessed = FALSE;
      break;
}

return( bProcessed );
}
```

This procedure handles two messages: WM_INITDIALOG and WM_COMMAND. When the program receives the WM_INITDIALOG message, it places the version number into a field of the dialog box. When the program receives a WM_COMMAND with the IDOK word parameter, it ends the dialog processing.

Processing the WM_CHAR Message

When TSMTermWndProc() receives a WM_CHAR message, it processes the message as shown in Listing 3.11. First, the character is sent to the remote system using TSMWriteComm(). Next, if the program is not in full-duplex mode, the character is either displayed on the screen in TTY emulation or sent to the TE_ProcessChars() function of the external emulation.

Processing the WM_COMM_CHARS Message

The WM_COMM_CHARS emulation is sent by TSMCOMM.DLL when it receives characters through the serial port. The characters are displayed on the screen by calling either TE_ProcessChars() for an external terminal emulation or TTYWriteScreen() for the internal TTY emulation. TTYWriteScreen() is presented in Listing 3.11.

Processing the WM_ERASEBKGND Message

The WM_ERASEBKGND message is only processed for the internal TTY terminal emulation. This message is sent when the background of the window has been erased. It resets the current row and column to the HOME position because the TTY emulation does not save the screen for redisplay.

Processing the WM_PAINT Message

The WM_PAINT message is processed only for the external terminal emulations. The TE_ProcessPaint() function is called when this message is received.

Processing the WM_CLOSE Message

The final message that TSMTermWndProc() handles is WM_CLOSE. The program receives this message when the application is being terminated. Therefore, the program does its cleanup during this message, as seen in Listing 3.11. First, it sends a HELP_QUIT indication to the Windows Help system, terminating the help application. Next, the program stops the external terminal emulation (if it is using one) by calling StopTerminalEmulation().

StopTerminalEmulation() calls the TE_Terminate() function of the external emulation and resets the terminal emulation global variable. Finally, it frees the terminal emulation DLL.

WM_CLOSE closes the communications port by calling TSMCloseComm(). It then destroys the window. Finally, **PostQuitMessage()** is called. This places a WM_QUIT message in the message queue, causing the message-processing loop and TSMTerm to terminate.

Summary

This chapter closely covered the ANSI terminal specification and ANSITERM.DLL, your program's implementation of that specification. The chapter also presented the first version of TSMTerm, both its overall structure and how the terminal emulation processing is built into the program. The next chapter adds event, error, and flow control processing to both the TSM Communications API and TSMTerm.

Errors, Events, and Flow Control

T he first versions of the TSM Communications API and TSMTerm have ignored errors for the most part and events completely. In this chapter, however, you'll examine

- Communications errors that Windows recognizes and how error processing can be added to your programs.

- Communications events that Windows recognizes and how event processing can be added to your programs.

- Flow control and how it can be added to your programs.

Communications Errors

The Windows communications driver detects a host of errors that the communications programmer needs to be aware of. There is a problem with Windows error handling—when an error occurs, Windows locks the communications port until the error is cleared by calling **GetCommError()**. This function should be called after every read from or write to a communications port. It also would be wise to call it during the message loop when you use the polling method of communications. **GetCommError()** returns an integer value that is a combination of error values, as listed in Table 4.1. A 0 return value indicates that no errors were detected.

Table 4.1. GetCommError() error values.

Value	Description
CE_BREAK	A BREAK condition has been detected on the communications line.
CE_CTSTO	Clear-To-Send timeout. The CTS line has been low for the period of time given by CtsTimeout in the DCB while a character has been waiting to be transmitted.
CE_DSRTO	Data-Set-Ready timeout. The DSR line has been low for the period of time given by DsrTimeout in the DCB while a character has been waiting to be transmitted.

continues

Table 4.1. continued

Value	Description
CE_FRAME	A hardware framing error occurred.
CE_MODE	The requested mode is not available. If this error occurs, it is the only valid error in the return value.
CE_OVERRUN	A hardware overrun error occurred.
CE_RLSDTO	Receive-Line-Signal-Detect timeout. The RLSD, more commonly known as Carrier Detect (CD), was low for the amount of time specified by RlsTimeout in the DCB while a character has been waiting to be transmitted.
CE_RXOVER	The input queue was out of room when a character was received.
CE_RXPARITY	A hardware parity error occurred.
CE_TXFULL	An attempt was made to write a character to the transmit queue while it was full.

Note: Windows defines other error values also. The values not shown in Table 4.1 are used for parallel communications. They are not needed for this book.

There are as many methods of processing errors as there are communications programs. The method you select for your program depends on the reliability needed from the communications link and the amount of information needed by the program's users. Your communications API and terminal program implement two methods of error handling. First, the program counts the number of errors that occur during the communications session. Second, the program displays each error as it occurs. These error-handling methods are called COUNT and DISPLAY.

TSMCOMM Modifications

Implementing the COUNT and DISPLAY error-handling methods requires modifications and additions to the TSM Communications API. These routines must be modified to call `GetCommError()` and process the information that the function returns. In addition, there must be a way for programmers to set which error-handling method they want to use. This functionality is provided by `TSMSetErrorProcessing()`, shown in Listing 4.1. This routine enables users to set either `COUNT` or `DISPLAY` mode. `TSMSetErrorProcessing()` accepts two parameters—the port ID and the error-handling mode (either the value `ERROR_COUNT` or `ERROR_DISPLAY`). These values are defined in TSMCOMM.H. First the function ensures that there's an open communications port and that the port IDs are the same. If not, the routine returns an error. Next, the function ensures that the error method is within range, again returning an error if the method is out of range. Finally, the error-processing method is stored in the global variable `nErrorHandling`. This global variable is initialized to `ERROR_COUNT` when the library is loaded.

Listing 4.1. TCSETERR.C `TSMSetErrorProcessing()` routine.

```
//
// TSM Communications API DLL
//
// tcseterr.c
//
// set error-processing type
//
// int FAR PASCAL _export TSMSetErrorProcessing( int nComId,
//                                                int nErrorType )
//
// parameters:
//    int   nComId      ID of comm port to write to
//    int   nErrorType  type of error processing required
//
// returns:
//    0  if successful
//    <0 if an error occurred
//


//
// system include files
//
#include <windows.h>
#ifdef _ _BORLANDC_ _
#pragma hdrstop
#endif
```

continues

Listing 4.1. continued

```c
//
// local include files
//
#include "tsmcomm.h"
#include "tcglobal.h"


//
// TSMSetErrorProcessing
//
int FAR PASCAL _export TSMSetErrorProcessing( int nComId,
                                              int nErrorType )
{
   //
   // make sure that there's a COM port open
   //
   if ( !hTSMCommInfo )
      return( IE_NOPEN );


   //
   // lock the CommInfo structure and ensure that the ComIds
   // are the same
   //
   lpTSMCommInfo = (LPTSMCOMMINFO)GlobalLock( hTSMCommInfo );
   if ( lpTSMCommInfo->ComId != nComId ) {
      GlobalUnlock( hTSMCommInfo );
      return( IE_NOPEN );
   }
   GlobalUnlock( hTSMCommInfo );


   //
   // make sure that the error-processing type is correct
   //
   if ( nErrorType < ERROR_COUNT ¦¦ nErrorType > ERROR_DISPLAY ) {
      //
      // argument out of range, so return an error
      //
      return( IE_DEFAULT );
   }


   //
   // set the error-processing type
   //
   nErrorHandling = nErrorType;
```

```
    //
    // return that everything worked
    //
    return( 0 );
}
```

The program also needs to be able to retrieve the current error-handling method. TSMGetErrorProcessing() returns this information. The routine starts by checking that a communications port has been opened and that the IDs are the same. It then returns the current processing method, either ERROR_COUNT or ERROR_DISPLAY. TSMGetErrorProcessing() is presented in Listing 4.2.

Listing 4.2. TCGETERR.C TSMGetErrorProcessing() routine.

```
//
// TSM Communications API DLL
//
// tcgeterr.c
//
// get error-processing type
//
// int FAR PASCAL _export TSMGetErrorProcessing( int nComId )
//
// parameters:
//    int    nComId      ID of comm port to write to
//
// returns:
//    >0   error processing type
//    <0   if an error is found
//

//
// system include files
//
#include <windows.h>
#ifdef _ _BORLANDC_ _
#pragma hdrstop
#endif

//
// local include files
//
#include "tsmcomm.h"
#include "tcglobal.h"
```

continues

Listing 4.2. continued

```
//
// TSMSetErrorProcessing
//
int FAR PASCAL _export TSMGetErrorProcessing( int nComId )
{
   //
   // check to make sure there's a COM port open
   //
   if ( !hTSMCommInfo )
      return( IE_NOPEN );

   //
   // lock the CommInfo structure and ensure that the ComIds
   // are the same
   //
   lpTSMCommInfo = (LPTSMCOMMINFO)GlobalLock( hTSMCommInfo );
   if ( lpTSMCommInfo->ComId != nComId ) {
      GlobalUnlock( hTSMCommInfo );
      return( IE_NOPEN );
   }
   GlobalUnlock( hTSMCommInfo );

   //
   // return the current error-processing type
   //
   return( nErrorHandling );
}
```

Now you need to add error checking after each read and write your program makes. Also, your program needs to check for errors during the message loop. These additions are made to the TSM Communications API routines. For error checking during transmission, modify the routine TSMWriteComm(). The addition is simple: call **GetCommError()** if **WriteComm()**, by returning a negative number, indicates that an error occurred. If the return value from **GetCommError()** is nonzero, TSMProcessCommError() is called, as shown in the following section of code taken from TSMWriteComm().

```
//
// get the error from Windows and process it
//
nCommError = GetCommError( nComId, NULL );
if ( nCommError )
   TSMProcessCommError( nComId, nCommError );
```

TSMProcessCommError() is an internal routine of TSMCOMM.DLL not available to the application programmer. It takes the port ID and the error value returned by **GetCommError()** as parameters, as shown in Listing 4.3.

Listing 4.3. TCPRCERR.C **TSMProcessCommError()** routine.

```
//
// TSM Communications API DLL
//
// tcprcerr.c
//
// process any errors that occur
//
// int TSMProcessCommError( int nComId, int nError )
//
// parameters:
//    int nComId  ID of comm port to write to
//    int nError  error flags returned by GetCommError()
//
// returns:
//    0  if successful
//    <0 if an error occurred
//


//
// system include files
//
#include <windows.h>
#ifdef __BORLANDC__
#pragma hdrstop
#endif


//
// local include files
//
#include "tsmcomm.h"
#include "tcglobal.h"


//
// TSMProcessCommError
//
#ifdef __BORLANDC__
#pragma argsused
#endif
int TSMProcessCommError( int nComId, int nError )
```

continues

Listing 4.3. continued

```c
{
    //
    // automatic variables
    //

    //
    // process the error based on the error-handling flag as set
    // by the user
    //
    switch ( nErrorHandling ) {
       case ERROR_COUNT:
          //
          // increment the global error variables
          //
          if ( nError & CE_MODE )
             nCEMode++;
          else {
             if ( nError & CE_BREAK )
                nCEBreak++;
             if ( nError & CE_CTSTO )
                nCECtsTO++;
             if ( nError & CE_DSRTO )
                nCEDsrTO++;
             if ( nError & CE_FRAME )
                nCEFrame++;
             if ( nError & CE_OVERRUN )
                nCEOverrun++;
             if ( nError & CE_RLSDTO )
                nCERlsdTO++;
             if ( nError & CE_RXOVER )
                nCERXOver++;
             if ( nError & CE_RXPARITY )
                nCERXParity++;
             if ( nError & CE_TXFULL )
                nCETXFull++;
          }
          break;

       case ERROR_DISPLAY:
          //
          // create the error string to be displayed
          //
          lstrcpy( szTemp1,
           "The following communications error(s) occurred:\n\n" );
          if ( nError & CE_MODE )
```

```
            lstrcat( szTemp1, "MODE ERROR" );
        else {
            if ( nError & CE_BREAK )
                lstrcat( szTemp1, "BREAK DETECTED\n\n" );
            if ( nError & CE_CTSTO )
                lstrcat( szTemp1, "CTS TIMEOUT\n\n" );
            if ( nError & CE_DSRTO )
                lstrcat( szTemp1, "DSR TIMEOUT\n\n" );
            if ( nError & CE_FRAME )
                lstrcat( szTemp1, "FRAMING ERROR\n\n" );
            if ( nError & CE_OVERRUN )
                lstrcat( szTemp1, "OVERRUN ERROR\n\n" );
            if ( nError & CE_RLSDTO )
                lstrcat( szTemp1, "RLSD (CD) TIMEOUT\n\n" );
            if ( nError & CE_RXOVER )
                lstrcat( szTemp1, "RECEIVE QUEUE OVERFLOW\n\n" );
            if ( nError & CE_RXPARITY )
                lstrcat( szTemp1, "PARITY ERROR\n\n" );
            if ( nError & CE_TXFULL )
                lstrcat( szTemp1, "TRANSMIT QUEUE FULL\n\n" );
        }

        //
        // display the error message
        //
        MessageBox( NULL, szTemp1, "TSMCOMM.DLL",
                    MB_ICONINFORMATION | MB_OK );
        break;

    default:
        //
        // increment the global error variables
        //
        if ( nError & CE_MODE )
            nCEMode++;
        else {
            if ( nError & CE_BREAK )
                nCEBreak++;
            if ( nError & CE_CTSTO )
                nCECtsTO++;
            if ( nError & CE_DSRTO )
                nCEDsrTO++;
            if ( nError & CE_FRAME )
                nCEFrame++;
            if ( nError & CE_OVERRUN )
                nCEOverrun++;
```

continues

Listing 4.3. continued

```
            if ( nError & CE_RLSDTO )
                nCERlsdTO++;
            if ( nError & CE_RXOVER )
                nCERXOver++;
            if ( nError & CE_RXPARITY )
                nCERXParity++;
            if ( nError & CE_TXFULL )
                nCETXFull++;
        }
        break;
    }


    //
    // return 0
    //
    return( 0 );
}
```

The routine starts by switching to the appropriate code based on the error-processing global variable. If the mode is COUNT, the error value is processed and the global count variables are incremented as necessary. If the mode is DISPLAY, an error message is concatenated in one of the temporary strings. The error message is then displayed using MessageBox(). Finally, if the global variable contains an invalid value, the error is processed and the counts are incremented as if the program was using COUNT mode. With the errors being detected and processed when you write characters to the communications port, error processing during character reception must be next.

Your program also must check for errors while it is receiving characters. This means a modification to TSMReadComm(). This particular modification also satisfies the need to check for errors during the message-processing loop. TSMReadComm() calls GetCommError() twice. The first call checks whether there are characters or errors in the receive queue. The next call to GetCommError() is after the call to ReadComm() if it indicates an error by returning a negative value. Both times, the function calls TSMProcessCommError() if the return from GetCommError() is not 0. Because the first call to GetCommError() is executed each time TSMReadComm() is called, this fulfills your need to check for errors during message processing.

Counting the number of errors that occur is pretty worthless if the application programmer can't retrieve those values. The function TSMGetErrorCount()

accomplishes this purpose. Shown in Listing 4.4, this function takes a port ID and a far pointer to an error-count structure, defined in Table 4.2, as parameters. TSMGetErrorCount() starts by ensuring that there's a port open and the ComIds match. It then fills in the error-count structure with the values of the global variables. Finally, execution returns to the calling program. This final addition to TSMCOMM.DLL completes adding simple error processing. The next discussion shows how to add error checking to TSMTerm.

Listing 4.4 TCGETECT.C TSMGetErrorCount() routine.

```
//
// TSM Communications API DLL
//
// tcgetect.c
//
// set error-processing type
//
// int FAR PASCAL _export TSMGetErrorCount( int nComId,
//                        LPCOMMERRORCOUNT lpCommErrorCount )
//
// parameters:
//    int               nComId          -  ID of COM port to
//                                          write to
//    LPCOMMERRORCOUNT  lpCommErrorCount - pointer to the
//                                          structure to fill
//                                          with the error
//                                          counts
//
// returns:
//    0  if successful
//    <0 if an error occurred
//


//
// system include files
//
#include <windows.h>
#ifdef __BORLANDC__
#pragma hdrstop
#endif


//
// local include files
//
```

continues

Listing 4.4 continued

```c
#include "tsmcomm.h"
#include "tcglobal.h"

//
// TSMSetErrorProcessing
//

int  FAR PASCAL _export TSMGetErrorCount( int nComId,
                             LPCOMMERRORCOUNT lpCommErrorCount )
{
    //
    // make sure that there's a COM port open
    //
    if ( !hTSMCommInfo )
        return( IE_NOPEN );

    //
    // lock the CommInfo structure and ensure that the ComIds
    // are the same
    //
    lpTSMCommInfo = (LPTSMCOMMINFO)GlobalLock( hTSMCommInfo );
    if ( lpTSMCommInfo->ComId != nComId ) {
        GlobalUnlock( hTSMCommInfo );
        return( IE_NOPEN );
    }
    GlobalUnlock( hTSMCommInfo );

    //
    // fill the comm error count structure
    //
    lpCommErrorCount->nCEMode     = nCEMode;
    lpCommErrorCount->nCEBreak    = nCEBreak;
    lpCommErrorCount->nCECtsTO    = nCECtsTO;
    lpCommErrorCount->nCEDsrTO    = nCEDsrTO;
    lpCommErrorCount->nCEFrame    = nCEFrame;
    lpCommErrorCount->nCEOverrun  = nCEOverrun;
    lpCommErrorCount->nCERlsdTO   = nCERlsdTO;
    lpCommErrorCount->nCERXOver   = nCERXOver;
    lpCommErrorCount->nCERXParity = nCERXParity;
    lpCommErrorCount->nCETXFull   = nCETXFull;

    //
    // return that everything worked
```

```
   //
   return( 0 );
}
```

Table 4.2. Error count structure fields.

Field name	Description
nCEMode	Number of MODE errors that have occurred
nCEBreak	Number of BREAKs that have been detected
nCECtsTO	Number of CTS timeouts that have occurred
nCEDsrTO	Number of DSR timeouts that have occurred
nCEFrame	Number of frame errors that have occurred
nCEOverrun	Number of overrun errors that have occurred
nCERlsdTO	Number of RLSD (CD) timeouts that have occurred
nCERXOver	Number of receive buffer overruns that have occurred
nCERXParity	Number of parity errors that have occurred
nCETXFull	Number of transmit queue full errors that have occurred

TSMTerm Modifications

Because TSMTerm is designed to be a simple, general-purpose communications program, your implementation of error checking follows this simplicity. The first addition to your application can be seen in Figure 4.1, which shows the new Preferences menu with the Error Handling Method item highlighted.

Selecting this menu item brings up the Error Handling Method dialog box, shown in Figure 4.2. This dialog box enables the user to choose between counting errors and displaying errors as they occur. The dialog procedure for this dialog box is ErrorMthdDialogProc(), which processes the WM_INITDIALOG command by setting the radio buttons based on a global variable that indicates the current error-handling method. The WM_COMMAND message also is processed. When the OK button is pressed, the routine reads the state of the radio buttons to get the new method. This method is then stored in the TSMTERM.INI

file and a TRUE indication is returned to the calling function. When the
CANCEL button is pressed, the dialog is ended and a FALSE is returned. Listing
4.5 presents `ErrorMthdDialogProc()`.

Figure 4.1.
TSMTerm
Preferences
Menu.

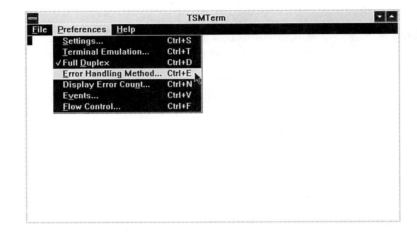

Figure 4.2.
Error
Handling
Method
dialog box.

Listing 4.5. TTERRMTH.C `ErrorMthdDialogProc()` routine.

```
//
// TSM Terminal Program
//
// tterrmth.c
//
// Error Handling Method dialog box routines
//
// BOOL FAR PASCAL _export ErrorMthdDialogProc( HWND hDlg,
//                       UINT wMsg, WPARAM wParam, LPARAM lParam )
//
// parameters:
//     HWND    hDlg      handle to the dialog window
```

```
//    UINT      wMsg      window message being sent
//    WPARAM    wParam    word parameter of the message
//    LPARAM    lParam    long parameter of the message
//
// returns:
//    TRUE  if the message has been processed
//    FALSE if the message is not processed
//


//
// system include files
//
#include <windows.h>
#pragma hdrstop

//
// local include files
//
#include "..\tsmcomm\tsmcomm.h"
#include "ttglobal.h"
#include "ttstring.h"
#include "tterrmth.h"


//
// ErrorMthdDialogProc
//
// RETURNS:
//    TRUE  if a new error method has been selected
//    FALSE if cancel was selected
//
#pragma argsused
BOOL FAR PASCAL _export ErrorMthdDialogProc( HWND hDlg,
                     UINT wMsg, WPARAM wParam, LPARAM lParam )
{
   //
   // automatic variables
   //
   BOOL  bProcessed = TRUE;
   char  szValue[20];

   //
   // process based on the message
   //
```

continues

Listing 4.5. continued

```c
switch( wMsg ) {
    case WM_INITDIALOG:
        //
        // set the radio button based on the error method's global
        // variable
        //
        if ( nErrorMethod == ERROR_COUNT )
            CheckRadioButton( hDlg, COUNT_RADIO, DISPLAY_RADIO,
                            COUNT_RADIO );
        else if ( nErrorMethod == ERROR_DISPLAY )
            CheckRadioButton( hDlg, COUNT_RADIO, DISPLAY_RADIO,
                            DISPLAY_RADIO );
        else {
            nErrorMethod = ERROR_COUNT;
            CheckRadioButton( hDlg, COUNT_RADIO, DISPLAY_RADIO,
                            COUNT_RADIO );
        }
        break;
    case WM_COMMAND:
        //
        // process based on the parameter
        //
        switch( wParam ) {
            case IDOK:
                //
                // get the communication method from the radio
                // buttons
                //
                if ( IsDlgButtonChecked( hDlg, COUNT_RADIO ) )
                    nErrorMethod = ERROR_COUNT;
                else if ( IsDlgButtonChecked( hDlg,
                                            DISPLAY_RADIO ) )
                    nErrorMethod = ERROR_DISPLAY;
                else
                    nErrorMethod = ERROR_COUNT;

                //
                // write the communication method to the .INI file
                //
                LoadString( hInst, IDS_INI_FILE_NAME, szTemp1,
                        sizeof( szTemp1 ) );
                LoadString( hInst, IDS_INI_SECTION_NAME, szTemp2,
                        sizeof( szTemp2 ) );
```

```
                    if ( nErrorMethod == ERROR_COUNT )
                        lstrcpy( szValue, "COUNT" );
                    else if ( nErrorMethod == ERROR_DISPLAY )
                        lstrcpy( szValue, "DISPLAY" );
                    else
                        lstrcpy( szValue, "COUNT" );
                    WritePrivateProfileString( szTemp2, "ErrorMethod",
                                                  szValue, szTemp1 );


                    //
                    // terminate the dialog box with a successful
                    // indication
                    //
                    EndDialog( hDlg, TRUE );
                    break;

                case IDCANCEL:
                    //
                    // terminate the dialog box with a cancel indication
                    //
                    EndDialog( hDlg, FALSE );
                    break;

                default:
                    //
                    // indicate that the message wasn't processed
                    //
                    bProcessed = FALSE;
                    break;
            }
            break;

        default:
            //
            // indicate that the message wasn't processed
            //
            bProcessed = FALSE;
            break;
    }

    //
    // return the result value
    //
    return( bProcessed );
}
```

The user's preference for the error-handling method is stored in the TSMTERM.INI file. This preference is read into the program during the WM_CREATE processing of TSMTermWndProc(). The following code fragment sets this default method:

```
//
// get the error-handling method from the .INI file
//
LoadString( hInst, IDS_INI_FILE_NAME, szTemp1,
           sizeof( szTemp1 ) );
LoadString( hInst, IDS_INI_SECTION_NAME, szTemp2,
           sizeof( szTemp2 ) );
GetPrivateProfileString( szTemp2, "ErrorMethod", "COUNT",
                        szValue, sizeof( szValue ), szTemp1 );
if ( !lstrcmp( szValue, "COUNT" ) )
   nErrorMethod = ERROR_COUNT;
else if ( !lstrcmp( szValue, "DISPLAY" ) )
   nErrorMethod = ERROR_DISPLAY;
else
   nErrorMethod = ERROR_COUNT;


//
// enable the selected error-handling method
//
TSMSetErrorProcessing( nComId, nErrorMethod );
```

First, the .INI filename and section name are loaded into the temporary string variables. Then **GetPrivateProfileString()** is called to get the value of the ErrorMethod setting. The setting defaults to COUNT if the value is not in the .INI file. The program then checks to see which error-handling method the user wants to use and sets the global variable appropriately. Finally, the program calls TSMSetErrorProcessing() to enable the correct error method. Setting the error-processing method to COUNT does not make much sense if the user can't get at the error counts.

There's a second item added to the **P**references menu, as shown in Figure 4.1. By selecting Display Error Cou**n**t, the user brings up the Communications Error Counts dialog box seen in Figure 4.3. The dialog procedure for this dialog box is ErrorCntDlgProc(), shown in Listing 4.6. The only complicated part of this processing is the WM_INITDIALOG message. This message gets the error count from TSMCOMM.DLL by calling TSMGetErrorCount(). ErrorCntDlgProc() processes each error count the same way. It converts the error count to a string value and then uses **SetDlgItemText()** to display the value in the dialog box. The WM_COMMAND processing checks for the OK button being pressed and ends the dialog with a TRUE return code. This completes the error checking and processing additions to TSMTerm. The next section looks at communications events and how to handle them.

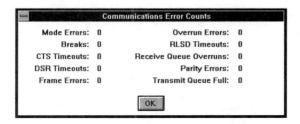

Figure 4.3.
Communications Error Counts dialog box.

Listing 4.6. TTERRCNT.C `ErrorCntDlgProc()` routine.

```
//
// TSM Terminal Program
//
// tterrcnt.c
//
// Communications Error Counts dialog box routines
//
// BOOL FAR PASCAL _export ErrorCntDialogProc( HWND hDlg,
//                     UINT wMsg, WPARAM wParam, LPARAM lParam )
//
// parameters:
//    HWND      hDlg      handle to the dialog window
//    UINT      wMsg      window message being sent
//    WPARAM    wParam    word parameter of the message
//    LPARAM    lParam    long parameter of the message
//
// returns:
//    TRUE  if the message has been processed
//    FALSE if the message has not been processed
//


//
// system include files
//
#include <windows.h>
#ifdef _ _BORLANDC_ _
#pragma hdrstop
#endif
```

continues

Listing 4.6. continued

```
//
// local include files
//
#include "..\tsmcomm\tsmcomm.h"
#include "ttglobal.h"
#include "tterrcnt.h"

//
// ErrorCntDialogProc
//
#ifdef __BORLANDC__
#pragma argsused
#endif
BOOL FAR PASCAL _export ErrorCntDialogProc( HWND hDlg, UINT wMsg,
                                    WPARAM wParam, LPARAM lParam )
{
    //
    // automatic variables
    //
    BOOL            bProcessed = TRUE;
    char            szValue[20];
    COMMERRORCOUNT CommErrorCount;

    //
    // process based on the message
    //
    switch( wMsg ) {
        case WM_INITDIALOG:
            //
            // get the error counts from TSMCOMM
            //
            TSMGetErrorCount( nComId,
                        (LPCOMMERRORCOUNT)&CommErrorCount );

            //
            // load the dialog fields with the values retrieved
            //
            wsprintf( szValue, "%d", CommErrorCount.nCEMode );
            SetDlgItemText( hDlg, MODE_TEXT, szValue );
            wsprintf( szValue, "%d", CommErrorCount.nCEBreak );
            SetDlgItemText( hDlg, BREAK_TEXT, szValue );
            wsprintf( szValue, "%d", CommErrorCount.nCECtsTO );
            SetDlgItemText( hDlg, CTSTO_TEXT, szValue );
```

```
            wsprintf( szValue, "%d", CommErrorCount.nCEDsrTO );
            SetDlgItemText( hDlg, DSRTO_TEXT, szValue );
            wsprintf( szValue, "%d", CommErrorCount.nCEFrame );
            SetDlgItemText( hDlg, FRAME_TEXT, szValue );
            wsprintf( szValue, "%d", CommErrorCount.nCEOverrun );
            SetDlgItemText( hDlg, OVERRUN_TEXT, szValue );
            wsprintf( szValue, "%d", CommErrorCount.nCERlsdTO );
            SetDlgItemText( hDlg, RLSDTO_TEXT, szValue );
            wsprintf( szValue, "%d", CommErrorCount.nCERXOver );
            SetDlgItemText( hDlg, RXOVER_TEXT, szValue );
            wsprintf( szValue, "%d", CommErrorCount.nCERXParity );
            SetDlgItemText( hDlg, PARITY_TEXT, szValue );
            wsprintf( szValue, "%d", CommErrorCount.nCETXFull );
            SetDlgItemText( hDlg, TXFULL_TEXT, szValue );
            break;

    case WM_COMMAND:
        //
        // process based on the parameter
        //
        switch( wParam ) {
            case IDOK:
                //
                // terminate the dialog with a successful
                // indication
                //
                EndDialog( hDlg, TRUE );
                break;

            default:
                //
                // indicate that the message wasn't processed
                //
                bProcessed = FALSE;
                break;
        }
        break;

    default:
        //
        // indicate that the message wasn't processed
        //
        bProcessed = FALSE;
        break;
}
```

continues

189

Listing 4.6. continued

```
//
// return the result value
//
return( bProcessed );
}
```

Communications Events

Windows provides communications programmers two event polling functions: `SetCommEventMask()` and `GetCommEventMask()`. First, you must determine which events you want to track. You then tell Windows about your selection using `SetCommEventMask()`. Once the events have been enabled, your program calls `GetCommEventMask()` to retrieve the event word for the device. By masking bits in this word, your program is able to determine which events occurred since the last time `GetCommEventMask()` was called. This is possible because the event word is cleared when `GetCommEventMask()` is called. The events that Windows enables you to track are listed in Table 4.3. The next discussion prepares you to add event support to the TSM Communications API.

Table 4.3. Trackable communications events.

Name	Description
EV_BREAK	Set when a break condition is detected.
EV_CTS	Set when the CTS line changes state from high to low or vice versa.
EV_CTSS	Indicates the current state of the CTS line.
EV_DSR	Set when the DSR line changes state.
EV_ERR	Set when a CE_FRAME, CE_OVERRUN, or CE_RXPARITY error occurs.
EV_RING	Indicates the current state of the RI line.
EV_RLSD	Set when the RLSD (CD) line changes state.
EV_RLSDS	Indicates the current state of the RLSD (CD) line.
EV_RXCHAR	Set when a character is placed in the receive queue.

Name	Description
EV_RXFLAG	Set when a special event character is received and placed in the receive queue.
EV_TXEMPTY	Set when the transmit queue is empty.

> **Caution:** You must read the event word using `GetEventMask()` to enable Windows to respond to more events.

TSMCOMM Modifications

Two functions add event-processing capabilities to the TSM Communications API. The first function, `TSMSetEvents()`, enables users to specify which events they want the program to process. The second, `TSMPollEvents()`, enables the program to determine which events have occurred. Each of these functions is covered in detail in the following paragraphs.

`TSMSetEvents()` indicates which events you are interested in processing. These events are the same as accepted by **SetCommEventMask()**. `TSMSetEvents()`, shown in Listing 4.7, takes the port ID and event mask as parameters. The event mask is a combination of the events listed in Table 4.3. This routine starts, as all other TSMCOMM.DLL routines do, by checking for an open port and making sure that the ComIds are the same. The function returns an error if either test fails. Next, the function calls **SetCommEventMask()** to tell Windows which events the user is interested in. Finally, `TSMSetEvents()` stores the event mask in a global variable for use in `TSMPollEvents()`.

Listing 4.7. TCSETEVT.C `TSMSetEvents()` routine.

```
//
// TSM Communications API DLL
//
// tcsetevt.c
//
// set events to be processed
//
```

continues

Listing 4.7. continued

```
// int FAR PASCAL _export TSMSetEvents( int nComId,
//                                      UINT uEvents )
//
// parameters:
//     int    nComId    ID of comm port to write to
//     UINT   uEvents   events to be processed
//
// returns:
//     0   if successful
//     <0 if an error occurred
//


//
// system include files
//
#include <windows.h>
#ifdef __BORLANDC__
#pragma hdrstop
#endif


//
// local include files
//
#include "tsmcomm.h"
#include "tcglobal.h"


//
// TSMSetEvents
//
int FAR PASCAL _export TSMSetEvents( int nComId, UINT uEvents )
{
   //
   // make sure there's a COM port open
   //
   if ( !hTSMCommInfo )
      return( IE_NOPEN );


   //
   // lock the CommInfo structure and ensure that the ComIds
   // are the same
   //
   lpTSMCommInfo = (LPTSMCOMMINFO)GlobalLock( hTSMCommInfo );
```

```
    if ( lpTSMCommInfo->ComId != nComId ) {
      GlobalUnlock( hTSMCommInfo );
      return( IE_NOPEN );
    }
    GlobalUnlock( hTSMCommInfo );

    //
    // set the communications event mask
    //
    SetCommEventMask( nComId, uEvents );

    //
    // save the events in a global variable
    //
    uCurrentEvents = uEvents;

    //
    // return that everything worked
    //
    return( 0 );
}
```

TSMPollEvents() enables users to get the events that have occurred since the last time they polled for events. TSMPollEvents() sends messages containing the event information. The function takes a port ID and a window handle as parameters. This window handle specifies which window receives the WM_COMM_EVENT messages generated by TSMPollEvents(). The word parameter of the WM_COMM_EVENT message indicates which event actually occurred. Listing 4.8 presents TSMPollEvents().

Listing 4.8. TCPLLEVT.C TSMPollEvents() routine.

```
//
// TSM Communications API DLL
//
// tcpllevt.c
//
// poll the event mask and send WM_COMM_EVENT messages to the
// specified window
//
// int FAR PASCAL _export TSMPollEvents( int nComId, HWND hWnd )
//
```

continues

Listing 4.8. continued

```
// parameters:
//    int    nComId    ID of COM port to write to
//    HWND   hWnd       window handle to receive the
//                      WM_COMM_EVENT messages
//
// returns:
//    0  if successful
//    <0 if an error occurred
//

//
// system include files
//
#include <windows.h>
#ifdef __BORLANDC__
#pragma hdrstop
#endif

//
// local include files
//
#include "tsmcomm.h"
#include "tcglobal.h"

//
// TSMPollEvents
//
int FAR PASCAL _export TSMPollEvents( int nComId, HWND hWnd )
{
   //
   // automatic variables
   //
   UINT  uEvents;

   //
   // make sure there's a COM port open
   //
   if ( !hTSMCommInfo )
      return( IE_NOPEN );
   //
   // lock the CommInfo structure and ensure that the ComIds
   // are the same
   //
```

```
        lpTSMCommInfo = (LPTSMCOMMINFO)GlobalLock( hTSMCommInfo );
        if ( lpTSMCommInfo->ComId != nComId ) {
            GlobalUnlock( hTSMCommInfo );
            return( IE_NOPEN );
        }
        GlobalUnlock( hTSMCommInfo );

        //
        // get the communications event mask
        //
        uEvents = GetCommEventMask( nComId, uCurrentEvents );

        //
        // see whether each type of event has occurred and send a
        // message to the specified window for each one that has
        //
        if ( uEvents & EV_BREAK )
            SendMessage( hWnd, WM_COMM_EVENT, EV_BREAK, 0l );
        if ( uEvents & EV_CTS )
            SendMessage( hWnd, WM_COMM_EVENT, EV_CTS, 0l );
        if ( uEvents & EV_CTSS )
            SendMessage( hWnd, WM_COMM_EVENT, EV_CTSS, 0l );
        if ( uEvents & EV_DSR )
            SendMessage( hWnd, WM_COMM_EVENT, EV_DSR, 0l );
        if ( uEvents & EV_ERR )
            SendMessage( hWnd, WM_COMM_EVENT, EV_ERR, 0l );
        if ( uEvents & EV_RING )
            SendMessage( hWnd, WM_COMM_EVENT, EV_RING, 0l );
        if ( uEvents & EV_RLSD )
            SendMessage( hWnd, WM_COMM_EVENT, EV_RLSD, 0l );
        if ( uEvents & EV_RLSDS )
            SendMessage( hWnd, WM_COMM_EVENT, EV_RLSDS, 0l );
        if ( uEvents & EV_RXCHAR )
            SendMessage( hWnd, WM_COMM_EVENT, EV_RXCHAR, 0l );
        if ( uEvents & EV_RXFLAG )
            SendMessage( hWnd, WM_COMM_EVENT, EV_RXFLAG, 0l );
        if ( uEvents & EV_TXEMPTY )
            SendMessage( hWnd, WM_COMM_EVENT, EV_TXEMPTY, 0l );

        //
        // return value showing that everything worked
        //
        return( 0 );
    }
```

This routine starts by ensuring that a port is open and that the IDs match. It then calls `GetCommEventMask()` to retrieve the event word for this port, automatically clearing the event word. The program checks for each event by ANDing the event word with the event mask. If the event has occurred, a `WM_COMM_EVENT` message is sent to the window specified by the parameters.

These two functions give your program the capability to specify and process the communications events that Windows makes available. Adding this event processing to TSMTerm is covered next.

TSMTerm Modifications

Event processing in communications programs can range from nonexistent to fairly complex. For TSMTerm, you will add simple event processing just to get the feel of how event processing works. The event processing you are adding does not do anything useful, but making functional event processing is a logical next step once you understand the example. You start adding event processing by adding the Events item to the **P**references menu, as shown in Figure 4.1. Selecting the Events menu item displays the Event Selection dialog box, shown in Figure 4.4.

Figure 4.4.
Event
Selection
dialog box.

```
┌────────────────────────────────────────────┐
│ ▄       Event Selection               ▀     │
├────────────────────────────────────────────┤
│ ☐ BREAK            ⊠ RLSD Change            │
│                                              │
│ ☐ CTS Change       ☐ Received Character     │
│                                              │
│ ☐ DSR Change       ☐ Received Event Character│
│                                              │
│ ⊠ Line Errors      ☐ Transmit Queue Empty   │
│                                              │
│ ☐ Ring Indicator   [  OK  ]  [ Cancel ]     │
└────────────────────────────────────────────┘
```

Listing 4.9 shows `EventSelectDialogProc()`, the window procedure for the Event Selection dialog box. This function processes two important messages. First, the `WM_INITDIALOG` message is processed. During this message the global variable `uCurrentEvents` is examined and the dialog's checkboxes are set accordingly. The important processing takes place during the `WM_COMMAND` message. If the OK button was pressed, the program clears the current event flag and re-creates it based on the checkboxes currently set. If a checkbox is checked, the program uses the OR operator to compare the current event flag and the event that the checkbox represents. After all the checkboxes have been processed, uCurrentEvents holds the proper value. The program then enables the events with a call to TSMSetEvents(). Finally, the program saves the event mask in the .INI file and returns execution to the calling program.

Listing 4.9. TTEVTSEL.C `EventSelectDialogProc()` routine.

```
//
// TSM Terminal Program
//
// ttevtsel.c
//
// Event Selection dialog box routines
//
// BOOL FAR PASCAL _export EventSelectDialogProc( HWND hDlg,
//                      UINT wMsg, WPARAM wParam, LPARAM lParam )
//
// parameters:
//    HWND      hDlg      handle to the dialog window
//    UINT      wMsg      window message being sent
//    WPARAM    wParam    word parameter of the message
//    LPARAM    lParam    long parameter of the message
//
// returns:
//    TRUE  if the message has been processed
//    FALSE if the message has not been processed
//

//
// system include files
//
#include <windows.h>
#ifdef __BORLANDC__
#pragma hdrstop
#endif

//
// local include files
//
#include "..\tsmcomm\tsmcomm.h"
#include "ttglobal.h"
#include "ttstring.h"
#include "ttevtsel.h"
```

continues

197

Listing 4.9. continued

```c
//
// EventSelectDialogProc
//
// RETURNS:
//    TRUE if new events have been selected
//    FALSE if cancel was selected
//
#ifdef __BORLANDC__
#pragma argsused
#endif
BOOL FAR PASCAL _export EventSelectDialogProc( HWND hDlg,
                    UINT wMsg, WPARAM wParam, LPARAM lParam )
{
    //
    // automatic variables
    //
    BOOL  bProcessed = TRUE;
    char  szValue[20];


    //
    // process based on the message
    //
    switch( wMsg ) {
      case WM_INITDIALOG:
        //
        // set the checkboxes for each selected event
        //
        if ( uCurrentEvents & EV_BREAK )
           CheckDlgButton( hDlg, BREAK_CB, 1 );
        if ( uCurrentEvents & EV_CTS )
           CheckDlgButton( hDlg, CTS_CB, 1 );
        if ( uCurrentEvents & EV_DSR )
           CheckDlgButton( hDlg, DSR_CB, 1 );
        if ( uCurrentEvents & EV_ERR )
           CheckDlgButton( hDlg, ERR_CB, 1 );
        if ( uCurrentEvents & EV_RING )
           CheckDlgButton( hDlg, RI_CB, 1 );
        if ( uCurrentEvents & EV_RLSD )
           CheckDlgButton( hDlg, RLSD_CB, 1 );
        if ( uCurrentEvents & EV_RXCHAR )
           CheckDlgButton( hDlg, RXCHAR_CB, 1 );
        if ( uCurrentEvents & EV_RXFLAG )
           CheckDlgButton( hDlg, RXFLAG_CB, 1 );
        if ( uCurrentEvents & EV_TXEMPTY )
```

```
                CheckDlgButton( hDlg, TXEMPTY_CB, 1 );
        break;

    case WM_COMMAND:
        //
        // process based on the parameter
        //
        switch( wParam ) {
            case IDOK:
                //
                // determine the new events value
                //
                uCurrentEvents = 0;
                if ( IsDlgButtonChecked( hDlg, BREAK_CB ) )
                    uCurrentEvents |= EV_BREAK;
                if ( IsDlgButtonChecked( hDlg,  CTS_CB ) )
                    uCurrentEvents |= EV_CTS;
                if ( IsDlgButtonChecked( hDlg,  DSR_CB ) )
                    uCurrentEvents |= EV_DSR;
                if ( IsDlgButtonChecked( hDlg,  ERR_CB ) )
                    uCurrentEvents |= EV_ERR;
                if ( IsDlgButtonChecked( hDlg,  RI_CB ) )
                    uCurrentEvents |= EV_RING;
                if ( IsDlgButtonChecked( hDlg,  RLSD_CB ) )
                    uCurrentEvents |= EV_RLSD;
                if ( IsDlgButtonChecked( hDlg,  RXCHAR_CB ) )
                    uCurrentEvents |= EV_RXCHAR;
                if ( IsDlgButtonChecked( hDlg,  RXFLAG_CB ) )
                    uCurrentEvents |= EV_RXFLAG;
                if ( IsDlgButtonChecked( hDlg,  TXEMPTY_CB ) )
                    uCurrentEvents |= EV_TXEMPTY;

                //
                // set the events in TSMCOMM.DLL
                //
                TSMSetEvents( nComId, uCurrentEvents );

                //
                // write the events mask to the .INI file
                //
                LoadString( hInst, IDS_INI_FILE_NAME, szTemp1,
                            sizeof( szTemp1 ) );
                LoadString( hInst, IDS_INI_SECTION_NAME, szTemp2,
                            sizeof( szTemp2 ) );
                wsprintf( szValue, "%u", uCurrentEvents );
```

continues

Listing 4.9. continued

```
                WritePrivateProfileString( szTemp2, "Events",
                                           szValue, szTemp1 );

            //
            // close the dialog box with a successful
            // indication
            //
            EndDialog( hDlg, TRUE );
            break;

        case IDCANCEL:
            //
            // close the dialog with a cancel indication
            //
            EndDialog( hDlg, FALSE );
            break;

        default:
            //
            // indicate that the message wasn't processed
            //
            bProcessed = FALSE;
            break;
        }
        break;

    default:
        //
        // indicate that the message wasn't processed
        //
        bProcessed = FALSE;
        break;
    }

    //
    // return the result value
    //
    return( bProcessed );
}
```

The next modification is an addition to the WM_CREATE processing to read the
event mask from the .INI file and call TSMSetEvents() to enable event processing. Finally, the program must have a way to process the events that occur. For

polled communications, add a call to `TSMPollEvents()` to your message loop after the routine has processed any incoming characters. This call sends `WM_COMM_EVENT` messages to the terminal window. `TSMTermWndProc()` processes these messages as shown in the code snippet that follows. This code comes from `TSMTermWndProc()` in the file TTWINDOW.C.

```
case WM_COMM_EVENT:
    //
    // process a communications event
    //
    switch ( wParam ) {
        case EV_BREAK:
            lstrcpy( szTemp1, "BREAK EVENT" );
            break;

        case EV_CTS:
            lstrcpy( szTemp1, "CTS CHANGED EVENT" );
            break;

        case EV_DSR:
            lstrcpy( szTemp1, "DSR CHANGED EVENT" );
            break;

        case EV_ERR:
            lstrcpy( szTemp1, "LINE STATUS ERROR EVENT" );
            break;

        case EV_RING:
            lstrcpy( szTemp1, "RING INDICATOR EVENT" );
            break;

        case EV_RLSD:
            lstrcpy( szTemp1, "RLSD (CD) CHANGED EVENT" );
            break;

        case EV_RXCHAR:
            lstrcpy( szTemp1, "CHARACTER RECEIVED EVENT" );
            break;

        case EV_RXFLAG:
            lstrcpy( szTemp1, "EVENT CHARACTER RECEIVED EVENT" );
            break;

        case EV_TXEMPTY:
            lstrcpy( szTemp1, "TRANSMIT QUEUE EMPTY EVENT" );
            break;
```

```
        default:
            lstrcpy( szTemp1, "UNKNOWN EVENT" );
            break;
    }

    //
    // display a message box containing the error message
    //
    MessageBox( hWndTerm, szTemp1, szTSMTerm,
                MB_ICONINFORMATION ¦ MB_OK );

    break;
```

This piece of code starts by using a `switch` statement to determine the type of event that occurred. For the simple example given here, each case copies a message into one of the temporary strings. `MessageBox()` then displays the event message on-screen, as seen in Figure 4.5. You now have error and event handling in TSMCOMM.DLL and TSMTerm. The next section looks at adding flow control to your program.

Figure 4.5.
Event
message
box.

Flow Control

Flow control is a method of stopping either the transmission or reception of characters. There are two widely accepted ways of achieving flow control: hardware flow control and XON/XOFF flow control. (XON/XOFF is software-based.) With either flow-control scheme, the basic function is the same. Using reception as an example, when the receive queue starts to fill, your program can stop the flow of incoming characters by either sending an XOFF character or setting RTS low. Then when the characters have been processed and the amount of data in the queue falls below a certain threshold, either RTS is reasserted or the XON character is sent and the incoming character flow continues. Windows provides methods for using either hardware or XON/XOFF for flow control. The next discussion covers adding flow control to the TSM Communications API.

> **Note:** COMM.DRV is responsible for implementing flow control. It takes care of watching the queues and either manipulating the control lines or sending the proper control code. The application programmer just needs to set the proper values in the DCB and call `SetCommState()`.

TSMComm Modifications

The COMM.DRV handles most of the details of flow control; the user just has to turn flow control on and off and specify which flow-control scheme to use. The last piece of functionality is setting the buffer-full and buffer-empty thresholds. The addition of two functions (listed in Table 4.4) can accomplish this. Each of these functions is covered in detail in the following paragraphs.

Table 4.4. Flow control functions.

Function	Description
TSMSetFlowControl()	Set the flow-control scheme.
TSMSetFCLimits()	Set the upper and lower thresholds for flow-control processing.

`TSMSetFlowControl()` enables the user to set either the incoming or outgoing flow control to the values listed in Table 4.5. The user cannot set both incoming and outgoing flow control at the same time. This routine starts by ensuring that there's an open port and the ComIds are the same. The routine gets the current state of the serial port using **GetCommState()**, which fills the DCB. The routine sets the fields of the DCB to use the appropriate flow control. It uses an `if` statement to select between incoming and outgoing flow control and a `switch` statement to process the different flow-control types, as seen in Listing 4.10. The routine completes by setting the new state of the serial port using **SetCommState()**.

Table 4.5. Flow-control settings.

Value	Description
FLOW_INCOMING	The user wants to set the incoming flow control.
FLOW_OUTGOING	The user wants to set the outgoing flow control.
FLOW_NONE	The user does not want to use flow control.
FLOW_HARDWARE	The user wants to use hardware flow control. The TSMCOMM.DLL uses CTS/RTS lines for hardware flow control.
FLOW_XONXOFF	The user wants to use XON/XOFF flow control.

Listing 4.10. TCSETFC.C TSMSetFlowControl() routine.

```
//
// TSM Communications API DLL
//
// tcsetfc.c
//
// set the flow-control scheme
//
// int TSMSetFlowControl( int nComId, WORD wDirection,
//                        WORD wFlowControl )
//
// parameters:
//    int  nComId       -   ID of port to set the flow control for
//    WORD wDirection   -   direction to set flow control for
//    WORD wFlowControl -   new flow-control setting
//
// returns:
//    0  if successful
//    <0 if an error occurs
//


//
// system include files
//
#include <windows.h>
#ifdef __BORLANDC__
#pragma hdrstop
#endif
```

```
//
// local include files
//
#include "tsmcomm.h"
#include "tcglobal.h"

//
// TSMSetFlowControl
//
int FAR PASCAL _export TSMSetFlowControl( int nComId,
                            WORD wDirection, WORD wFlowControl )
{
   //
   // automatic variables
   //
   LPDCB lpDCB;
   int   nResult;

   //
   // make sure there's a COM port open
   //
   if ( !hTSMCommInfo )
      return( IE_NOPEN );

   //
   // lock the CommInfo structure and ensure that the ComIds
   // are the same
   //
   lpTSMCommInfo = (LPTSMCOMMINFO)GlobalLock( hTSMCommInfo );
   if ( lpTSMCommInfo->ComId != nComId ) {
      GlobalUnlock( hTSMCommInfo );
      return( IE_NOPEN );
   }

   //
   // lock the DCB structure
   //
   lpDCB = (LPDCB)GlobalLock( lpTSMCommInfo->hDCB );

   //
   // get the current port settings
   //
   GetCommState( nComId, lpDCB );
```

continues

Listing 4.10. continued

```c
//
// set the appropriate fields for the flow control specified
//
if ( wDirection == FLOW_INCOMING ) {
    //
    // handle incoming flow control
    //
    switch( wFlowControl ) {
        case FLOW_NONE:
            lpDCB->fDtrflow = 0;
            lpDCB->fRtsflow = 0;
            lpDCB->fInX = 0;
            break;

        case FLOW_HARDWARE:
            lpDCB->fDtrflow = 0;
            lpDCB->fRtsflow = 1;
            lpDCB->fInX = 0;
            break;

        case FLOW_XONXOFF:
            lpDCB->fDtrflow = 0;
            lpDCB->fRtsflow = 0;
            lpDCB->fInX = 1;
            break;

        default:
            lpDCB->fDtrflow = 0;
            lpDCB->fRtsflow = 0;
            lpDCB->fInX = 0;
            break;
    }
} else {
    //
    // handle outgoing flow control
    //
    switch( wFlowControl ) {
        case FLOW_NONE:
            lpDCB->fOutxCtsFlow = 0;
            lpDCB->fOutxDsrFlow = 0;
            lpDCB->fOutX = 0;
            break;
```

```
        case FLOW_HARDWARE:
            lpDCB->fOutxCtsFlow = 1;
            lpDCB->fOutxDsrFlow = 0;
            lpDCB->fOutX = 0;
            break;

        case FLOW_XONXOFF:
            lpDCB->fOutxCtsFlow = 0;
            lpDCB->fOutxDsrFlow = 0;
            lpDCB->fOutX = 1;
            break;

        default:
            lpDCB->fOutxCtsFlow = 0;
            lpDCB->fOutxDsrFlow = 0;
            lpDCB->fOutX = 0;
            break;
    }
}

//
// set the new flow-control setting
//
nResult = SetCommState( lpDCB );

//
// unlock both the DCB and the CommInfo structures
//
GlobalUnlock( lpTSMCommInfo->hDCB );
GlobalUnlock( hTSMCommInfo );

//
// return the result
//
return( nResult );
}
```

The function TSMSetFCLimits() enables the user to specify the thresholds for starting and ending flow control. The routine accepts three parameters, a ComId, a bottom value, and a top value. The top value specifies how many characters should be left unused in the queue when flow control is asserted. The bottom value indicates how many characters should remain in the queue when flow control is turned off. Listing 4.11 shows the TSMSetFCLimits() routine.

Listing 4.11. TCFCLIM.C `TSMSetFCLimits()` routine.

```c
//
// TSM Communications API DLL
//
// tcfclim.c
//
// set the flow-control scheme
//
// int TSMSetFCLimits( int nComId, WORD wBottom , WORD wTop )
//
// parameters:
//    int  nComId   -  ID of port to set the flow control for
//    WORD wBottom  -  restart threshold
//    WORD wTop     -  stop threshold
//
// returns:
//    0  if successful
//    <0 if an error occurs
//


//
// system include files
//
#include <windows.h>
#ifdef _ _BORLANDC_ _
#pragma hdrstop
#endif


//
// local include files
//
#include "tsmcomm.h"
#include "tcglobal.h"


//
// TSMSetFCLimits
//
int FAR PASCAL _export TSMSetFCLimits( int nComId, WORD wBottom,
                                       WORD wTop )
{
   //
   // automatic variables
   //
   LPDCB lpDCB;
   int   nResult;
```

```
//
// make sure there's a COM port open
//
if ( !hTSMCommInfo )
   return( IE_NOPEN );


//
// lock the CommInfo structure and ensure that the ComIds
// are the same
//
lpTSMCommInfo = (LPTSMCOMMINFO)GlobalLock( hTSMCommInfo );
if ( lpTSMCommInfo->ComId != nComId ) {
   GlobalUnlock( hTSMCommInfo );
   return( IE_NOPEN );
}


//
// lock the DCB structure
//
lpDCB = (LPDCB)GlobalLock( lpTSMCommInfo->hDCB );


//
// get the current port settings
//
GetCommState( nComId, lpDCB );


//
// set the appropriate fields for the flow-control limits
//
lpDCB->XoffLim = wTop;
lpDCB->XonLim = wBottom;


//
// set the new flow-control setting
//
nResult = SetCommState( lpDCB );


//
// unlock both the DCB and the CommInfo structures
//
GlobalUnlock( lpTSMCommInfo->hDCB );
GlobalUnlock( hTSMCommInfo );
```

continues

209

Listing 4.11. continued

```
//
// return the result
//
return( nResult );
}
```

This routine ensures that there's a legal port and retrieves the current settings for that port. It then sets the XonLim and XoffLim fields of the DCB using the bottom and top values, respectively. Finally, the routine sets the port's new state and returns. Now you can add flow control to TSMTerm.

TSMTerm Modifications

A **F**low Control menu item has been added to the **P**references menu, shown in Figure 4.1. Selecting this item brings up the Flow Control dialog box. This box enables the user to set the flow control for incoming and outgoing characters separately. Each type of transmission has three choices: no flow control, hardware flow control, and XON/XOFF flow control. Figure 4.6 shows the Flow Control dialog box.

Figure 4.6.
Flow
Control
dialog box.

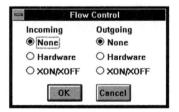

The processing of this dialog box mirrors that of the other dialog boxes covered already, so the specifics aren't covered here. By selecting OK, TSMSetFlowControl() is called twice: once for incoming flow control and once for outgoing flow control.

Summary

This chapter looked at how Windows handles errors, events, and flow control. You saw how to add each of these capabilities to the TSM Communications API and the TSMTerm program. The next chapter looks at message-based communications.

Message-Based
Communications

A s you saw in Chapter 2, "Windows Communications Basics," Windows 3.1 enables both a polled communications scheme and a message-based communications scheme. This message-based scheme relies on the WM_COMMNOTIFY message. Unfortunately, this message is not supported by Windows 3.0. In this chapter you

☐ receive an overview of message-based communications.

☐ add message-based communications to the TSM Communications API.

☐ add the choice of polled or message-based communications to TSMTerm.

Message-Based Communications Overview

The EnableCommNotification() function enables the message-based communications scheme. When this function is called, users can set the limits at which communications messages are sent. They set the number of characters that must be received for a CN_RECEIVE message to be sent. However, the CN_RECEIVE message is sent if fixed timeout—approximately 100 milliseconds for Windows 3.1—occurs. Users also can set the number of characters that should remain in the transmit queue when the CN_TRANSMIT message is sent. CN_TRANSMIT is not sent if the number of characters in the queue never exceeds the set value. Finally, the user also can receive CN_EVENT messages. These messages are enabled by calling SetCommEventMask(), in addition to enabling the communications messages.

All three messages—CN_RECEIVE, CN_TRANSMIT, and CN_EVENT—are the low word of the long parameter to the WM_COMMNOTIFY message. Table 5.1 lists the parameters to WM_COMMNOTIFY.

Table 5.1. WM_COMMNOTIFY parameters.

Parameter	Description
wParam	Communications port ID that the message pertains to.
LOWORD(lParam)	The notification type message, a combination of CN_RECEIVE, CN_TRANSMIT, and CN_EVENT.
HIWORD(lParam)	Unused.

The major requirement of the message-based communications scheme is the processing of these three communications notifications. Adding the capability to process these messages in the TSM Communications API is examined in the next section.

Modifications to TSMCOMM.DLL

In Chapter 2, "Windows Communications Basics," you developed the function TSMEnablePolling() to put the API in polled communications mode. To enable message-based communications, you must add the function TSMEnableMessages(). This function, shown in Listing 5.1, starts by ensuring that there's an open port and that the port IDs match. The routine returns an error if either is not true. It then enables the WM_COMMNOTIFY message with a call to EnableCommNotification(), using the arbitrary value of 32 as both the CN_RECEIVE and CN_TRANSMIT limits. Finally, the function sets the global variable bPollComm to FALSE, indicating that the program is using message-based communications.

Listing 5.1. TCENBMSG.C TSMEnableMessages() routine.

```
//
// TSM Communications API DLL
//
// tcenbmsg.c
//
// enable messages as the current method of communications
```

```
//
// int TSMEnableMessages( int nComId, HWND hWnd )
//
// parameters:
//     int nComId - ID of port to enable messages for
//     Hwnd hWnd - window to receive WM_COMMNOTIFY messages
// returns:
//     0 if successful
//     <0 if an error occurs
//
// system include files
//
#include <windows.h>
#ifdef __BORLANDC__
#pragma hdrstop
#endif


//
// local include files
//
#include "tsmcomm.h"
#include "tcglobal.h"


//
// TSMEnableCommMessages
//
BOOL FAR PASCAL _export TSMEnableMessages( int nComId,
                                           HWND hWndComm )
{
   //
   // automatic variables
   //
   BOOL  bResult;

   //
   // make sure there's a COM port open
   //
   if ( !hTSMCommInfo )
      return( IE_NOPEN );

   //
   // lock the CommInfo structure and ensure that the ComIds
   // are the same
   //
   lpTSMCommInfo = (LPTSMCOMMINFO)GlobalLock( hTSMCommInfo );
```

continues

Listing 5.1. continued

```
if ( lpTSMCommInfo->ComId != nComId ) {
    GlobalUnlock( hTSMCommInfo );
    return( IE_NOPEN );
}
GlobalUnlock( hTSMCommInfo );

//
// enable Windows WM_COMMNOTIFY messages
//
bResult = EnableCommNotification( nComId, hWndComm, 32, 32 );

//
// set the polled communications flag to FALSE
//
bPolledComm = FALSE;

//
// return the result
//
return( bResult );
}
```

You also must modify `TSMEnablePolled()`, turning off the communication messages if they were enabled. Your program accomplishes this by checking the `bPolledComm` flag; if it is not set, your program calls `EnableCommNotification()` with a NULL window handle. This makes Windows disable all `WM_COMMNOTIFY` messages for the current window. By calling `TSMEnableMessages()`, your program enables Windows to send the `WM_COMMNOTIFY` message. The next section looks at processing this message.

Processing the WM_COMMNOTIFY Message

A `WM_COMMNOTIFY` message from Windows really could be one of three messages. The `CN_EVENT` message is sent when an event, enabled by `SetCommEventMask()`, occurs. The `CN_RECEIVE` message is sent when there are more characters in the reception queue than the limit set with `EnableCommNotification()`. The last message, `CN_TRANSMIT`, is sent when the number of characters in the transmission queue has exceeded and now is less

than the number of characters specified in the call to EnableCommNotification().
Listing 5.2 presents TSMProcessCommNotify(), which handles the processing
of these messages.

> **Tip:** The notification type sent with the WM_COMMNOTIFY message is an
> OR'd combination of CN_EVENT, CN_RECEIVE, and CN_TRANSMIT. You
> use a bitwise AND to test for each of these notification types.

Listing 5.2. TCPRCCN.C TSMProcessCommNotify() routine.

```
//
// TSM Communications API DLL
//
// tcprccn.c
//
// process the WM_COMMNOTIFY message
//
// int  FAR PASCAL _export TSMProcessCommNotify( int nComId,
//                             int nNotification, HWND hWnd )
//
// parameters:
//    int   nComId   -  ID of COM port to write to
//    HWND  hWnd     -  window handle to receive the
//                      WM_COMM_EVENT messages
//
// returns:
//    0  if successful
//    <0 if an error occurs
//

//
// system include files
//
#include <windows.h>
#ifdef __BORLANDC__
#pragma hdrstop
#endif
#include <string.h>

//
```

continues

Listing 5.2. continued

```
// local include files
//
#include "tsmcomm.h"
#include "tcglobal.h"


//
// TSMProcessCommNotify
//
int  FAR PASCAL _export TSMProcessCommNotify( int nComId,
                                    int nNotification, HWND hWnd )

{
   //
   // automatic variables
   //
   int          nTransSize,
                nCurrTrans;
   LPTRANSLIST  lpTransHead;
   LPSTR        lpCurrent,
                lpStart;
   HANDLE       hDeleteBlock;

   //
   // make sure there's a COM port open
   //
   if ( !hTSMCommInfo )
      return( IE_NOPEN );


   //
   // lock the CommInfo structure and ensure that the ComIds
   // are the same
   //
   lpTSMCommInfo = (LPTSMCOMMINFO)GlobalLock( hTSMCommInfo );
   if ( lpTSMCommInfo->ComId != nComId ) {
      GlobalUnlock( hTSMCommInfo );
      return( IE_NOPEN );
   }
   GlobalUnlock( hTSMCommInfo );

   //
   // process based on the notification type
   //
   if ( nNotification & CN_EVENT )
      //
      // process the events that have occurred
      //
```

```
    TSMPollEvents( nComId, hWnd );

if ( nNotification & CN_RECEIVE )
    //
    // process the characters that have been received
    //
    TSMReadComm( nComId, hWnd );

if ( nNotification & CN_ATRANSMIT )
    //
    // process the characters on the transmit linked list
    // until the list is empty
    //
    while ( hTransHead ) {
        //
        // lock the head of the list for transmission
        //
        lpTransHead = (LPTRANSLIST)GlobalLock( hTransHead );
        nTransSize  = lpTransHead->nDataSize;
        //
        // write the characters from the head
        //
        nCurrTrans = WriteComm( nComId, &lpTransHead->cData,
                                nTransSize );
        if ( nCurrTrans != nTransSize ) {
            //
            // the complete block was not transferred, so
            // update the linked-list entry and break from
            // the loop
            //
            if ( nCurrTrans < 0 )
                nCurrTrans = -nCurrTrans;
            lpCurrent = &lpTransHead->cData + nCurrTrans;
            lpStart = &lpTransHead->cData;
            _fmemcpy( lpStart, lpCurrent,
                      (nTransSize - nCurrTrans ) );
            lpTransHead->nDataSize = nTransSize - nCurrTrans;
            GlobalUnlock( hTransHead );
            break;
        } else {
            //
            // the whole block was sent.
            // Remove it from the linked list.
            //
            hDeleteBlock = hTransHead;
```

continues

Listing 5.2. continued

```
            hTransHead = lpTransHead->hNextBlock;
            GlobalUnlock( hDeleteBlock );
            GlobalFree( hDeleteBlock );
    }
}


//
// return message that everything worked okay
//
return ( 0 );
}
```

This routine starts by checking whether a port is open and the ComIds match, returning an error if either test fails. The message is then processed based on the communications notification located in the low word of the long parameter. After the message processing, the routine returns 0, indicating that no errors occurred. The processing for the CN_EVENT notification is simple. The routine calls TSMPollEvents() to process the event mask and to send the appropriate event messages. For the CN_RECEIVE message, the program calls TSMReadComm() to read the characters from the reception queue and send them as a WM_COMM_CHARS message. Processing the CN_TRANSMIT message is more complicated and is covered fully next.

Message-Based Transmission

The only tricky part of message-based communications is character transmission, and it only gets tricky if the transmission queue fills. To start the transmission processing, you modify TSMWriteComm(), adding a check to see whether the program is using polled communications. If your program is using polled communications, there is no change in the way characters are processed. If your program is not using polled communications, it must be using message-based communications, and the program processes the characters as follows. First, the routine checks whether there are characters waiting to be transmitted on the transmission linked list. This linked list is a series of structures, defined in Table 5.2, that hold characters awaiting transmission. If characters are already in this linked list, new characters are added to the tail of the list with a call to TSMAddTransmitBlock().

Table 5.2. Transmission linked-list structure.

Field	Description
hNextBlock	The handle of the next block in the linked list. The tail of the list has a NULL in this field.
nDataSize	The number of characters in this block that need to be transmitted.
cData	The first character awaiting transmission. The remaining data follows this character but is not included in the formal structure definition.

If the linked list is not empty, the program attempts to transmit the characters by calling WriteComm(). If this function does not transmit all the characters, the leftover characters are added to the linked list with a call to TSMAddTransmitBlock(). The complete TSMWriteComm() function is presented in Listing 5.3. TSMAddTransmitBlock() is included in Listing 5.3 also.

Listing 5.3. TCWRTCOM.C TSMWriteComm() and TSMAddTransmitBlock() routines.

```
//
// TSM Communications API DLL
//
// tcwrtcom.c
//
// write characters to the communications port
//
// int FAR PASCAL _export TSMWriteComm( int nComId, int nCount,
//                                  LPCSTR lpOutChars )
//
// parameters:
//     int nComId       -  ID of COM port to write to
//     int nCount       -  number of characters to write
//     LPCSTR lpOutChars - far pointer to the characters to be
//                         written
//
// returns:
//     0  if successful
//     <0 if an error occurred
//
```

continues

Listing 5.3. continued

```c
//
// system include files
//
#include <windows.h>
#ifdef __BORLANDC__
#pragma hdrstop
#endif

//
// local include files
//
#include "tsmcomm.h"
#include "tcglobal.h"

//
// TSMWriteComm
//
int FAR PASCAL _export TSMWriteComm( int nComId, int nCount,
                                     LPCSTR lpOutChars )
{
   //
   // automatic variables
   //
   LPSTR szCurrent;
   int   nTotalSent = 0,
         nCurrentSent,
         nCommError = 0;

   //
   // make sure there's a COM port open
   //
   if ( !hTSMCommInfo )
      return( IE_NOPEN );

   //
   // lock the CommInfo structure and ensure that the ComIds
   // are the same
   //
   lpTSMCommInfo = (LPTSMCOMMINFO)GlobalLock( hTSMCommInfo );
   if ( lpTSMCommInfo->ComId != nComId ) {
      GlobalUnlock( hTSMCommInfo );
      return( IE_NOPEN );
   }
   GlobalUnlock( hTSMCommInfo );
```

```
//
// determine which communications method is in use
//
if ( bPolledComm ) {
   //
   // handle polled communications transmission
   //
   // set the current pointer to the start of the string and
   // set the starting value of nTotalSent
   //
   szCurrent = (LPSTR)lpOutChars;

   //
   // loop until all the characters have been sent
   //
   while ( nTotalSent < nCount ) {
      //
      // try to send all remaining characters
      //
      nCurrentSent = WriteComm( nComId, szCurrent,
                                ( nCount - nTotalSent ) );

      //
      // check whether an error occurred
      //
      if ( nCurrentSent < 0 ) {
         //
         // get the error from Windows and process it
         //
         nCommError = GetCommError( nComId, NULL );
         if ( nCommError )
            TSMProcessCommError( nComId, nCommError );
         nCurrentSent = -nCurrentSent;
      }

      //
      // update the current string pointer and the total
      // number of characters sent
      //
      szCurrent += nCurrentSent;
      nTotalSent += nCurrentSent;
   }
} else {
```

continues

Listing 5.3. continued

```
         //
         // handle message-based transmission
         //
         if ( hTransHead ) {
           //
           // there is already data to be transmitted
           // add this data to the end of the linked list
           //
           TSMAddTransmitBlock( lpOutChars, nCount );
         } else {
           //
           // write the buffer to the output queue. If it succeeds
           // the routine is done.
           //
           if ( (nCurrentSent = WriteComm( nComId, lpOutChars,
                                        nCount ) ) < 0 ) {
             //
             // not all the characters were transmitted, so add the
             // rest of the characters to the linked list
             //
             TSMAddTransmitBlock( lpOutChars + nCurrentSent,
                                  nCount - nCurrentSent );
           }
         }
     }


     //
     // return the current error value
     //
     return( nCommError );
}

//
// TSMAddTransmitBlock
//
// returns:
//     TRUE  - if block was added to the linked list
//     FALSE - if block was NOT added to the linked list
//
BOOL  TSMAddTransmitBlock( LPSTR lpOutChars, int nCount )
{
   //
   // automatic variables
   //
```

```
    int         nBlockSize;
    HANDLE      hMemBlock;
    LPTRANSLIST lpMemBlock;
    LPTRANSLIST lpTransTail;

    //
    // not all the characters were transmitted. Allocate a global
    // memory block to hold the remaining characters and copy the
    // characters to it.
    //
    // this memory block has the structure:
    //     HANDLE - next memory block on the linked list
    //     int    - size of data
    //     data   - transmission data
    //
    nBlockSize = sizeof( TRANSLIST ) + nCount - 1;
    hMemBlock = GlobalAlloc( GMEM_MOVEABLE, (DWORD)nBlockSize );
    if ( !hMemBlock )
        return( FALSE );
    lpMemBlock = (LPTRANSLIST)GlobalLock( hMemBlock );
    if ( !lpMemBlock ) {
        GlobalFree( hMemBlock );
        return( FALSE );
    }
    lpMemBlock->hNextBlock = NULL;
    lpMemBlock->nDataSize = nCount;
    lstrcpy( &lpMemBlock->cData, lpOutChars );
    GlobalUnlock( hMemBlock );

    //
    // link this memory block into the linked list
    //
    if ( hTransTail ) {
        lpTransTail = (LPTRANSLIST)GlobalLock( hTransTail );
        lpTransTail->hNextBlock = hMemBlock;
        GlobalUnlock( hTransTail );
        hTransTail = hMemBlock;
    } else {
        hTransHead = hTransTail = hMemBlock;
    }

    //
    // return a TRUE indicating the everything worked
    return( TRUE );
}
```

TSMAddTransmitBlock() adds characters to the transmission linked list. This routine starts by allocating a block of memory to hold the linked list structure and the characters. The size of this block is the size of the linked list structure plus the number of characters to save minus one. The minus one comes from the one character included in the linked list structure. The next block handle is set to NULL because this block becomes the tail of the linked list. The size of the data is set and the characters to be held are copied to the block. Finally, the routine adds this block to the end of the linked list by locking the current tail and setting its next block handle to the block just created. Then the tail handle is set to the new block.

Now that the characters have been added to the linked list, the program must transmit these characters during the CN_TRANSMIT notification processing, seen in Listing 5.2. This processing starts with a while loop that terminates when the linked list is empty. Next, the routine locks the head of the linked list and gets the number of characters that need to be transmitted from this list. It then writes the characters to the port using WriteComm(). If all of the characters were transmitted, the routine removes the block from the head of the linked list, unlocking and freeing it also. If not all of the characters were transmitted, the routine calculates the number of characters that remain to be transmitted and copies the remaining characters to the start of the data buffer. It then unlocks the memory block and breaks from the while loop, terminating the processing of the CN_TRANSMIT notification. Now that TSMCOMM.DLL supports message-based communications, you can add the capability to choose the communications method used in TSMTerm.

Additions to TSMTERM.EXE

Figure 5.1 shows the addition of a Communications Method item to the Preferences menu. This item enables the user to access the Communications Method dialog box. This box enables the user to select either polled communications or message-based communications, as seen in Figure 5.2.

The processing for this dialog box takes place in the procedure CommMthdDialogProc(). This processing is straightforward with the only notable feature being that it sets the global variable bPolledComm to TRUE if the user selects polled communications and FALSE if the user selects message-based. If this procedure returns a TRUE, the menu processing calls either TSMEnablePolled() or TSMEnableMessages() as appropriate.

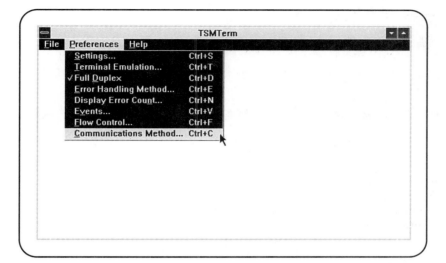

Figure 5.1.
New
Prefer-
ences
menu.

Figure 5.2.
Communi-
cations
Method
dialog box.

You also must modify the WM_CREATE message processing to read the communications flag from the .INI file and call the appropriate TSM Communications API function. This code is shown in the sample that follows.

```
//
// get the communication method setting from the .INI file
//
LoadString( hInst, IDS_INI_FILE_NAME, szTemp1,
            sizeof( szTemp1 ) );
LoadString( hInst, IDS_INI_SECTION_NAME, szTemp2,
            sizeof( szTemp2 ) );
GetPrivateProfileString( szTemp2, "PolledComm", "TRUE", szValue,
                         sizeof( szValue ), szTemp1 );
if ( !lstrcmp( szValue, "TRUE" ) )
   bPolledComm = TRUE;
else if ( !lstrcmp( szValue, "FALSE" ) )
   bPolledComm = FALSE;
```

```
else
   bPolledComm = TRUE;

//
// enable the selected communications method
//
if ( bPolledComm)
   TSMEnablePolling( nComId );
else
   TSMEnableMessages( nComId, hWnd );
```

The largest change in TSMTerm is in the message-processing loop. Listing 5.4 shows the new WinMain(), which includes the modified message-processing loop. The first thing to notice is that the loop is enclosed in a larger while statement that determines whether the program should terminate, so the communications method can be changed during program execution. Next, an if statement determines which message loop to execute. If the user has selected polled communications, the message loop is the same as discussed in Chapter 3, "Terminal Emulation."

Listing 5.4. TSMTERM.C Modified WinMain() routine.

```
//
// TSM Terminal program
//
// tsmterm.c
//
// main entry point for TSM Terminal
//
// int PASCAL WinMain( HANDLE hInstance, HANDLE hPrevInstance,
//                     LPSTR lpCmdLine, int nCmdShow )
//
// parameters:
//     HANDLE    hInstance       instance handle for this instance
//                               of TSMTERM
//     HANDLE    hPrevInstance   instance handle of a previous
//                               instance
//     LPSTR     lpCmdLine       far pointer to the command line
//     int       nCmdShow        initial show window command
//
// returns:
//     0     if successful
//     NULL  if an error occurs
//
```

```
//
// system include files
//
#include <windows.h>
#ifdef __BORLANDC__
#pragma hdrstop
#endif

//
// local include files
//
#include "..\tsmcomm\tsmcomm.h"
#include "tsmterm.h"
#define GLOBAL_DEF
#include "ttglobal.h"
#undef  GLOBAL_DEF
#include "ttstring.h"

//
// WinMain
//
#ifdef __BORLANDC__
#pragma argsused
#endif
int PASCAL WinMain( HANDLE hInstance, HANDLE hPrevInstance,
                    LPSTR lpCmdLine, int nCmdShow )
{
   //
   // automatic variables
   //
   WNDCLASS WndClass;
   BOOL     fContinue;
   BOOL     fProgramCont;
   MSG      msg;
   int      nResult;

   //
   // save the instance handle in a global variable
//
   hInst = hInstance;

   //
   // load the application name to a global variable
   //
   LoadString( hInst, IDS_TSMTERM, szTSMTerm,
               sizeof( szTSMTerm ) );
```

continues

Listing 5.4. continued

```
//
// check whether another instance already exists and
// terminate if it does
//
if ( hPrevInstance ) {
   //
   // get the error message string
   //
   LoadString( hInst, IDS_1INSTANCE, szTemp1,
               sizeof( szTemp1 ) );

   //
   // display a message box with the error message
   //
   MessageBox( NULL, szTemp1, szTSMTerm,
               MB_ICONSTOP | MB_OK );

   //
   // return a value indicating the program did not start
   //
   return( NULL );
}

//
// check for Windows version 3.0 or above
//
if ( LOWORD(LOBYTE(GetVersion())) < 3 ) {
   //
   // get the error message string
   //
   LoadString( hInst, IDS_WRONGVERSION, szTemp1,
               sizeof( szTemp1 ) );

   //
   // display the error message
   //
   MessageBox( NULL, szTemp1, szTSMTerm,
               MB_ICONSTOP | MB_OK );

   //
   // return a value indicating the program did not start
   //
   return( NULL );
}
```

```
//
// register the Window class
//
WndClass.style          =   CS_HREDRAW ¦ CS_VREDRAW;
WndClass.lpfnWndProc    =   TSMTermWndProc;
WndClass.cbClsExtra     =   0;
WndClass.cbWndExtra     =   0;
WndClass.hInstance      =   hInst;
WndClass.hIcon          =   LoadIcon( hInst, szTSMTerm );
WndClass.hCursor        =   LoadCursor( NULL, IDC_ARROW );
WndClass.hbrBackground  =   (HBRUSH)(COLOR_WINDOW + 1);
WndClass.lpszMenuName   =   szTSMTerm;
WndClass.lpszClassName  =   szTSMTerm;
if ( !RegisterClass( &WndClass ) ) {
   //
   // the class did not register correctly.
   // Display an error and exit the program.
   //
   LoadString( hInst, IDS_REGCLASSERR, szTemp1,
               sizeof( szTemp1 ) );
   MessageBox( NULL, szTemp1, szTSMTerm,
               MB_ICONSTOP ¦ MB_OK );
   return( NULL );
}

//
// create a window based on the class just registered
//
hWndTerm = CreateWindow( szTSMTerm, szTSMTerm,
                         WS_OVERLAPPEDWINDOW, CW_USEDEFAULT,
                         CW_USEDEFAULT, CW_USEDEFAULT,
                         CW_USEDEFAULT, HWND_DESKTOP,
                         NULL, hInst, NULL );
if ( !hWndTerm ) {
    //
   // the window was not created correctly. Display an error
   // message if it did not fail because of a communications
   // failure.
   //
   if ( !bCommFailedErr ) {
      LoadString( hInst, IDS_CREATEWINERR, szTemp1,
                  sizeof( szTemp1 ) );
      MessageBox( NULL, szTemp1, szTSMTerm,
                  MB_ICONSTOP ¦ MB_OK );
   }
```

continues

Listing 5.4. continued

```
        // exit the program
    //
    return( NULL );
}


//
// load the keyboard accelerators
//
hAccelerators = LoadAccelerators( hInst, szTSMTerm );


//
// show the window based on the nCmdShow parameter
//
ShowWindow( hWndTerm, nCmdShow );
UpdateWindow( hWndTerm );


//
// loop until program should be terminated
//
fProgramCont = TRUE;
while ( fProgramCont ) {
    //
    // determine whether the program should use
    // polling or message-based communications
    //
    if ( bPolledComm ) {
        //
        // message-processing loop
        //
        fContinue = TRUE;
        while ( fContinue && bPolledComm ) {
            //
            // check for a message in the queue
            //
            if ( PeekMessage( &msg, NULL, 0, 0, PM_REMOVE ) ) {
                //
                // there is a message. Check whether it is a
                // WM_QUIT message.
                //
                if ( msg.message != WM_QUIT ) {
                    //
                    // it is a "normal" message, so process it
                    //
```

```
                       if ( !TranslateAccelerator( hWndTerm,
                                       hAccelerators, &msg ) ) {
                           TranslateMessage( &msg );
                           DispatchMessage( &msg );
                       }
                  } else {
                      //
                      // process the WM_QUIT message
                      //
                      fContinue = FALSE;
                      fProgramCont = FALSE;
                      nResult = msg.wParam;
                  }
              } else {
                  //
                  // no message; call
                  // TSMReadComm() to do polled mode
                  // communications receiving.
                  //
                  TSMReadComm( nComId, hWndTerm );

                  //
                  // check the events also
                  //
                  TSMPollEvents( nComId, hWndTerm );
              }
          }
      } else {
          //
          // message-based communications message loop
          //
          while ( (nResult = GetMessage( &msg, NULL, 0, 0 ) ) ) {
              //
              // process the message
              //
              if ( !TranslateAccelerator( hWndTerm, hAccelerators,
                                    &msg ) ) {
                  TranslateMessage( &msg );
                  DispatchMessage( &msg );
              }

              //
              // make sure program is using message-based
              // communications
              //
```

continues

Listing 5.4. continued

```
            if ( bPolledComm ) {
                nResult = 1;
                break;
            }
        }
        if ( !nResult ) {
            fProgramCont = FALSE;
            nResult = msg.wParam;
        }
    }
}

//
// return the result from the WM_QUIT message
//
return( nResult );
}
```

If the program is using message-based communications, the message-processing loop is normal with one exception—it can terminate from two occurrences: the reception of a WM_QUIT message or a break caused by changing from message-based to polled communications. The routine sets nResult to 1 to indicate a communications method change and to 0 for WM_QUIT. The routine checks this value after the loop has terminated to determine whether the program should terminate or switch communications modes.

Summary

In this chapter you looked at message-based communications and added this capability to the TSM Communications API. You also added a dialog box to TSMTerm that enables users to select which communications method they want to use. Now that you have completed the TSM Communications API, you can look at communicating with your modem.

Modem
Communications

o this point, the book has covered communicating through the serial port of the computer, generally discussing how to manage communications with a remote computer. However, this communication generally takes place using modems. With the basics developed so far, now you can look at communicating with the modem, having it place calls to remote systems and hang up the phone when appropriate. In this chapter you

☐ Examine modem communications and the standard modem-communications command set.

☐ Develop a generalized modem-communications API.

☐ Add a dialing directory to TSMTerm using the modem-communications API.

Modem Communications

For most serial communications, your computer does not connect directly to another computer; it works through its modem, which communicates with another modem through the telephone system. That modem then connects directly with the remote PC. Figure 6.1 shows this relationship. To make the modem dial the telephone number, respond correctly to the remote modem, and hang up the telephone, your computer must send commands to the modem.

Figure 6.1.
PC-to-PC
connection
with modems.

Local Modem   Modem Remote
PC   PC

Unlike terminal manufacturers, modem manufacturers have standardized a single command set for controlling modems. The manufacturer Hayes Microcomputer Products developed this command set, known as the AT or

Hayes command set. This chapter examines the AT command set implemented by US Robotics on the Courier HST Dual Standard modem. This modem has become a popular choice for BBS communications throughout the country.

All AT commands have the same basic structure, as shown in Figure 6.2. Each command starts with the command prefix AT, which you can think of as meaning ATtention. This is followed by a series of commands. Each command comprises either a single character or a single character preceded by the ampersand (&), such as &C, which controls the modem's usage of the Carrier Detect line. The command line is terminated by a carriage return (0x0D).

Figure 6.2.
AT command structure.

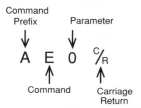

The modem's response to this command line is controlled by four AT commands. These commands, E, Q, V, and X, control whether the modem echoes back the command, returns a result, (number or verbal), and the amount of information contained in the result. Each of these commands is discussed in detail later in this section.

> **Note:** Every modem has two distinct modes in which it operates. The first, command mode, enables you to send AT commands to control the modem's operation. The second, online mode, is entered when your computer connects with another system. In online mode, all data sent to the modem is passed to the remote system. In this mode, the modem does not recognize AT commands. The only command the modem recognizes is the Escape (+++) command, covered later in this section.

Now that you know the basic format of AT commands, look at a subset of the AT commands recognized by the Courier HST Dual Standard Modem. This book divides the commands into several categories: control commands, dial and answer commands, and interface commands. Each of these categories is covered in the following sections.

Control Commands

The control commands enable you to change the modem's operating characteristics. These characteristics all affect local operation of the modem. The interface commands deal with the operation of the modem in connecting with remote systems. Table 6.1 lists the control commands. Note that the small n denotes a numeric parameter. Each command is covered in the following paragraphs.

Table 6.1. Control commands.

Command	Description
Z	Reset the modem to the default configuration.
En	Control the local command mode echo.
Qn	Control whether a result is returned.
Vn	Control whether the result is a numeric value or a verbal description.
Xn	Control the set of responses to use for the result code.
Mn	Control the modem's speaker.

The Z command resets the modem to its default settings. This enables you to bring the modem into a known state. This command does not take any parameters.

The E command controls whether the modem echoes to the screen any characters you type while you're using command mode. E turns local echo off, whereas E1 turns it on.

The Q command controls the quiet mode of the modem. When you use quiet mode, the modem doesn't send result codes back to the computer. Q0 turns quiet mode off, enabling result codes to be sent to the system. Q1 turns quiet mode on, and Q2 turns quiet mode on while the modem is in answer mode.

The V command controls the form of the result code. V0 selects numeric mode for the result codes. The numeric result is followed by a carriage return but no line feed. V1 selects verbal mode. In verbal mode the return code is an English message, such as CONNECT, preceded and followed by a carriage return and a line feed.

The x command controls the set of result codes available to be returned to the system. The x command ranges from X0 to X7. Table 6.2 lists the result codes for each of the eight x command levels.

Table 6.2. X result code sets.

Verbal	Numeric	X0	X1	X2	X3	X4	X5	X6	X7
OK	0	Y	Y	Y	Y	Y	Y	Y	Y
CONNECT	1	Y	Y	Y	Y	Y	Y	Y	Y
RING	2	Y	Y	Y	Y	Y	Y	Y	Y
NO CARRIER	3	Y	Y	Y	Y	Y	Y	Y	Y
ERROR	4	Y	Y	Y	Y	Y	Y	Y	Y
CONNECT 1200	5		Y	Y	Y	Y	Y	Y	Y
NO DIAL TONE	6		Y			Y		Y	Y
BUSY	7				Y	Y	Y	Y	Y
NO ANSWER	8				Y	Y	Y	Y	Y
CONNECT 2400	10		Y	Y	Y	Y	Y	Y	Y
RINGING	11						Y	Y	Y
VOICE	12						Y	Y	
CONNECT 9600	13		Y	Y	Y	Y	Y	Y	Y
CONNECT 4800	18		Y	Y	Y	Y	Y	Y	Y
CONNECT 7200	20		Y	Y	Y	Y	Y	Y	Y
CONNECT 12000	21		Y	Y	Y	Y	Y	Y	Y
CONNECT 14400	25		Y	Y	Y	Y	Y	Y	Y
CONNECT 16800	43		Y	Y	Y	Y	Y	Y	Y

The M command controls the modem's use of its internal speaker. M0 turns the speaker off, so you do not hear what is happening on the phone line. M1 turns the speaker on from the time a dial command is issued until a carrier is detected. M2 turns the speaker on continuously. M3 turns the speaker on after the number has been dialed and stays on until a carrier is detected.

Dial and Answer Commands

You use the dial and answer commands to place a call through the modem or answer an incoming call with the modem. These commands also include the escape command for going back to command mode and the online command to move back to online mode. Finally, a command is included to hang up the phone. Table 6.3 lists the dial and answer commands and the following paragraphs discuss each.

Table 6.3. Dial and answer commands.

Command	Description
D	Control dialing the phone.
A	Control answering the phone.
H	Control the on-hook status of the phone.
+++	Escape to command mode from online mode.
O	Return to online mode.

The D command enables you to control the dialing of a phone number by the modem. This command includes a parameter that indicates type of dialing as well as the number to be dialed. The parameter also can include characters that cause the modem to wait for a specified amount of time to continue. The command ATDT9,5551234 tells the modem that using Touch-Tone dialing, dial a 9, wait for two seconds, and then dial 555-1234. The dialing types available are T for Touch-Tone dialing and P for pulse (rotary) dialing. In addition to the two-second delay caused by the comma (,), the slash (/) causes a 125-millisecond delay. The phone number can include dashes (-) without causing any problems.

Whereas the D command enables your computer to place outgoing calls, the A command forces the modem to answer the phone even if no call has been detected. The A command takes no parameters.

The H command controls the hook status of the modem, whether the phone line is on or off the hook. H0 causes the line to go on-hook, hanging up the call. H1 causes the line to go off-hook.

When your computer has dialed a call and connected with a remote system, the modem goes from command mode to online mode. In online mode, the modem recognizes the Escape (+++) command only. To invoke the escape command, wait one second after characters have been sent, then type three plus signs and wait another second. The modem returns to command mode and sends an OK result code. At this point you can issue AT commands to the modem, but your computer is still connected with the remote system.

The O command enables you to go back to online mode after you have used the Escape (+++) command to move to command mode. The O command does not take any parameters.

Interface Commands

The interface commands enable you to specify how the modem deals with the remote environment. These commands include controlling the RS-232 control lines and setting the flow control methods. Table 6.4 lists the interface commands.

Table 6.4. Interface commands.

Command	Description
&Dn	Control how the modem uses DTR.
&Cn	Control how the modem uses CD.
&Sn	Control how the modem uses DSR
&Hn	Control the transmit data flow control.
&Rn	Control the received data hardware flow control.
&In	Control the received data software flow control.

The &D command controls how the modem interprets the DTR line. &D0 overrides the DTR line and enables the modem to operate as if it is always on. &D2 selects normal DTR operation—the computer must set DTR high for the modem to accept commands. In this mode, dropping DTR causes the modem to disconnect an active call.

The &C command determines how the modem uses the carrier detect (CD) signal sent to the computer. &C0 forces the CD line to stay high all the time. &C1

causes the modem to set the CD line high when it detects a carrier from the remote system and to drop the CD line low when no carrier is present.

The &S command controls when the modem signals the computer using the DSR line. &S0 sets the DSR line high at all times. &S1 causes DSR to be set high after the modem detects the remote modem's answer or after the modem answers an incoming call.

The &H command controls the type of flow control used by the modem to stop the data flow from your program. The Courier HST Dual Standard Modem stops the data flow when its buffer is 90 percent full and restarts it when the buffer has dropped to 50 percent full. &H0 disables transmit data flow control. &H1 enables hardware flow control. The modem uses the CTS line to signal flow control in this mode. &H2 enables software flow control. The software flow control method is XON/XOFF.

The &R command controls the hardware flow control applied to the received data stream. This flow control consists of dropping the RTS line to stop the flow of data and setting it high again to restart the data. &R0 is used by synchronous communications and does not apply to asynchronous calls. &R1 causes the modem to ignore the state of RTS, thereby disabling hardware flow control. &R2 enables hardware flow control.

The &I command controls the software flow control used for the received data. XON/XOFF is used as the software flow control method. &I0 disables software flow control. &I1 causes the modem to act on the XON/XOFF characters transmitted and also send them to the remote system. &I2 causes the modem to act on the XON/XOFF characters but remove them from the data stream being transmitted.

With an understanding of the types of commands that the modem accepts and the modem's responses to those commands, now you can look at developing a Modem Interface API.

Modem Interface API

To simplify your usage of the modem, you can develop a Modem Interface API. This API should enable you to enter the specific commands to initialize the modem, dial a number, and hang up an active call. Table 6.5 lists the functions that this chapter defines for your API, and the following discussions cover each command in detail. With these commands, you can add a dialing directory to TSMTerm.

Table 6.5. Modem Interface API functions.

Function	Description
ModemInitialize()	Initialize the Modem Interface API.
ModemTerminate()	Terminate the use of the Modem Interface API.
ModemSettings()	Enable the user to enter command, connect, and failed connect response strings.
ModemSendInitString()	Send the initialization string to the modem and wait for its response.
ModemDial()	Send a dial command to the modem and check for a response that indicates a successful connection or a response that indicates a failed attempt.
ModemHangup()	Hang up an active call using either a command string entered in the settings dialog box or a hardware method.

DLL Entry and Exit Routines

The Modem Interface API resides in the dynamic link library, MODEM.DLL. As with all DLLs, MODEM.DLL must have a **LibMain()** and a **WEP()**. These routines are contained in the files MODEM.C and MDWEP.C, respectively. You have already covered DLL entry and exit procedures, so you do not need to cover them in detail again. Instead, you can get right to the meat of the API.

ModemInitialize()

The ModemInitialize() routine initializes the global variables used in the remaining API routines. As seen in Listing 6.1, ModemInitialize() receives two parameters: a port ID and a far pointer to the name of an .INI file. This file stores the modem command and response strings. The routine starts by ensuring that there's a port initialized for modem usage. At this point, MODEM.DLL only enables communications with a single modem at a time.

Listing 6.1. MDINIT.C `ModemInitialize()` routine.

```
//
// Modem Interface DLL
//
// mdinit.c
//
// Modem Interface DLL initialization routine
//
// int FAR PASCAL _export ModemInitialize( int nComId,
//                                          LPCSTR szINIFile )
//
// parameters:
//     int      nComId      port that the modem is connected to
//     LPCSTR   szINIFile    far pointer to a zero-terminated .INI
//                           filename
//
// returns:
//     0     if initialization succeeded
//     <0    if initialization failed
//


//
// system include files
//
#include <windows.h>
#ifdef __BORLANDC__
#pragma hdrstop
#endif


//
// local include files
//
#include "modem.h"
#include "mdglobal.h"
#include "mdstring.h"


//
// ModemInitialize
//
#ifdef __BORLANDC__
#pragma argsused
#endif
int FAR PASCAL _export ModemInitialize( int nComId,
                                         LPCSTR szINIFile )
```

continues

Listing 6.1. continued

```
{
   //
   // automatic variables
   //

   //
   // check to ensure that a port is open
   // for modem operations
   //
   if ( nGlobalComId != -1 )
      return( IE_OPEN );

   //
   // save the com port ID
   //
   nGlobalComId = nComId;

   //
   // save the .INI filename
   //
   if ( szINIFile )
      lstrcpy( szINIFileName, szINIFile );
   else {
      LoadString( hLibInst, IDS_DEFAULTINIFILE, szTemp1,
                  sizeof( szTemp1 ) );
      lstrcpy( szINIFileName, szTemp1 );
   }

   //
   // return that the initialization worked
   //
   return( 0 );
}
```

If the program hasn't already initialized a modem, the routine stores the port ID in a global variable. Other API routines use this variable to check the validity of the port IDs passed to those functions. Next, the program saves the name of the .INI file used to save the modem commands and responses. If the .INI filename pointer is NULL, the program uses the default .INI file, MODEM.INI. Finally, the routine returns 0, indicating the initialization worked.

ModemTerminate()

Because the Modem Interface API enables only one modem to be used by the routines at a time, your program needs a way to end its usage of the API. ModemTerminate() can make the API available for another task. ModemTerminate() ensures that a modem is initialized and that the port ID received as a parameter is the same as the ID stored in the global variable. If either of these tests fails, the routine returns an error message. If both tests pass, the program sets the global ID variable to -1, indicating that the API is available for use. The routine clears the .INI filename and returns 0, indicating that the termination was successful. Listing 6.2 presents ModemTerminate().

Listing 6.2. MDTERM.C ModemTerminate() routine.

```
//
// Modem Interface DLL
//
// mdterm.c
//
// Modem Interface DLL termination routine
//
// int FAR PASCAL _export ModemTerminate( int nComId )
//
// parameters:
//    int       nComId      port that the modem is connected to
//
// returns:
//    0    if initialization succeeded
//    <0   if initialization failed
//


//
// system include files
//
#include <windows.h>
#ifdef __BORLANDC__
#pragma hdrstop
#endif

//
// local include files
//
#include "modem.h"
```

continues

Listing 6.2. continued

```c
#include "mdglobal.h"

//
// ModemTerminate()
//
int FAR PASCAL _export ModemTerminate( int nComId )
{
   //
   // ensure that a port is open
   //
   if ( nGlobalComId == -1 )
      return( IE_NOPEN );

   //
   // ensure that the IDs are the same
   //
   if( nGlobalComId != nComId )
      return( IE_NOPEN );

   //
   // clear the COM port ID
   //
   nGlobalComId = -1;

   //
   // clear the .INI filename
   //
   szINIFileName[ 0 ] = '\0';

   //
   // return value to show that the initialization worked
   //
   return( 0 );
}
```

ModemSettings()

Although the AT command set is the standard for communicating with modems, most modems have specific commands that enable you to access that particular modem's advanced features. ModemSettings() displays a dialog box, seen in Figure 6.3, that enables the user to enter the commands used by the API.

The Modem Settings dialog box enables the user to enter the command strings for initializing, dialing (both a prefix and a suffix), and hanging up the modem. Each of these commands should end with a ^M, which is converted into a carriage return before being sent to the modem. The default initialization command is ATZ^M. The default dialing prefix is ATDT and dialing suffix is ^M. The default modem hang-up command is ATH0^M.

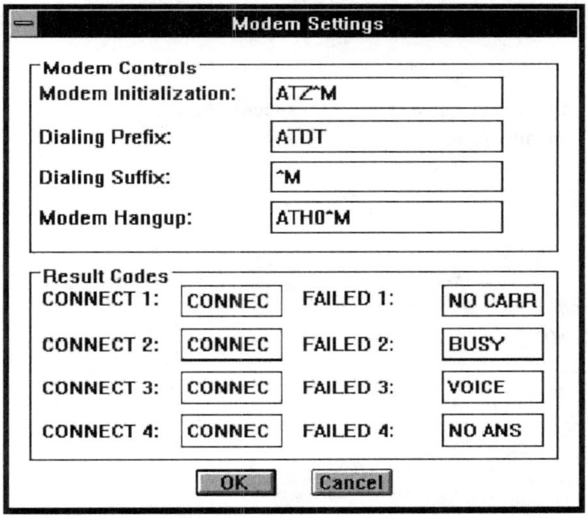

Figure 6.3.
Modem
Settings
dialog box.

The user can enter four connection strings also. These are the result codes returned by the modem, indicating that the connection was successful. The defaults for these fields are CONNECT 1200, CONNECT 2400, CONNECT 9600, and CONNECT 14400. The remaining four fields enable you to specify the result codes returned by the modem indicating that the connect failed. The defaults for these fields are NO CARRIER, BUSY, VOICE, and NO ANSWER.

Listing 6.3 presents the ModemSettings() routine and the accompanying dialog box procedure. ModemSettings() starts by checking the port ID for a match, returning an error if the test fails. The routine then loads the name of the Settings dialog box from the string table and starts the box.

Listing 6.3. MDSETTNG.C ModemSettings() routine.

```
//
// Modem Interface DLL
//
// mdsettng.c
//
// Modem Interface DLL Settings dialog box routines
//
// int FAR PASCAL _export ModemSettings( int nComId )
//
// parameters:
//    int      nComId       port that the modem is connected to
//
// returns:
//    0    if the settings dialog was successful
//    <0   if an error occurs
//


//
// system include files
//
#include <windows.h>
#ifdef __BORLANDC__
#pragma hdrstop
#endif


//
// local include files
//
#include "modem.h"
#include "mdglobal.h"
#include "mdstring.h"
#include "mdsettng.h"


//
// local function prototypes
//
BOOL FAR PASCAL _export ModemSettingsDialogProc( HWND hDlg,
                    UINT wMsg, WPARAM wParam, LPARAM lParam );


//
// ModemSettings()
//
int FAR PASCAL _export ModemSettings( int nComId, HWND hWnd )
{
```

```
    //
    // automatic variables
    //

    //
    // ensure that a port is open
    //
    if ( nGlobalComId == -1 )
       return( IE_NOPEN );

    //
    // ensure that the IDs are the same
    //
    if( nGlobalComId != nComId )
       return( IE_NOPEN );

    //
    // run the Modem Settings dialog box
    //
    LoadString( hLibInst, IDS_SETTINGS_DIALOG, szTemp1,
                sizeof( szTemp1 ) );
    DialogBox( hLibInst, szTemp1, hWnd, ModemSettingsDialogProc );

    //
    // return that everything worked
    //
    return( 0 );
}


//
// BOOL FAR PASCAL _export ModemSettingsDialogProc( HWND hDlg,
//                    UINT wMsg, WPARAM wParam, LPARAM lParam )
//
// parameters:
//    HWND      hDlg      handle to the dialog window
//    UINT      wMsg      window message being sent
//    WPARAM    wParam    word parameter of the message
//    LPARAM    lParam    long parameter of the message
//
// returns:
//    TRUE  if the message is processed
//    FALSE if the message is not processed
//
//
// ModemSettingsDialogProc
```

continues

Listing 6.3. continued

```
//
#ifdef __BORLANDC__
#pragma argsused
#endif
BOOL FAR PASCAL _export ModemSettingsDialogProc( HWND hDlg,
                       UINT wMsg, WPARAM wParam, LPARAM lParam )
{
   //
   // automatic variables
   //
   BOOL  bProcessed = TRUE;


   //
   // process based on the message
   //
   switch( wMsg ) {
      case WM_INITDIALOG:
         //
         // load the edit fields from the data in the .INI file
         //
         LoadString( hLibInst, IDS_INISECTION, szTemp1,
                    sizeof( szTemp1 ) );
         GetPrivateProfileString( szTemp1, "InitString", "ATZ^M",
                    szTemp2, sizeof( szTemp2 ), szINIFileName );
         SendDlgItemMessage( hDlg, INIT_EDIT, EM_LIMITTEXT,
                                              MAX_COMMAND, 0L );
         SetDlgItemText( hDlg, INIT_EDIT, szTemp2 );
         GetPrivateProfileString( szTemp1, "DialPrefix", "ATDT",
                    szTemp2, sizeof( szTemp2 ), szINIFileName );
         SendDlgItemMessage( hDlg, PREFIX_EDIT, EM_LIMITTEXT,
                             MAX_COMMAND, 0L );
         SetDlgItemText( hDlg, PREFIX_EDIT, szTemp2 );
         GetPrivateProfileString( szTemp1, "DialSuffix", "^M",
                    szTemp2, sizeof( szTemp2 ), szINIFileName );
         SendDlgItemMessage( hDlg, SUFFIX_EDIT, EM_LIMITTEXT,
                             MAX_COMMAND, 0L );
         SetDlgItemText( hDlg, SUFFIX_EDIT, szTemp2 );
         GetPrivateProfileString( szTemp1, "HangUp", "ATH0^M",
                    szTemp2, sizeof( szTemp2 ), szINIFileName );
         SendDlgItemMessage( hDlg, HANGUP_EDIT, EM_LIMITTEXT,
                             MAX_COMMAND, 0L );
         SetDlgItemText( hDlg, HANGUP_EDIT, szTemp2 );
         GetPrivateProfileString( szTemp1, "Connect1",
```

```
                            "CONNECT 1200", szTemp2,
                            sizeof( szTemp2 ), szINIFileName );
SendDlgItemMessage( hDlg, CONN1_EDIT, EM_LIMITTEXT,
                    MAX_RESULT, 0L );
SetDlgItemText( hDlg, CONN1_EDIT, szTemp2 );
GetPrivateProfileString( szTemp1, "Connect2",
                            "CONNECT 2400", szTemp2,
                            sizeof( szTemp2 ), szINIFileName );
SendDlgItemMessage( hDlg, CONN2_EDIT, EM_LIMITTEXT,
                    MAX_RESULT, 0L );
SetDlgItemText( hDlg, CONN2_EDIT, szTemp2 );
GetPrivateProfileString( szTemp1, "Connect3",
                            "CONNECT 9600", szTemp2,
                            sizeof( szTemp2 ), szINIFileName );
SendDlgItemMessage( hDlg, CONN3_EDIT, EM_LIMITTEXT,
                    MAX_RESULT, 0L );
SetDlgItemText( hDlg, CONN3_EDIT, szTemp2 );
GetPrivateProfileString( szTemp1, "Connect4",
                            "CONNECT 14400", szTemp2,
                            sizeof( szTemp2 ), szINIFileName );
SendDlgItemMessage( hDlg, CONN4_EDIT, EM_LIMITTEXT,
                    MAX_RESULT, 0L );
SetDlgItemText( hDlg, CONN4_EDIT, szTemp2 );
GetPrivateProfileString( szTemp1, "Fail1", "NO CARRIER",
            szTemp2, sizeof( szTemp2 ), szINIFileName );
SendDlgItemMessage( hDlg, FAIL1_EDIT, EM_LIMITTEXT,
                    MAX_RESULT, 0L );
SetDlgItemText( hDlg, FAIL1_EDIT, szTemp2 );
GetPrivateProfileString( szTemp1, "Fail2", "BUSY",
            szTemp2, sizeof( szTemp2 ), szINIFileName );
SendDlgItemMessage( hDlg, FAIL2_EDIT, EM_LIMITTEXT,
                    MAX_RESULT, 0L );
SetDlgItemText( hDlg, FAIL2_EDIT, szTemp2 );
GetPrivateProfileString( szTemp1, "Fail3", "VOICE",
            szTemp2, sizeof( szTemp2 ), szINIFileName );
SendDlgItemMessage( hDlg, FAIL3_EDIT, EM_LIMITTEXT,
                    MAX_RESULT, 0L );
SetDlgItemText( hDlg, FAIL3_EDIT, szTemp2 );
GetPrivateProfileString( szTemp1, "Fail4", "NO ANSWER",
            szTemp2, sizeof( szTemp2 ), szINIFileName );
SendDlgItemMessage( hDlg, FAIL4_EDIT, EM_LIMITTEXT,
                    MAX_RESULT, 0L );
SetDlgItemText( hDlg, FAIL4_EDIT, szTemp2 );
break;
```

continues

Listing 6.3. continued

```
case WM_COMMAND:
   //
   // process based on the parameter
   //
   switch( wParam ) {
      case IDOK:
         //
         // get the modem strings from the dialog fields
         // and add them to the .INI file
         //
         LoadString( hLibInst, IDS_INISECTION, szTemp1,
                                 sizeof( szTemp1 ) );
         GetDlgItemText( hDlg, INIT_EDIT, szTemp2,
                         sizeof( szTemp2 ) );
         WritePrivateProfileString( szTemp1, "InitString",
                                 szTemp2, szINIFileName );
         GetDlgItemText( hDlg, PREFIX_EDIT, szTemp2,
                         sizeof( szTemp2 ) );
         WritePrivateProfileString( szTemp1, "DialPrefix",
                                 szTemp2, szINIFileName );
         GetDlgItemText( hDlg, SUFFIX_EDIT, szTemp2,
                         sizeof( szTemp2 ) );
         WritePrivateProfileString( szTemp1, "DialSuffix",
                                 szTemp2, szINIFileName );
         GetDlgItemText( hDlg, HANGUP_EDIT, szTemp2,
                         sizeof( szTemp2 ) );
         WritePrivateProfileString( szTemp1, "HangUp",
                                 szTemp2, szINIFileName );
         GetDlgItemText( hDlg, CONN1_EDIT, szTemp2,
                         sizeof( szTemp2 ) );
         WritePrivateProfileString( szTemp1, "Connect1",
                                 szTemp2, szINIFileName );
         GetDlgItemText( hDlg, CONN2_EDIT, szTemp2,
                         sizeof( szTemp2 ) );
         WritePrivateProfileString( szTemp1, "Connect2",
                                 szTemp2, szINIFileName );
         GetDlgItemText( hDlg, CONN3_EDIT, szTemp2,
                         sizeof( szTemp2 ) );
         WritePrivateProfileString( szTemp1, "Connect3",
                                 szTemp2, szINIFileName );
         GetDlgItemText( hDlg, CONN4_EDIT, szTemp2,
                         sizeof( szTemp2 ) );
         WritePrivateProfileString( szTemp1, "Connect4",
                                 szTemp2, szINIFileName );
```

```
                GetDlgItemText( hDlg, FAIL1_EDIT, szTemp2,
                            sizeof( szTemp2 ) );
                WritePrivateProfileString( szTemp1, "Fail1",
                                szTemp2, szINIFileName );
                GetDlgItemText( hDlg, FAIL2_EDIT, szTemp2,
                            sizeof( szTemp2 ) );
                WritePrivateProfileString( szTemp1, "Fail2",
                                szTemp2, szINIFileName );
                GetDlgItemText( hDlg, FAIL3_EDIT, szTemp2,
                            sizeof( szTemp2 ) );
                WritePrivateProfileString( szTemp1, "Fail3",
                                szTemp2, szINIFileName );
                GetDlgItemText( hDlg, FAIL4_EDIT, szTemp2,
                            sizeof( szTemp2 ) );
                WritePrivateProfileString( szTemp1, "Fail4",
                                szTemp2, szINIFileName );


            //
            // terminate the dialog with an OK indication
            //
            EndDialog( hDlg, TRUE );
            break;

        case IDCANCEL:
            //
            // terminate the dialog with a cancel indication
            //
            EndDialog( hDlg, FALSE );
            break;

        default:
            //
            // indicate that the message wasn't processed
            //
            bProcessed = FALSE;
            break;
    }
    break;

default:
    //
    // indicate that the message wasn't processed
    //
    bProcessed = FALSE;
    break;
```

continues

255

Listing 6.3. continued

```
    }

    //
    // return the result value
    //
    return( bProcessed );
}
```

The processing for the Modem Settings dialog box is performed by `ModemSettingsDialogProc()`, as seen in Listing 6.3. The major processing for this dialog box is performed during the `WM_INITDIALOG` message and the `WM_COMMAND` message with an `IDOK` control ID. The `WM_INITDIALOG` message processing starts by getting the .INI file section name from the string table. The .INI filename was set during `ModemInitialize()`. The routine then gets the modem-initialization command from the .INI file using **`GetPrivateProfileString()`**. Next, the function limits the number of characters that the edit control enables in the string by sending an `EM_LIMITTEXT` message to the edit control. Finally, the modem-initialization string is placed in the edit control with a call to **`SetDlgItemText()`**. These three steps are repeated for the remaining fields in the dialog box.

When the user clicks the OK button, the program receives a `WM_COMMAND` message with an `IDOK` control ID. At this point, the user has completed editing the modem-command and -results strings. The program has to take the updated strings and put them in the .INI file. For each field in the dialog box, the program calls **`GetDlgItemText()`** to retrieve the updated command or result string. The program then calls **`WritePrivateProfileString()`** to save the string in the .INI file. When all the fields have been processed, **`EndDialog()`** returns a TRUE to the calling routine.

ModemSendInitString()

This routine initializes the modem. It takes the string the user entered in the Modem Initialization field of the Modem Settings dialog box and sends it to the modem. It then waits for a result from the modem. `ModemSendInitString()` is shown in Listing 6.4 and discussed in detail in the following paragraphs.

Listing 6.4. MDSNDIS.C `ModemSendInitString()` routine.

```
//
// Modem Interface DLL
//
// mdsndis.c
//
// Modem Interface DLL Send Modem Init String
//
// int FAR PASCAL _export ModemSendInitString( int nComId,
//                                             HWND hWnd )
//
// parameters:
//    int      nComId   port that the modem is connected to
//    HWND     hWnd     window handle of the terminal window
//
// returns:
//    0     if initialization succeeded
//    <0    if initialization failed
//


//
// system include files
//
#include <windows.h>
#ifdef __BORLANDC__
#pragma hdrstop
#endif


//
// local include files
//
#include "..\tsmcomm\tsmcomm.h"
#include "modem.h"
#include "mdglobal.h"
#include "mdstring.h"
#include "mdsettng.h"


//
// ModemSendInitString
//
int FAR PASCAL _export ModemSendInitString( int nComId,
                                            HWND hWnd )
{
    //
```

continues

Listing 6.4. continued

```
// automatic variables
  //
  char        szOK[5],
              szError[8],
              cChar;  BOOL        fOrigPolled,
              fContinue;
  int         nResult = 0,
              nOK,
              nError,
              nOKLimit,
              nErrorLimit,
              nInChar;
  DWORD       dwStart;

  //
  // ensure that a port is open
  //
  if ( nGlobalComId == -1 )
     return( IE_NOPEN );

  //
  // ensure that the IDs are the same
  //
  if( nGlobalComId != nComId )
     return( IE_NOPEN );

  //
  // get the initialization string from the .INI file
  //
  LoadString( hLibInst, IDS_INISECTION, szTemp1,
              sizeof( szTemp1 ) );
  GetPrivateProfileString( szTemp1, "InitString", "ATZ^M",
                    szTemp2, sizeof( szTemp2 ), szINIFileName );

  //
  // convert the initialization string
  //
  ModemConvertString( szTemp2 );

  //
  // initialize the variables
  //
  lstrcpy( szOK, "OK\r\n" );
  lstrcpy( szError, "ERROR\r\n" );
```

```
nOK = 0;
nError = 0;
fContinue = TRUE;
nOKLimit = lstrlen( szOK );
nErrorLimit = lstrlen( szError );

//
// set the communications to polled
//
fOrigPolled = TSMGetPollingEnabled( nComId );
if ( !fOrigPolled )
   TSMEnablePolling( nComId );

//
// write the initialization string to modem
//
TSMWriteComm( nComId, lstrlen( szTemp2 ), szTemp2 );

//
// get the starting tick count
//
dwStart = GetTickCount();

//
// loop until through or a TO occurs
//
while ( fContinue ) {
   if ( ( nInChar = TSMReadCommChar( nComId ) ) > 0 ) {
      cChar = nInChar;
      if ( cChar == szOK[ nOK ] ) {
         nOK++;
         if ( nOK == nOKLimit ) {
            nResult = 0;
            fContinue = FALSE;
            continue;
         }
      } else {
         nOK = 0;
      }
      if ( cChar == szError[ nError ] ) {
         nError++;
         if ( nError == nErrorLimit ) {
            nResult = 1;
            fContinue = FALSE;
            continue;
```

continues

Listing 6.4. continued

```
              }
          } else {
            nError = 0;
          }       }


    //
    // check for a timeout
    //
    if ( dwStart + 6000 < GetTickCount() ) {
       nResult = 1;
       fContinue = FALSE;
    }
  }

  //
  // restore the original communications method
  //
  if ( !fOrigPolled )
     TSMEnableMessages( nComId, hWnd );

  //
  // return the result
  //
  return( nResult );
}


//
// ModemConvertString
//
void ModemConvertString( LPSTR szString )
{
  //
  // automatic variables
  //
  int   nIn  = 0,
        nOut = 0;

  //
  // loop through this string converting ^M to \r
  //
  while ( szString[ nIn ] ) {
     //
     // is this character a ^?
     //
```

```
        if ( szString[ nIn ] == '^' ) {
            if ( szString[ nIn + 1 ] == 'M' ) {
                szString[ nOut ] = '\r';
                nIn++;
            }
        }

        //
        // update the pointers
        //
        nIn++;
        nOut++;
    }

    //
    // add a null at the end
    //
    szString[ nOut ] = '\0';
}
```

ModemSendInitString() starts by performing the standard port ID checks, returning an error if either test fails. It then gets the modem-initialization string from the .INI file. The routine calls ModemConvertString() to change the ^M to a carriage return (0x0D). Next, it initializes the variables used to wait for the result code from the modem, saving the current communications method and setting the method of polling if it is not already. Finally, the program sends the initialization command to the modem using TSMWriteComm().

With this routine two assumptions are made: The modem is not in quiet mode, and the result codes are verbal. If either of these conditions is not true, ModemSendInitString() does not work. The routine uses three variables to check for the OK result code and another three variables to check for the ERROR result code. In both cases the first variable is a character array that contains the string followed by a carriage return and line feed. The second variable is an integer that indicates the current character in the array and the final variable is an integer equal to the length of the string.

The routine continues by getting the tick count from Windows. This is the number of timer ticks that have occurred since Windows started, the starting time for timeout checking. Next, a loop begins and continues until the routine matches one of the result codes or a timeout occurs.

The loop starts by calling TSMReadCommChar() to get a single character from the received-character queue. If a character was received, it is converted from an integer to a character and checked against the OK string character that the program is trying to match. If they are the same, the routine increments its current-character counter. It then checks whether the current-character counter has reached the end of the string. If it has, the routine sets the result to 0 and the loop continuation flag to FALSE and continues to the next iteration of the while loop. If the character received and the current OK character do not match, the current OK character is set back to the start of the string. The routine then performs the same checking for the ERROR result code except for setting the result to 1 if it matches the ERROR code.

If neither result code terminates the loop, the routine checks for a timeout. The program has a hard-coded, six-second, timeout period. The program checks whether the starting time tick plus 6000 is less than the current tick count. If it is, over six seconds have elapsed and the program sets the result code to 1 and the loop continuation flag to FALSE. When the routine exits the while loop, it returns the communication method back to its original setting and returns the result to the calling program.

ModemDial()

ModemDial() enables users to place a call to another computer using the modem. It takes the dialing prefix, the dialing suffix (both from the Modem Settings dialog box), and the phone number it receives as a parameter and combines them into a single dialing command, as shown in Figure 6.4. This composite command is then used to command the modem to dial.

ModemDial() starts by ensuring that a port is initialized and that the IDs are the same. The routine then gets the dialing prefix and suffix from the .INI file and combines them with the telephone number to form the actual dialing command. This command is passed to ModemConvertString(), which changes any ^M to carriage returns. Several global variables to be used by the Dialing dialog box are initialized, and pointers to the remote system's name and telephone number are saved as well as the window handle of the terminal window. Finally, the program starts the Dialing dialog box. This code is shown in Listing 6.5. ModemDial() exits, returning the dialing result code, when control returns from DialingDialogProc().

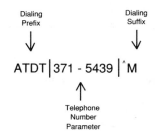

Figure 6.4.
Dialing
command
structure.

Listing 6.5. MDDIAL.C `ModemDial()` routine.

```
//
// Modem Interface DLL
//
// mddial.c
//
// Modem Interface DLL dialing routines
//
// int FAR PASCAL _export ModemDial( int nComId, LPCSTR szName,
//                                   LPCSTR szNumber, HWND hWnd )
//
// parameters:
//     int      nComId    port that the modem is connected to
//     LPCSTR   szName     name of the system being dialed
//     LPCSTR   szNumber   far pointer to the telephone number to
//                         dial
//     HWND     hWnd       handle of the terminal window
//
// returns:
//     DIAL_CONNECT   if dial was successful
//     DIAL_FAIL      if one of the fail codes was recognized
//     DIAL_CANCEL    if user presses the CANCEL button
//     DIAL_TIMEOUT   if 45 seconds pass without recognizing a
//                    connect or fail code
//


//
// system include files
//
#include <windows.h>
#ifdef __BORLANDC__
#pragma hdrstop
#endif
```

continues

Listing 6.5. continued

```
//
// local include files
//
#include "..\tsmcomm\tsmcomm.h"
#include "modem.h"
#include "mdglobal.h"
#include "mdstring.h"
#include "mdsettng.h"
#include "mddial.h"

//
// local function prototypes
//
BOOL FAR PASCAL _export DialingDialogProc( HWND hDlg, UINT wMsg,
                                  WPARAM wParam, LPARAM lParam );

//
// local global variables
//
int       nTimerCount;
LPCSTR    lpDispName;
LPCSTR    lpDispNumber;
int       nConnCurr[4];
int       nConnLimit[4];
int       nFailCurr[4];
int       nFailLimit[4];
char      szConnects[4][21];
char      szFails[4][21];
BOOL      fOrigPolled;
int       nDialResult;
HWND      hWndTerm;

//
// ModemDial
//
#ifdef __BORLANDC__
#pragma argsused
#endif
int FAR PASCAL _export ModemDial( int nComId, LPCSTR szName,
                                  LPCSTR szNumber, HWND hWnd )
{
   //
   // automatic variables
   //
```

```
char  szPrefix[61],
      szSuffix[61];

//
// ensure that a port is open
//
if ( nGlobalComId == -1 )
   return( IE_NOPEN );

//
// ensure that the IDs are the same
//
if( nGlobalComId != nComId )
   return( IE_NOPEN );

//
// get the dialing prefix and suffix strings from the .INI file
//
LoadString( hLibInst, IDS_INISECTION, szTemp1,
            sizeof( szTemp1 ) );
GetPrivateProfileString( szTemp1, "DialPrefix", "ATDT",
                szPrefix, sizeof( szPrefix ), szINIFileName );
GetPrivateProfileString( szTemp1, "DialSuffix", "^M",
                szSuffix, sizeof( szSuffix ), szINIFileName );

//
// combine the prefix, the number, and the suffix
//
lstrcpy( szTemp2, szPrefix );
lstrcat( szTemp2, szNumber );
lstrcat( szTemp2, szSuffix );

//
// convert the initialization string
//
ModemConvertString( szTemp2 );

//
// point the display variables to the name and number
//
lpDispName = szName;
lpDispNumber = szNumber;

//
// store the window handle
//
```

Listing 6.5. continued

```
   hWndTerm = hWnd;

   //
   // start the dialing dialog box
   //
   LoadString( hLibInst, IDS_DIALING_DIALOG, szTemp1,
               sizeof( szTemp1 ) );
   DialogBox( hLibInst, szTemp1, hWnd, DialingDialogProc );

   //
   // return the result
   //
   return( nDialResult );
}


//
// BOOL FAR PASCAL _export DialingDialogProc( HWND hDlg,
//                       UINT wMsg, WPARAM wParam, LPARAM lParam )
//
// parameters:
//    HWND      hDlg     handle to the dialog window
//    UINT      wMsg     window message being sent
//    WPARAM    wParam   word parameter of the message
//    LPARAM    lParam   long parameter of the message
//
// returns:
//    TRUE  if the message has been processed
//    FALSE if the message is not processed
//
#ifdef __BORLANDC__
#pragma argsused
#endif
BOOL FAR PASCAL _export DialingDialogProc( HWND hDlg, UINT wMsg, WPARAM
                                           wParam, LPARAM lParam )
{
   //
   // automatic variables
   //
   BOOL  bProcessed = TRUE;
   char  szValue[20];
   int   i, j;
   LPSTR lpCurrChar;
```

```
//
// process based on the message
//
switch( wMsg ) {
   case WM_INITDIALOG:
      //
      // load the connect and fail strings from the .INI file
      //
      LoadString( hLibInst, IDS_INISECTION, szTemp1,
                                    sizeof( szTemp1 ) );
      GetPrivateProfileString( szTemp1, "Connect1",
                          "CONNECT 1200", szConnects[0],
                    sizeof( szConnects[0] ), szINIFileName );
      GetPrivateProfileString( szTemp1, "Connect2",
                          "CONNECT 2400", szConnects[1],
                    sizeof( szConnects[1] ), szINIFileName );
      GetPrivateProfileString( szTemp1, "Connect3",
                          "CONNECT 9600", szConnects[2],
                    sizeof( szConnects[2] ), szINIFileName );
      GetPrivateProfileString( szTemp1, "Connect4",
                          "CONNECT 19200", szConnects[3],
                    sizeof( szConnects[3] ), szINIFileName );
      GetPrivateProfileString( szTemp1, "Fail1", "NO CARRIER",
            szFails[0], sizeof( szFails[0] ), szINIFileName );
      GetPrivateProfileString( szTemp1, "Fail2", "BUSY",
            szFails[1], sizeof( szFails[1] ), szINIFileName );
      GetPrivateProfileString( szTemp1, "Fail3", "VOICE",
            szFails[2], sizeof( szFails[2] ), szINIFileName );
      GetPrivateProfileString( szTemp1, "Fail4", "NO ANSWER",
            szFails[3], sizeof( szFails[3] ), szINIFileName );

      //
      // initialize the current and limit offsets
      //
      for ( i = 0; i < 4; i++ ) {
         nConnCurr[ i ] = 0;
         nConnLimit[ i ] = lstrlen( szConnects[ i ] );
         nFailCurr[ i ] = 0;
         nFailLimit[ i ] = lstrlen( szFails[ i ] );
      }

      //
      // display the system name and number
      //
      SetDlgItemText( hDlg, NAME_TEXT, lpDispName );
      SetDlgItemText( hDlg, NUMBER_TEXT, lpDispNumber );
```

continues

Listing 6.5. continued

```
        //
        // set the communications to polled
        //
        fOrigPolled = TSMGetPollingEnabled( nGlobalComId );
        if ( !fOrigPolled )
           TSMEnablePolling( nGlobalComId );

        //
        // write the dialing command to the modem
        //
        TSMWriteComm( nGlobalComId, lstrlen( szTemp2 ),
                      szTemp2 );

        //
        // start a timer
        //
        nTimerCount = 0;
        wsprintf( szTemp1, "%d", nTimerCount );
        SetDlgItemText( hDlg, COUNT_TEXT, szTemp1 );
        SetTimer( hDlg, 0, 1000, NULL );

        //
        // read characters from the COM port
        //
        TSMReadComm( nGlobalComId, hDlg );
        break;

    case WM_COMMAND:
        //
        // process based on the parameter
        //
        switch( wParam ) {
           case IDCANCEL:
              //
              // user pressed the CANCEL button
              //
              // write a character to the port to terminate
              // dialing
              //
              TSMWriteComm( nGlobalComId, 1, "\r" );

              //
              // set the result code, send a WM_CLOSE, and end
```

```
                        // the dialog with a FALSE
                        //
                        nDialResult = DIAL_CANCEL;
                        SendMessage( hDlg, WM_CLOSE, 0, 0l );
                        EndDialog( hDlg, FALSE );
                        break;

                default:
                    //
                    // indicate that this message wasn't processed
                    //
                    bProcessed = FALSE;
                    break;
            }
            break;

        case WM_TIMER:
            //
            // process the timer tick
            //
            // increment the count and display it
            //
            nTimerCount++;
            wsprintf( szTemp1, "%d", nTimerCount );
            SetDlgItemText( hDlg, COUNT_TEXT, szTemp1 );

            //
            // check for a time-out
            //
            if ( nTimerCount == 45 ) {
                //
                // routine has waited 45 seconds--a time-out
                //
                // write a character to the port to terminate dialing
                //
                TSMWriteComm( nGlobalComId, 1, "\r" );

                //
                // set the result code, send a WM_CLOSE and end the
                // dialog with a FALSE
                //
                nDialResult = DIAL_TIMEOUT;
                SendMessage( hDlg, WM_CLOSE, 0, 0l );
                EndDialog( hDlg, FALSE );
            }
```

continues

Listing 6.5. continued

```
            //
            // read characters from the communications port
            //
            TSMReadComm( nGlobalComId, hDlg );
            break;

        case WM_CLOSE:
            //
            // this is a fake WM_CLOSE that just does
            // termination things
            //

            //
            // kill the timer
            //
            KillTimer( hDlg, 0 );

            //
            // restore the original communications method
            //
            if ( !fOrigPolled )
                TSMEnableMessages( nGlobalComId, hWndTerm );
            break;

        case WM_COMM_CHARS:
            //
            // process the characters received from the modem
            //
            for ( i = 0, lpCurrChar = (LPSTR)lParam; i < wParam;
                i++, lpCurrChar++ ) {
                //
                // check the connect messages
                //
                for ( j = 0; j < 4; j++ ) {
                    if ( *lpCurrChar ==
                            szConnects[ j ][ nConnCurr[ j ] ] ) {
                        nConnCurr[j]++;
                        if ( nConnCurr[j] == nConnLimit[j] ) {
                            nDialResult = DIAL_CONNECT;
                            SendMessage( hDlg, WM_CLOSE, 0, 0l );
                            EndDialog( hDlg, TRUE );
                        }
                    } else {
```

```
                        nConnCurr[j] = 0;
                    }
                }

                //
                // check the fail messages
                //
                for ( j = 0; j < 4; j++ ) {
                    if ( *lpCurrChar == szFails[j][nFailCurr[j]] ) {
                        nFailCurr[j]++;
                        if ( nFailCurr[j] == nFailLimit[j] ) {
                            nDialResult = DIAL_FAIL;
                            SendMessage( hDlg, WM_CLOSE, 0, 0l );
                            EndDialog( hDlg, FALSE );
                        }
                    } else {
                        nFailCurr[j] = 0;
                    }
                }

                //
                // send the character to the terminal
                //
                SendMessage( hWndTerm, WM_COMM_CHARS, 1,
                            (LONG)lpCurrChar );
            }
            break;

        default:
            //
            // indicate that this message wasn't processed
            //
            bProcessed = FALSE;
            break;
    }

    //
    // return the result value
    //
    return( bProcessed );
}
```

The Dialing dialog box, seen in Figure 6.5, is displayed to give the user an indication that the dialing process is proceeding. This shows the name of the system the computer is calling, the number dialed, and the number of seconds that the computer has waited for a connection. The real purpose of this dialog is to process the incoming characters for the result codes while still maintaining the multitasking nature of Windows. The function DialingDialogProc() processes the messages for this dialog box. Each message that it handles is discussed in the following paragraphs.

Figure 6.5.
Dialing
dialog box.

The first message processed by DialingDialogProc() is the WM_INITDIALOG message. The routine starts processing this message by loading the connect and fail result codes from the .INI file into separate character arrays. The current character pointer and the limits are set. These character arrays and integer offsets are used for result-code matching, similar to the code in ModemSendInitString(). The routine then uses **SetDlgItemText()** to display the system name and number that it is dialing.

The routine continues WM_INITDIALOG processing by getting the current communications method and setting the communications method to polled if it was message-based. Then the function writes to the modem the dialing command constructed earlier. At this time, the routine initializes and displays the timer counter and starts a Windows timer using **SetTimer()**. This timer expires every second. Finally, the routine calls TSMReadComm() to process the incoming characters.

The timer started during the WM_INITDIALOG command expires every second. When it does, the program receives a WM_TIMER message. The processing of this message starts by incrementing the timer counter and displaying its new value. The program then checks for a timeout by testing whether the timer counter equals 45. If it does, a timeout occurs, and the program writes a carriage return to the port to terminate dialing. Next, the program sets the dialing result code to `DIAL_TIMEOUT` and sends the dialog box a `WM_CLOSE` message, ending the dialog with a `FALSE` return code. If a timeout has not occurred, the program reads characters from the communications port.

When the program reads characters from the serial port during the `WM_INITDIALOG` or `WM_TIMER` messages, it receives a `WM_COMM_CHARS` message that points to the characters received. The program processes `WM_COMM_CHARS` by trying to match the incoming characters with one of the connect or fail result codes. This is done by looping through each character received. The `for` loop initializes a far pointer to the first character received and updates that pointer for each character in the buffer. Another `for` loop checks the current communications character against each connect message in turn. If the character does not match the connect message, the current match character is set back to the first character of the connect string. If the character does match the connect message, the current match character is incremented to the next character in the connect string. The program then checks whether it has reached the limit on this string; if the program has reached the limit, it has connected successfully. When a connection is successful, the program sets the dialing result code to `DIAL_CONNECT`, sends the dialog box a `WM_CLOSE` message, and terminates the dialog box with a `TRUE` indication.

The `WM_COMM_CHARS` processing continues by checking the fail messages in the same manner as the connect messages. If the routine matches one of the fail result codes, it sets the dialing result to `DIAL_FAIL`, sends a `WM_CLOSE` message to the dialog box, and terminates the dialog box with a `FALSE` indication. Finally, the program sends the current character to the terminal emulation window so it can be displayed on the screen.

The dialog box also contains a CANCEL button. When the user clicks this button, the program receives a `WM_COMMAND` message with a `IDCANCEL` control ID. To process the `WM_COMMAND` message, the program first writes a carriage return to the modem to cancel the dialing process. Next, it sets the dialing result code to `DIAL_CANCEL`, sends a `WM_CLOSE` message, and ends the dialog with a `FALSE` indication.

Each time the program ends the dialog box, the program sends a `WM_CLOSE` message to itself. A dialog box does not normally receive a `WM_CLOSE` message; the program is using the message to do the necessary termination for the dialog procedure. The first item taken care of in the `WM_CLOSE` processing is the timer. The routine kills the timer that was started back in the `WM_INITDIALOG` message. Next, the program restores the communications back to its original method.

ModemHangup()

Because you now can dial another system using your modem, you also need to be able to hang it up. ModemHangup() offers you the choice of two methods for hanging up the modem.

1. Sending an Escape command followed by the Modem Hangup command specified in the Modem Settings dialog box.

2. Dropping DTR to force a modem hang-up.

ModemHangup() starts by ensuring that it has received the correct port ID, returning an error if this is not the case. The routine checks whether it is doing a software or hardware hang-up. If the routine is doing a software hang-up, the processing continues in the same manner as the ModemSendInitString() processing. This section doesn't cover the processing in detail, just the following differences. The routine sends two commands and waits for two responses. First, the routine sends the Escape (+++) command to change from online mode to command mode. Second, the routine sends the hang-up command.

The code in Listing 6.6 demonstrates processing for a hardware hang-up. First, the routine drops the DTR to a low state using **EscapeCommFunction()**. This function directly manipulates the serial port's RS-232 control lines. Next, the routine waits for 100 milliseconds. Dropping DTR for over 50 milliseconds causes most modems to hang up if a call is active. The routine then raises DTR high with another call to **EscapeCommFunction()**.

Listing 6.6. MDHANGUP.C ModemHangup() routine.

```
//
// Modem Interface DLL
//
// mdhangup.c
//
// Modem Interface DLL hang-up modem routines
//
// int FAR PASCAL _export ModemHangup( int nComId,
//                                 BOOL bSoftware, HWND hWnd )
//
// parameters:
//    int   nComId     port that the modem is connected to
//    BOOL  bSoftware  TRUE if software hang-up,
//                     FALSE for hardware hang-up
```

```
//     HWND   hWnd        window handle of terminal window
//
// returns:
//     0     if hang-up succeeded
//     <0    if hang-up failed
//


//
// system include files
//
#include <windows.h>
#ifdef __BORLANDC__
#pragma hdrstop
#endif

//
// local include files
//
#include "..\tsmcomm\tsmcomm.h"
#include "modem.h"
#include "mdglobal.h"
#include "mdstring.h"
#include "mdsettng.h"


//
// ModemHangup
//
int FAR PASCAL _export ModemHangup( int nComId, BOOL bSoftware,
                                    HWND hWnd )
{
   //
   // automatic variables
   //
   char      szOK[5],
             szError[8],
             cChar;
   BOOL      fOrigPolled,
             fContinue;
   int       nResult = 0,
             nOK,
             nError,
             nOKLimit,
             nErrorLimit,
             nInChar;
   DWORD     dwStart;
```

continues

Listing 6.6. continued

```
//
// ensure that a port is open
//
if ( nGlobalComId == -1 )
   return( IE_NOPEN );

//
// ensure that the IDs are the same
//
if( nGlobalComId != nComId )
   return( IE_NOPEN );

//
// determine whether it is a hardware or software hang-up
//
if ( bSoftware ) {
   //
   // do a software hang-up
   //
   // set the communications to polled
   //
   fOrigPolled = TSMGetPollingEnabled( nComId );
   if ( !fOrigPolled )
      TSMEnablePolling( nComId );

   //
   // initialize the variables
   //
   lstrcpy( szOK, "OK\r\n" );
   nOK = 0;
   fContinue = TRUE;
   nOKLimit = lstrlen( szOK );

   //
   // wait for 1 second
   //
   dwStart = GetTickCount();
   while ( dwStart + 1000 > GetTickCount() )
      ;

   //
   // write the hang-up string to modem
   //
   TSMWriteComm( nComId, 3, "+++" );
```

```
//
// get the starting tick count
//
dwStart = GetTickCount();

//
// loop until through or until a timeout occurs
//
while ( fContinue ) {
   if ( ( nInChar = TSMReadCommChar( nComId ) ) > 0 ) {
      cChar = nInChar;
      if ( cChar == szOK[ nOK ] ) {
         nOK++;
         if ( nOK == nOKLimit ) {
            fContinue = FALSE;
            continue;
         }
      } else {
         nOK = 0;
      }
   }

   //
   // check for a timeout
   //
   if ( dwStart + 3000 < GetTickCount() ) {
      nResult = IE_DEFAULT;
      fContinue = FALSE;
   }
}

//
// if nResult is 1, the program did not get
// the okay and should quit
//
if ( nResult == IE_DEFAULT ) {
   //
   // restore the original communications method
   //
   if ( !fOrigPolled )
      TSMEnableMessages( nComId, hWnd );

   //
   // return the error indication
   //
```

continues

Listing 6.6. continued

```
        return( nResult );
    }

    //
    // get the hang-up string from the .INI file
    //
    LoadString( hLibInst, IDS_INISECTION, szTemp1,
                sizeof( szTemp1 ) );
    GetPrivateProfileString( szTemp1, "HangUp", "ATH^M",
                    zTemp2, sizeof( szTemp2 ), szINIFileName );

    //
    // convert the hang-up string
    //
    ModemConvertString( szTemp2 );

    //
    // initialize the variables
    //
    lstrcpy( szOK, "OK\r\n" );
    lstrcpy( szError, "ERROR\r\n" );
    nOK = 0;
    nError = 0;
    fContinue = TRUE;
    nOKLimit = lstrlen( szOK );
    nErrorLimit = lstrlen( szError );

    //
    // write the hang-up string to the modem
    //
    TSMWriteComm( nComId, lstrlen( szTemp2 ), szTemp2 );

    //
    // get the starting tick count
    //
    dwStart = GetTickCount();

    //
    // loop until through or until a timeout occurs
    //
    while ( fContinue ) {
        if ( ( nInChar = TSMReadCommChar( nComId ) ) > 0 ) {
            cChar = nInChar;
            if ( cChar == szOK[ nOK ] ) {
```

```
        nOK++;
        if ( nOK == nOKLimit ) {
            //
            // OK has been received; terminate the loop
            //
            fContinue = FALSE;

            //
            // hang-up--send a FAKE NO CARRIER to
            // the screen
            //
            SendMessage( hWnd, WM_COMM_CHARS, 12,
                        (LONG)(LPSTR)"NO CARRIER\r\n" );
            continue;
        }
    } else {
        nOK = 0;
    }
    if ( cChar == szError[ nError ] ) {
        nError++;
        if ( nError == nErrorLimit ) {
            //
            // the ERROR message has been received
            //
            nResult = IE_DEFAULT;
            fContinue = FALSE;
            continue;
        }
    } else {
        nError = 0;
    }
}


//
// check for a timeout
//
if ( dwStart + 6000 < GetTickCount() ) {
    nResult = IE_DEFAULT;
    fContinue = FALSE;
}
}
//
// restore the original communications method
//
if ( !fOrigPolled )
```

continues

Listing 6.6. continued

```
        TSMEnableMessages( nComId, hWnd );
    } else {
        //
        // do a hardware hang-up by dropping DTR
        //
        // drop DTR
        //
        EscapeCommFunction( nComId, CLRDTR );

        //
        // wait for 100 milliseconds
        //
        dwStart = GetTickCount();
        while ( dwStart + 100 > GetTickCount() )
            ;

        //
        // raise DTR again
        //
        EscapeCommFunction( nComId, SETDTR );
    }

    //
    // return the result
    //
    return( nResult );
}
```

Now that you have a basic Modem Interface API, you can add the capability to place calls to TSMTerm.

Adding Modem Control to TSMTerm

TSMTerm is a general-purpose communications package, so it needs to be able to communicate with the modem for initialization, dialing, and hanging up. Fortunately, the Modem Interface API just developed meets these requirements. Figure 6.6 shows the modification made to the TSMTerm menu for the addition of modem control. This chapter adds a Dialing Directory entry to the main menu as well as a Modem Commands drop-down menu.

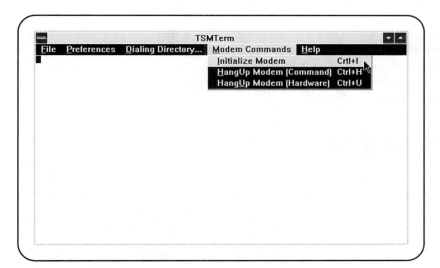

Figure 6.6.
TSMTerm menu with modem API support.

Modem Commands

The Modem Commands drop-down menu includes three menu items. These items—Initialize Modem, HangUp Modem (Command), and HangUp Modem (Hardware)—map directly to Modem Interface API calls. The code fragment below, from `TSMTermWindowProc()`, process each of these menu items.

```
case IDM_MODEM_INIT:
   if ( ModemSendInitString( nComId, hWnd ) )
      MessageBox( hWnd, "Modem Initialization Failed", szTSMTerm,
                  MB_ICONINFORMATION ¦ MB_OK );
   else
      MessageBox( hWnd, "Modem Initialized", szTSMTerm,
                  MB_ICONINFORMATION ¦ MB_OK );
   break;

case IDM_MODEM_HANGUP_SOFT:
```

```
      ModemHangup( nComId, TRUE, hWnd );
      break;

   case IDM_MODEM_HANGUP_HARD:
      ModemHangup( nComId, FALSE, hWnd );
      break;
```

When the user selects one of these menu items, the program calls the appropriate Modem Interface API function. When the program attempts to initialize the modem, a message box tells the user whether the initialization was successful. These menu items give the program most of the modem functionality it needs, except for the capability to dial the modem.

Dialing Directory

When the program needs to dial the modem, it could prompt the user to enter the phone number each time, but this would be an inconvenience. I can never remember the numbers of all the bulletin boards I call. The solution: Have the program keep track of those numbers by adding a dialing directory to your program. Users enter the name, number, and communication parameters for the systems they call. As was shown in Figure 6.6, the dialing directory is selected by clicking the Dialing Directory main menu item. When users select that menu item, the Dialing Directory dialog box, as shown in Figure 6.7, appears.

DialingDirDialogProc() handles the processing for this dialog box. The main

Figure 6.7.
TSMTerm
Dialing
Directory
dialog box.

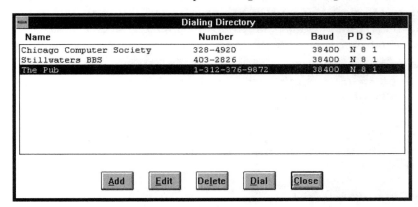

control of this dialog box is a listbox that displays the dialing directory entries. Users can select entries in this listbox by clicking them with the mouse. The other controls are all buttons that either do something separate from the selected listbox item, such as ADD and CLOSE, or act on the selected listbox item, which can be EDIT, DELETE, and DIAL. Each of the messages that `DialingDirDialogProc()` processes is discussed in the following paragraphs.

The `WM_INITDIALOG` message initializes the dialog box. The routine starts by sending a `WM_SETFONT` message, telling the listbox to use the `SYSTEM_FIXED_FONT` for its display. Next, the routine sets the tab stop locations in the listbox. These locations are designed so that the string added to and retrieved from the listbox has the format shown in Figure 6.8. By using the tab characters as field separators, the routine can break apart the string easily. Setting the tabs requires sending the `LB_SETTABSTOPS` message to the listbox with a pointer to an array containing the tab stops.

Finally, the program calls `ReadDialingDir()` to get the dialing directory entries

Tab Separators

Name \t Number \t Baud \t Parity \t Data Bits \t Stop Bits

Figure 6.8.
Dialing
directory
entry
format.

from the .INI file and copy them into the listbox. This routine and `DialingDirDialogProc()` are presented in Listing 6.7. `ReadDialingDir()` is straightforward and is not discussed in detail here. However, because of the method used to store the directory entries in the .INI file, the program can have only 63 directory entries.

Listing 6.7. TTDIALDR.C `DialingDirDialogProc()` routine.

```
//
// TSM Terminal Program
//
// ttdialdr.c
//
// dialing directory routines
//
// BOOL FAR PASCAL _export DialingDirDialogProc( HWND hDlg,
//                    UINT wMsg, WPARAM wParam, LPARAM lParam )
```

continues

Listing 6.7. continued

```
//
// parameters:
//    HWND     hDlg      handle to the dialog window
//    UINT     wMsg      window message being sent
//    WPARAM   wParam    word parameter of the message
//    LPARAM   lParam    long parameter of the message
//
// returns:
//    TRUE   if the message is processed
//    FALSE  if the message is not processed
//


//
// system include files
//
#include <windows.h>
#ifdef __BORLANDC__
#pragma hdrstop
#endif
#include <string.h>


//
// local include files
//
#include "..\tsmcomm\tsmcomm.h"
#include "..\modem\modem.h"
#include "tsmterm.h"
#include "ttglobal.h"
#include "ttstring.h"
#include "ttdialdr.h"


//
// local function prototypes
//
void SaveDialingDir( HWND hDlg );
void ReadDialingDir( HWND hDlg );


//
// DialingDirDialogProc
//
// RETURNS:
//    TRUE   if number was dialed correctly
//    FALSE  if close was selected
//
```

```
#ifdef __BORLANDC__
#pragma argsused
#endif
BOOL FAR PASCAL _export DialingDirDialogProc( HWND hDlg,
                    UINT wMsg, WPARAM wParam, LPARAM lParam )
{
    //
    // automatic variables
    //
    BOOL    bProcessed = TRUE,
            bResult    = FALSE;
    int     TabStops[5];
    LPSTR   szName, szNumber, szBaud, szParity, szDataBits,
            szStopBits;
    WORD    wTemp;
    FARPROC lpDialogBox;

    //
    // process based on the message
    //
    switch( wMsg ) {
        case WM_INITDIALOG:
            //
            // set up the listbox to use a fixed font
            //
            SendDlgItemMessage( hDlg, DIALING_LIST, WM_SETFONT,
                    GetStockObject( SYSTEM_FIXED_FONT ), FALSE );

            //
            // set up the tab stops in the listbox
            //
            TabStops[0] = 128;
            TabStops[1] = 216;
            TabStops[2] = 244;
            TabStops[3] = 252;
            TabStops[4] = 260;
            SendDlgItemMessage( hDlg, DIALING_LIST, LB_SETTABSTOPS,
                        5, (LONG)(int FAR *)TabStops );

            //
            // read the dialing directory from the .INI file
            //
            ReadDialingDir( hDlg );
            break;
```

continues

285

Listing 6.7. continued

```
case WM_COMMAND:
    //
    // process based on the parameter
    //
    switch( wParam ) {
        case ADD_BUTTON:
            //
            // set the new entry flag to TRUE and store the
            // dialog box handle
            //
            bNewDDEntry = TRUE;
            hDDDlg = hDlg;

            //
            // start the Add/Edit Dialing Entry dialog box
            //
            lpDialogBox = MakeProcInstance( DialingDirEditDialogProc,
                                            hInst );
            LoadString( hInst, IDS_DIALING_DIR_EDIT, szTemp1,
                        sizeof( szTemp1 ) );
            DialogBox( hInst, szTemp1, hDlg, lpDialogBox );
            FreeProcInstance( lpDialogBox );
            break;

        case EDIT_BUTTON:
            //
            // get the current selection number
            //
            nDDCurrent = (int) SendDlgItemMessage( hDlg,
                        DIALING_LIST, LB_GETCURSEL, 0, 0l );

            //
            // if there is no selection, display a message
            // box
            //
            if ( nDDCurrent == LB_ERR ) {
                MessageBox( hDlg,
                        "An entry must be selected for editing",
                        szTSMTerm, MB_ICONINFORMATION | MB_OK );
                break;
            }

            //
```

```
        // set the new entry flag to TRUE and store the
        // dialog box handle
        //
        bNewDDEntry = FALSE;
        hDDDlg = hDlg;


        //
        // start the Add/Edit Dialing Entry dialog box
        //
        lpDialogBox = MakeProcInstance( DialingDirEditDialogProc,
                                        hInst );
        LoadString( hInst, IDS_DIALING_DIR_EDIT, szTemp1,
                    sizeof( szTemp1 ) );
        DialogBox( hInst, szTemp1, hDlg,
                   lpDialogBox );
        FreeProcInstance( lpDialogBox );
        break;

    case DELETE_BUTTON:
        //
        // get the current selection number
        //
        nDDCurrent = (int) SendDlgItemMessage( hDlg,
                        DIALING_LIST, LB_GETCURSEL, 0, 0l );

        //
        // if there is no selection, display a message
        // box
        //
        if ( nDDCurrent == LB_ERR ) {
            MessageBox( hDlg,
                "An entry must be selected to be deleted",
                szTSMTerm, MB_ICONINFORMATION | MB_OK );
            break;
        }

        //
        // delete this entry
        //
        SendDlgItemMessage( hDlg, DIALING_LIST,
                        LB_DELETESTRING, nDDCurrent, 0l );
        SendDlgItemMessage( hDlg, DIALING_LIST,
                        LB_SETCURSEL, nDDCurrent, 0l );
        break;
```

continues

Listing 6.7. continued

```
case DIAL_BUTTON:
   //
   // get the current selection number
   //
   nDDCurrent = (int) SendDlgItemMessage( hDlg,
                DIALING_LIST, LB_GETCURSEL, 0, 0l );

   //
   // if there is no selection, display a message
   // box
   //
   if ( nDDCurrent == LB_ERR ) {
      MessageBox( hDlg,
              "An entry must be selected for dialing",
              szTSMTerm, MB_ICONINFORMATION ¦ MB_OK );
      break;
   }

   //
   // save the dialing directory in the .INI file
   //
   SaveDialingDir( hDlg );

   //
   // get the current items text
   //
   SendDlgItemMessage( hDlg, DIALING_LIST,
           LB_GETTEXT, nDDCurrent, (LONG)szTemp1 );

   //
   // set up pointers to the name and number
   //
   szName = szTemp1;
   szNumber = _fstrchr( szTemp1, '\t' );
   *szNumber = '\0';
   szNumber++;
   szBaud = _fstrchr( szNumber, '\t' );
   *szBaud = '\0';
   szBaud++;
   szParity = _fstrchr( szBaud, '\t' );
   *szParity = '\0';
   szParity++;
   szDataBits = _fstrchr( szParity, '\t' );
   *szDataBits = '\0';
```

```
szDataBits++;
szStopBits = _fstrchr( szDataBits, '\t' );
*szStopBits = '\0';
szStopBits++;

//
// set the baud rate
//
if ( !lstrcmp(szBaud, "110") )
   wTemp = CBR_110;
else if ( !lstrcmp(szBaud, "300") )
   wTemp = CBR_300;
else if ( !lstrcmp(szBaud, "600") )
   wTemp = CBR_600;
else if ( !lstrcmp(szBaud, "1200") )
   wTemp = CBR_1200;
else if ( !lstrcmp(szBaud, "2400") )
   wTemp = CBR_2400;
else if ( !lstrcmp(szBaud, "4800") )
   wTemp = CBR_4800;
else if ( !lstrcmp(szBaud, "9600") )
   wTemp = CBR_9600;
else if ( !lstrcmp(szBaud, "19200") )
   wTemp = CBR_19200;
else if ( !lstrcmp(szBaud, "38400") )
   wTemp = CBR_38400;
else if ( !lstrcmp(szBaud, "56000") )
   wTemp = CBR_56000;
else if ( !lstrcmp(szBaud, "128000") )
   wTemp = CBR_128000;
else if ( !lstrcmp(szBaud, "256000") )
   wTemp = CBR_256000;
else
   wTemp = CBR_2400;
TSMSetBaudRate( nComId, wTemp );

//
// set the parity
//
if ( !lstrcmp(szParity, "N") )
   wTemp = NOPARITY;
else if ( !lstrcmp(szParity, "E") )
   wTemp = EVENPARITY;
else if ( !lstrcmp(szParity, "O") )
   wTemp = ODDPARITY;
```

continues

289

Listing 6.7. continued

```
                    else if ( !lstrcmp(szParity, "M") )
                       wTemp = MARKPARITY;
                    else if ( !lstrcmp(szParity, "S") )
                       wTemp = SPACEPARITY;
                    else
                       wTemp = NOPARITY;
                    TSMSetParity( nComId, wTemp );

                    //
                    // set the data bits
                    //
                    TSMSetDataBits( nComId, szDataBits[0] - '0' ) ;

                    //
                    // set the stop bits
                    //
                    if ( !lstrcmp(szStopBits, "1") )
                       wTemp = ONESTOPBIT;
                    else if ( !lstrcmp(szStopBits, "1.5") )
                       wTemp = ONE5STOPBITS;
                    else if ( !lstrcmp(szStopBits, "2") )
                       wTemp = TWOSTOPBITS;
                    else
                       wTemp = ONESTOPBIT;
                    TSMSetStopBits( nComId, wTemp );

                    //
                    // dial the modem
                    //
                    if ( ModemDial( nComId, szName, szNumber,
                                    hWndTerm ) == DIAL_CONNECT )
                       bResult = TRUE;

                    //
                    // terminate the dialog with a dial indication
                    //
                    EndDialog( hDlg, bResult );

                    break;

                case CLOSE_BUTTON:
                    //
                    // save the dialing directory in the .INI file
                    //
                    SaveDialingDir( hDlg );
```

```
                //
                // terminate the dialog with a close indication
                //
                EndDialog( hDlg, FALSE );
                break;

            default:
                //
                // indicate that the message wasn't processed
                //
                bProcessed = FALSE;
                break;
        }
        break;

    default:
        //
        // indicate that the message wasn't processed
        //
        bProcessed = FALSE;
        break;
    }

    //
    // return the result's value
    //
    return( bProcessed );
}

//
// SaveDialingDir
//
void SaveDialingDir( HWND hDlg )
{
    //
    // automatic variables
    //
    int   nNumberItems, i;
    char  szFileName[ 64 ];
    char  szSection[ 32 ];
    LPSTR szCurrent;

    //
    // get the number of items in the listbox
    //
```

CHAPTER 6

Listing 6.7. continued

```
            nNumberItems = SendDlgItemMessage( hDlg, DIALING_LIST,
                                    LB_GETCOUNT, 0, 0l );

    //
    // make sure there are items in the dialing directory
    //
    if ( nNumberItems ) {
        //
        // get the .INI filename and dialing directory section name
        //
        LoadString( hInst, IDS_INI_FILE_NAME, szFileName,
                    sizeof(szFileName) );
        LoadString( hInst, IDS_INI_DIALING_SECTION, szSection,
                    sizeof(szSection) );

        //
        // delete the whole dialing directory section
        //
        WritePrivateProfileString( szSection, NULL, NULL,
                                   szFileName );

        //
        // loop through all the entries
        //
        for ( i = 0; i < nNumberItems; i++ ) {
            //
            // get the current item
            //
            SendDlgItemMessage( hDlg, DIALING_LIST, LB_GETTEXT, i,
                                (LONG)szTemp1 );

            //
            // convert the tabs to ¦s
            //
            szCurrent = _fstrchr( szTemp1, '\t' );
            while ( szCurrent ) {
                *szCurrent = '¦';
                szCurrent = _fstrchr( szCurrent, '\t' );
            }

            //
            // create the item name for the .INI file
            //
```

292

```
        wsprintf( szTemp2, "Number%d", i );

        //
        // write it to the .INI file
        //
        WritePrivateProfileString( szSection, szTemp2, szTemp1,
                            szFileName );
    }
  }
}

//
// ReadDialingDir
//
void ReadDialingDir( HWND hDlg )
{
  //
  // automatic variables
  //
  char  szFileName[ 64 ];
  char  szSection[ 32 ];
  LPSTR szCurrent,
        szTab;

  //
  // get the .INI filename and dialing directory section name
  //
  LoadString( hInst, IDS_INI_FILE_NAME, szFileName,
            sizeof(szFileName) );
  LoadString( hInst, IDS_INI_DIALING_SECTION, szSection,
            sizeof( szSection ) );

  //
  // get all the directory entries from the .INI file
  //
  GetPrivateProfileString( szSection, NULL, "", szTemp1,
                        sizeof(szTemp1), szFileName );

  //
  // continue until the routine finds an empty string
  //
  szCurrent = szTemp1;
  while ( *szCurrent ) {
```

continues

Listing 6.7. continued

```
//
// read this entry from the .INI file
//
GetPrivateProfileString( szSection, szCurrent,
  "¦¦2400¦N¦8¦1", szTemp2, sizeof(szTemp2), szFileName );

//
// convert the ¦s to tabs
//
szTab = _fstrchr( szTemp2, '¦' );
while ( szTab ) {
    *szTab = '\t';
    szTab = _fstrchr( szTab, '¦' );
}

//
// add the string to the dialing directory listbox
//
SendDlgItemMessage( hDlg, DIALING_LIST, LB_ADDSTRING, 0,
                    (LONG)szTemp2 );

//
// point to the next item name
//
szCurrent = _fstrchr( szCurrent, '\0' );
szCurrent++;
    }
}
```

The only other message that DialingDirDialogProc() processes is the WM_COMMAND message. The routine receives WM_COMMAND whenever one of the buttons is clicked. Each button causes different processings, which are covered in the following paragraphs.

Pressing the CLOSE button sends WM_COMMAND with a control ID of CLOSE_BUTTON. Receiving this ID, the program saves to the .INI file the entries currently in the dialing directory listbox. SaveDialingDir() is straightforward and won't be discussed in detail. The program continues the CLOSE_BUTTON processing by terminating the dialog box with a FALSE return value, which means that the dialing directory did not successfully dial a number before terminating.

ADD_BUTTON and EDIT_BUTTON perform basically the same processing. First, both routines set the global variable bNewDDEntry to TRUE for ADD and FALSE for EDIT.

Next, they save the dialog box handle in a global variable, and EDIT also saves the index of the currently selected listbox entry. If no entry is selected, the routine displays an error message and terminates processing. Next, both buttons start the Add/Edit Dialing Entry dialog box, as shown in Figure 6.9. `DialingDirEditDialogProc()`, in the file TTDDEDT.C, processes this dialog box. It is straightforward dialog box control manipulation and won't be discussed completely here. A couple of things about it should be noted, however. First, the global variable `bNewDDEntry` determines whether the fields are filled with default values or an entry is to be read from the dialing directory listbox to fill the fields. If an entry is to be read, the variables `hDDDlg` and `nDDCurrent` define the dialog box and entry number respectively. When the user clicks OK, `DialingDirEditDialogProc()` stores the entry back into the listbox, either using `LB_ADDSTRING` for new entries or `LB_DELETESTRING` and `LB_INSERTSTRING` for modified entries.

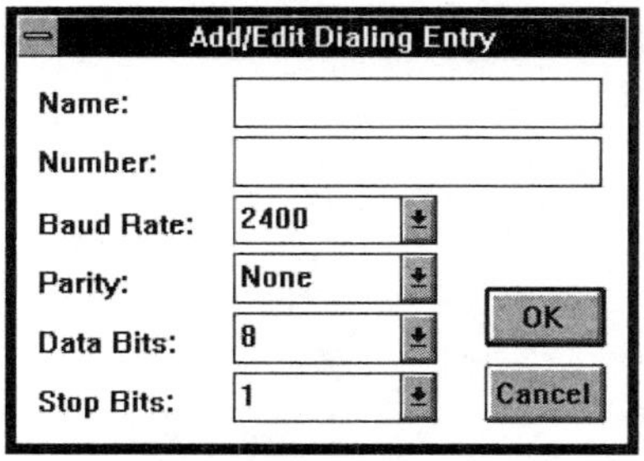

Figure 6.9.
Add/Edit
Dialing
Entry
dialog box.

`DialingDirDialogProc()` processes the `DELETE_BUTTON` control ID by getting the index of the current listbox entry. If no entry is selected, the routine displays a message box containing an error message. If an entry has been selected, the routine deletes the entry by sending a `LB_DELETESTRING` message to the listbox.

Finally, the `DIAL_BUTTON` is also processed by the `WM_COMMAND` message processing. When this button is pressed, the program retrieves the current entry from the listbox, displaying an error if no entry has been selected. Next, the listbox entries text is retrieved from the listbox using the `LB_GETTEXT` message. Once the program has this text string, it processes the string, changing the tabs to NULL characters and initializing pointers to each part of the entry.

With the pointer initialized, the program calls the TSM Communications API routines to set up the request communications parameters. Finally, the program calls `ModemDial()` to place the call. If `ModemDial()` returns `DIAL_CONNECT`, the dialog box ends with a `TRUE` return value. If the routine returns any other value, the dialog box ends with a `FALSE` return value.

Summary

This chapter explored ways of communicating with modems and examined the AT command set. You developed a Modem Interface API to enable easy access to the modem functions of dialing and hang-up as well as modem initialization. Finally, you added modem control to TSMTerm and developed a dialing directory to store information about the systems you call most often. The last piece of the communications programming puzzle, file transfer, is covered in the next chapter.

File Transfer

SMTerm now has the capability to dial into remote systems and electronic bulletin boards (BBSs). One of the main reasons people gain access to BBSs is to download software. Multitudes of software packages are available if you can transfer them from the remote computer to your own. This is the function of file transfer software. This chapter covers:

- The XMODEM file transfer protocol.

- Developing a dynamic link library to perform XMODEM transfers.

- Adding file transfer functions to TSMTerm.

XMODEM File Transfer Protocol

The purpose of any file transfer protocol is to enable files to be copied error-free between systems. One of the first file transfer protocols for microcomputer was XMODEM, developed by Ward Christenson in 1977 in response to a personal need to transfer data between microcomputers. XMODEM has become a standard file transfer protocol supported by virtually every communications package on the market today.

XMODEM allows the transfer of 8-bit data across asynchronous (serial) communications lines. The protocol is receiver-driven; the system receiving the file causes the transfer to start and requests the type of error detection to be used. XMODEM uses several terms and special characters, defined in Table 7.1.

Table 7.1. XMODEM terms and characters.

Term	Description
Download	To receive a file from a remote system.
Upload	To send a file to a remote system.

continues

Table 7.1. continued

Term	Description
Transmitter	The system that is sending a file to another system. If you download a file from a BBS, the BBS system is the transmitter.
Receiver	The system that is receiving a file from another system. If you download a file from a BBS, your system is the receiver.
SOH	Start of Header character. Has the value 0x01.
EOT	End of Transmission character. Has the value 0x04.
ACK	Acknowledgment character. Has the value 0x06.
NAK	Negative acknowledgment character. Has the value 0x16.
CAN	Cancel character. Has the value 0x18.

The XMODEM Packet

The basic structure of XMODEM is the *packet*. Depending on the error-detection method you use, an XMODEM packet consists of either 132 or 133 characters. Figure 7.1 shows the layout of the XMODEM packet.

The first byte is an SOH character; it is followed by a sequence number. The sequence numbers start at 1 and increase by 1 with each packet until they reach 255. The next packet after 255 is 0.

The next byte of the packet is the *ones complement* of the sequence number, which can be calculated with the formula: complement = (255 AND sequence) XOR 255. Following the complemented sequence number is the data. Each XMODEM packet contains exactly 128 data characters. This restriction to an exact number of characters is one of the weaknesses of XMODEM.

Caution: If the file being transferred isn't a multiple of 128, extra data is transmitted and stored as part of the file. This isn't significant for executable files that know how long they are, but it can cause garbage characters to show up at the end of text files.

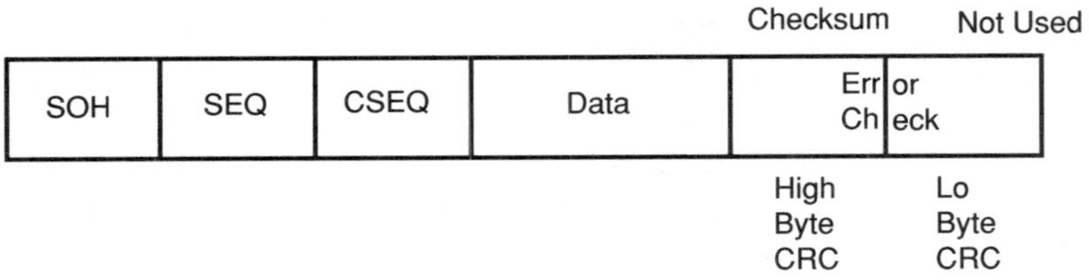

Figure 7.1. XMODEM packet.

The last field of the XMODEM packet is the error-checking value. XMODEM supports two types of error checking: checksum and cyclical redundancy check (CRC). When *checksum* is used, the error-checking value is 1 byte, and the packet length is 132 characters. When *CRC* is used, the error-checking value is 2 bytes, and the packet length is 133 characters.

XMODEM Error Checking

The original version of XMODEM used a checksum byte for error detection. This checksum is calculated by adding the 128 data bytes together and immediately discarding any overflow from the single byte sum. For example, if the first 3 bytes of the data are decimal 254, 4, and 6, the checksum after these 3 bytes is 8. Unfortunately, this error-detection method allows some types of errors to escape detection.

CRC error detection was added to the XMODEM protocol to drastically reduce the chance of any error going undetected. The CRC calculation is a complicated subject that is beyond the scope of this book. For a thorough discussion of CRCs, read the *C Programmer's Guide to Serial Communications* by Joe Campbell. The CRC routines used in this chapter are adapted from routines developed by Peter Boswell in his paper "Xmodem, CRC Xmodem, Wxmodem File Transfer Protocols."

XMODEM Transmission

The flowchart in Figure 7.2 shows the basic flow of an XMODEM transmission without taking timeouts into consideration. When a system transmits a file

using XMODEM, it must first determine which file to transfer and then wait for the protocol start-up character from the receiver. If the letter C is received as the start-up character, the transmitting system uses CRC error detection; if the character received is NAK, the system uses checksum error detection. If CAN is received, the transfer is terminated. Any other characters received are ignored. The transmitter waits a maximum of one minute for a start-up character it recognizes. If none is received, the transfer terminates.

Figure 7.2.
Flowchart of the XMODEM file transmission process.

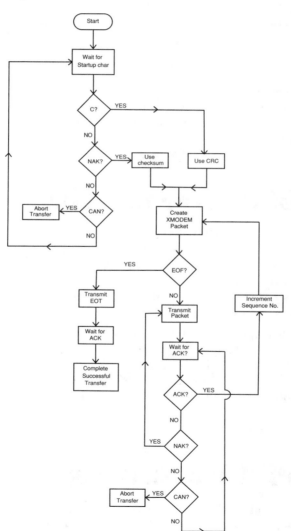

When the transmitter receives a start-up character, it enters the main loop of the protocol. The transmitter creates an XMODEM packet by reading 128 bytes of data from the file; adding the SOH, the sequence number, and the complemented sequence number to the beginning of the data; and adding the appropriate error-detection value to the end. The XMODEM packet is then transmitted, and the receiver returns an acknowledgment character. If the acknowledgment character is NAK, the transmitting system resends the packet and awaits another acknowledgment. If CAN is received, the system aborts the transfer. If an acknowledgment character isn't received within 10 seconds, the packet is retransmitted.

When the ACK is received, the transmitting system increments the sequence number, remembering to wrap at 255, and creates the next XMODEM packet. When all the data are successfully transmitted, the transmitter sends an EOT character to the receiver. The receiver then sends a final ACK and completes the transmission. Figure 7.3 illustrates the flow of packets and acknowledgments between the transmitter and the receiver.

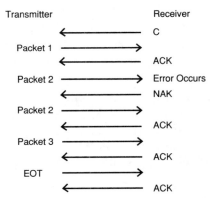

Figure 7.3. XMODEM packet/ acknowledgment flow.

XMODEM Reception

The tasks performed by the receiver in the XMODEM protocol are more complicated than those of the transmitter. Figure 7.4 shows the basic flowchart of XMODEM reception, and the following summarizes the process:

1. The receiver starts by determining where to store the incoming data.

2. The receiver transmits a C to request CRC error detection.

3. The receiver waits for the SOH of the first XMODEM packet. If the receiver doesn't receive an SOH within 10 seconds, it resends the C.

4. After three tries, the receiving system reverts to checksum error detection and sends an NAK. This too is tried three times before the receiver terminates the reception.

5. When it gets the first SOH, the receiver enters the main receiver loop. It receives the XMODEM packet and, if an EOT was received, sends an ACK and successfully terminates the transmission.

6. The receiver checks whether it received a CAN and, if so, aborts the transmission.

7. The receiving system checks whether the sequence number and the ones complement of the sequence number match. If not, the receiver sends an NAK and returns to receive the next XMODEM packet.

8. The receiver determines whether the packet has the sequence number it expected. If not—and if the packet has the previous sequence number—the receiver sends an ACK and goes back to receive the next packet. If the packet has neither the present nor the previous sequence number, the receiver aborts the transmission.

9. The receiver checks the error-detection value to determine whether it is checksum or CRC. If the value it calculates for the data received and the value received in the packet don't match, it sends an NAK and goes back to receive the next packet.

10. If the receiver hasn't found any errors by now, the packet has been received without errors. The receiving system saves the data, sends an ACK to the transmitter, and increments the expected sequence number before going back to receive the next packet. If it doesn't receive a packet within 10 seconds, it sends an NAK and waits for the next packet.

XMODEM Errors and Timeouts

The receiving system must limit the number of consecutive errors or timeouts it tolerates before terminating the transfer. If no limits were set, it might attempt a doomed transfer indefinitely. XMODEM sets this limit at 10 consecutive errors or timeouts before the transfer is aborted. An exception to this limit is the receiver's start-up, when only three timeouts are accepted before the receiver switches from CRC to checksum error detection. The transmitter's start-up is also an exception, with a single one-minute timeout before the process is aborted.

With this basic understanding of the XMODEM protocol, in the next section
you can begin its implementation.

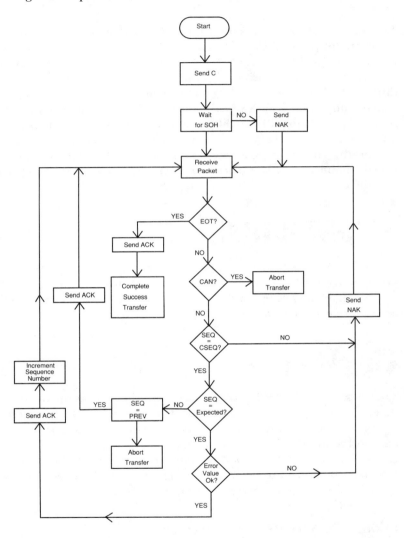

Figure 7.4.
Flowchart of
XMODEM
reception
process.

Implementing XMODEM

The XMODEM protocol is implemented in a dynamic link library named, appropriately, XMODEM.DLL. This library provides two entry points, called `FT_Transmit()` and `FT_Receive()`. Using generic function names enables you to use other file transfer protocols in place of XMODEM by simply loading a different DLL that uses the same function names and parameters. `FT_Transmit()`, which sends a file using XMODEM, accepts four parameters: the port ID to use, a far pointer to a fully qualified filename, a far pointer to just the filename and extension, and the window handle of the terminal window. `FT_Receive()` accepts the same four parameters for receiving a file. The following discussions examine in detail both of these functions as well as the DLL-specific files and the error-detection value calculations.

XMODEM.DLL

As with all DLLs, XMODEM.DLL requires both `LibMain()` and `WEP()` routines. For XMODEM.DLL these are contained in XMODEM.C and XMDMWEP.C. They are like the `LibMain()` and `WEP()` routines discussed in earlier chapters and aren't discussed here in detail.

CheckSum()

The original XMODEM protocol uses an 8-bit checksum value for error detection. The `CheckSum()` routine calculates this value, which is used by both `FT_Transmit()` and `FT_Receive()`. `CheckSum()` takes a far pointer to the 128 bytes of data and returns an 8-bit checksum. It calculates the checksum by setting the checksum byte to 0 and adding the data bytes to it. Because C allows calculations to overflow without causing an error, the checksum byte contains the correct value. `CheckSum()` is given in Listing 7.1.

Listing 7.1. XMDMCSUM.C `CheckSum()` routine.

```
//
// XMODEM file transfer DLL
//
// xmdmcsum.c
```

```
//
// calculate the XMODEM checksum
//
// BYTE CheckSum( LPCSTR lpData )
//
// parameters:
//    LPCSTR   lpData    far pointer to 128 bytes of data for
//                       checksum calculation
//
// returns:
//    the calculated checksum
//


//
// system include files
//
#include <windows.h>
#ifdef __BORLANDC__
#pragma hdrstop
#endif

//
// local include files
//
#include "xmodem.h"
#include "xmdmglob.h"
#include "xmdmchar.h"

//
// CheckSum
//
BYTE CheckSum( LPCSTR lpData )
{
   //
   // automatic variables
   //
   int   i;
   BYTE  bCheckSum = 0;

   //
   // loop through all 128 characters
   //
```

continues

Listing 7.1. continued

```
    for ( i = 0; i < 128; i++ )
        bCheckSum += lpData[ i ];
    //
    // return the checksum value
    //
    return( bCheckSum );
}
```

CalcCRC16()

The newer XMODEM protocols use a CRC value for error detection. This is a 16-bit code. CalcCRC16(), shown in Listing 7.2, calculates this CRC code and returns it as an unsigned integer value. This routine uses a lookup table method for CRC calculation. This method is faster than a true calculation method of CRC determination. For further information, see the references given earlier.

Listing 7.2. XMDMCRC.C CalcCRC16() routine.

```
//
// XMODEM File Transfer DLL
//
// xmdmcrc.c
//
// calculate the XMODEM CRC-16.
// adapted from routine written by Peter Boswell
//
// unsigned int CalcCRC16( LPCSTR lpData )
//
// parameters:
//    LPCSTR    lpData    far pointer to the 128 bytes of data for
//                        CRC calculation
//
// returns:
//    unsigned 16-bit CRC value
//


//
// system include files
//
```

```
#include <windows.h>
#ifdef __BORLANDC__
#pragma hdrstop
#endif

//
// local include files
//
#include "xmodem.h"
#include "xmdmglob.h"
#include "xmdmchar.h"

//
// CRC Table
//
static int CrcTable[256] = {
   0, 4129, 8258, 12387, 16516, 20645, 24774, 28903,
   -32504,-28375,-24246,-20117,-15988,-11859,-7730,-3601,
   4657, 528, 12915, 8786, 21173, 17044, 29431, 25302,
   -27847,-31976,-19589,-23718,-11331,-15460,-3073,-7202,
   9314, 13379, 1056, 5121, 25830, 29895, 17572, 21637,
   -23190,-19125,-31448,-27383,-6674,-2609,-14932,-10867,
   13907, 9842, 5649, 1584, 30423, 26358, 22165, 18100,
   -18597,-22662,-26855,-30920,-2081,-6146,-10339,-14404,
   18628, 22757, 26758, 30887, 2112, 6241, 10242, 14371,
   -13876,-9747,-5746,-1617,-30392,-26263,-22262,-18133,
   23285, 19156, 31415, 27286, 6769, 2640, 14899, 10770,
   -9219,-13348,-1089,-5218,-25735,-29864,-17605,-21734,
   27814, 31879, 19684, 23749, 11298, 15363, 3168, 7233,
   -4690,-625,-12820,-8755,-21206,-17141,-29336,-25271,
   32407, 28342, 24277, 20212, 15891, 11826, 7761, 3696,
   -97,-4162,-8227,-12292,-16613,-20678,-24743,-28808,
   -28280,-32343,-20022,-24085,-12020,-16083,-3762,-7825,
   4224, 161, 12482, 8419, 20484, 16421, 28742, 24679,
   -31815,-27752,-23557,-19494,-15555,-11492,-7297,-3234,
   689, 4752, 8947, 13010, 16949, 21012, 25207, 29270,
   -18966,-23093,-27224,-31351,-2706,-6833,-10964,-15091,
   13538, 9411, 5280, 1153, 29798, 25671, 21540, 17413,
   -22565,-18438,-30823,-26696,-6305,-2178,-14563,-10436,
   9939, 14066, 1681, 5808, 26199, 30326, 17941, 22068,
   -9908,-13971,-1778,-5841,-26168,-30231,-18038,-22101,
   22596, 18533, 30726, 26663, 6336, 2273, 14466, 10403,
   -13443,-9380,-5313,-1250,-29703,-25640,-21573,-17510,
   19061, 23124, 27191, 31254, 2801, 6864, 10931, 14994,
   -722,-4849,-8852,-12979,-16982,-21109,-25112,-29239,
```

continues

Listing 7.2. continued

```
   31782, 27655, 23652, 19525, 15522, 11395, 7392, 3265,
   -4321,-194,-12451,-8324,-20581,-16454,-28711,-24584,
   28183, 32310, 20053, 24180, 11923, 16050, 3793, 7920
};

//
// CalcCRC16
//
unsigned int CalcCRC16( LPCSTR lpData )
{
    //
    // automatic variables
    //
    unsigned int    i, j, crc;
    unsigned char   crch1;

    //
    // initialize the crc to 0
    //
    crc = 0;

    //
    // loop through all 128 characters
    //
    for ( i = 0; i < 128; i++ ) {
        crch1 = crc >> 8;
        crch1 = crch1   ^ lpData[i];
        crc = crc << 8;
        crc = crc ^ CrcTable[ crch1 ];
    }

    //
    // return the crc
    //
    return( crc );
}
```

FT_Transmit()

Now that you have calculated the error-detection values, you can begin implementation of the XMODEM protocol. The XMODEM implementation uses a finite state machine (FSM) model. The states of the FSM are listed in Table 7.2. The FT_Transmit() routine starts a dialog box to perform the actual transfer, which is the same program structure used for modem dialing. FT_Receive() operates in the same way.

Table 7.2. XMODEM transmit FSM states.

State	Description
EXPECT_INIT	Awaiting the initial start-up character, either a C or an NAK from the receiver.
EXPECT_ACK	Have transmitted a packet and expect an acknowledgment from the receiver.
EXPECT_FINAL_ACK	Have transmitted the EOT and expect a final acknowledgment from the receiver.

FT_Transmit() starts by initializing the special communications characters used by XMODEM. It saves the pointer to the full filename and the short filename; then it saves the window handle of the terminal window. All these assignments initialize global variables that are used by the dialog procedure. After this initialization, FT_Transmit gets the dialog box name from the string table and starts the dialog box. The XMODEM Transmission dialog box, shown in Figure 7.5, displays the short filename along with statistics about this transfer. The dialog box includes a CANCEL button for stopping the transmission. When the dialog box terminates, the transfer result global variable is returned to the calling program.

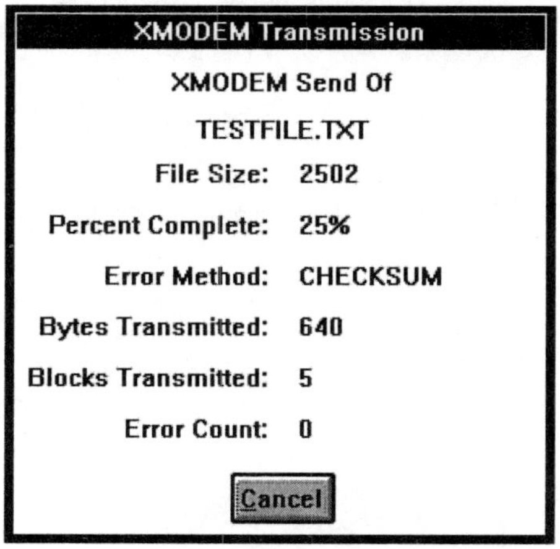

Figure 7.5. XMODEM Transmission dialog box.

TransmitDialogProc() processes the messages for the XMODEM Transmission dialog box. This routine implements the XMODEM transmission protocol. Each of the messages processed by TransmitDialogProc() (Listing 7.3) is discussed in the following paragraphs.

Listing 7.3. XMDMTRAN.C FT_Transmit() routine.

```
//
// XMODEM File Transfer DLL
//
// xmdmtran.c
//
// transmit a file via XMODEM
//
// int FAR PASCAL _export FT_Transmit( int nComId, LPCSTR lpFile,
//                          LPCSTR lpFileTitle, HWND hWnd )//
//
// parameters:
//    int     nComId       communications port to use for
//                         transfer
//    LPCSTR  lpFile       far pointer to a fully qualified
//                         filename
//    LPCSTR  lpFileTitle  far pointer to just the filename
//                         and extension
//    HWND    hWnd         window handle of the terminal
//                         window
//
// returns:
//    FT_SUCCESS           if the transmission succeeds
//    FT_LOCAL_CANCEL      if the local user cancels the
//                         transmission
//    FT_REMOTE_CANCEL     if the remote system cancels the
//                         transmission
//    FT_TIMEOUT           if the transmission is aborted due
//                         to timeouts
//    FT_DISK_ERROR        if the transmission is aborted due
//                         to a disk error
//

//
// system include files
//
#include <windows.h>
```

```
#ifdef __BORLANDC__
#pragma hdrstop
#endif

//
// local include files
//
#include "..\tsmcomm\tsmcomm.h"
#include "xmodem.h"
#include "xmdmglob.h"
#include "xmdmstrg.h"
#include "xmdmtran.h"
#include "xmdmchar.h"

//
// local function prototypes
//
BOOL FAR PASCAL _export TransmitDialogProc( HWND hDlg, UINT wMsg,
                            WPARAM wParam, LPARAM lParam );
void                    UpdateTransCounts( HWND hDlg );
void                    RestartTransTimer( HWND hDlg );
void                    TransmitDataBlock( HWND hDlg );

//
// local 'global' variables
//
static LPCSTR     lpFullFileName;
static LPCSTR     lpDispFileName;
static HWND       hWndTerm;
static int        nTransferResult,
                  nGlobalComId,
                  nDataTimerCount,
                  nFSMState,
                  nDataCount,
                  nReadStatus;
static LONG       lByteCount,
                  lBlockCount,
                  lErrorCount,
                  lFileSize;
static OFSTRUCT   OFStruct;
static HFILE      hTransmitFile;
static char       cCAN,
                  cACK,
```

continues

Listing 7.3. continued

```
                   cNAK,
                   cSOH,
                   cEOT,
                   szXMData[133];
static BOOL        fOrigPolled,
                   bPollTimer,
                   bDataTimer,
                   fCRC;
static BYTE        bSeq,
                   bCheck;
static UINT        uCRCValue;

//
// XModemReceive
//
int FAR PASCAL _export FT_Transmit( int nComId, LPCSTR lpFile,
                                    LPCSTR lpFileTitle, HWND hWnd )
{
   //
   // initialize the communications characters
   //
   cSOH = SOH;
   cACK = ACK;
   cNAK = NAK;
   cCAN = CAN;
   cEOT = EOT;

   //
   // point the display variables to the name and number
   //
   lpFullFileName = lpFile;
   lpDispFileName = lpFileTitle;
   //
   // store the window handle
   //
   hWndTerm = hWnd;

   //
   // store the port ID
   //
   nGlobalComId = nComId;
```

```
    //
    // start the XMODEM Transmission dialog box
    //
    LoadString( hLibInst, IDS_TRANSMIT_DIALOG, szTemp1,
                sizeof( szTemp1 ) );
    DialogBox( hLibInst, szTemp1, hWnd, TransmitDialogProc );

    //
    // return the result
    //
    return( nTransferResult );
}



//
// BOOL FAR PASCAL _export TransmitDialogProc( HWND hDlg,
//                    UINT wMsg, WPARAM wParam, LPARAM lParam )
//
// parameters:
//    HWND      hDlg      handle to the dialog window
//    UINT      wMsg      window message being sent
//    WPARAM    wParam    word parameter of the message
//    LPARAM    lParam    long parameter of the message
//
// returns:
//    TRUE  if the message has been processed
//    FALSE if the message is not processed
//
//
#ifdef _ _BORLANDC_ _
#pragma argsused
#endif
BOOL FAR PASCAL _export TransmitDialogProc( HWND hDlg, UINT wMsg,
                                  WPARAM wParam, LPARAM lParam )
{
    //
    // automatic variables
    //
    BOOL  bProcessed = TRUE;
    int   i;
    LPSTR lpCurrChar;

    //
    // process based on the message
```

continues

Listing 7.3. continued

```
//
switch( wMsg ) {
  case WM_INITDIALOG:
    //
    // open the file that we are transmitting
    //
    hTransmitFile = OpenFile( lpFullFileName, &OFStruct,
                                  OF_READ ¦ OF_PROMPT );
    if ( hTransmitFile == HFILE_ERROR ) {
      //
      // the file can't be opened so quit with an error
      //
      nTransferResult = FT_DISK_ERROR;
      EndDialog( hDlg, FALSE );
    }

    //
    // display the filename
    //
    SetDlgItemText( hDlg, T_NAME_TEXT, lpDispFileName );

    //
    // display and save the file size
    //
    lFileSize = _llseek( hTransmitFile, 0, 2 );
    wsprintf( szTemp1, "%ld", lFileSize );
    SetDlgItemText( hDlg, T_FILE_SIZE_TEXT, szTemp1 );
    _llseek( hTransmitFile, 0, 0 );

    //
    // initialize the counts
    //
    lByteCount = lBlockCount = lErrorCount = 0;

    //
    // update the counts in the window
    //
    UpdateTransCounts( hDlg );

    //
    // initialize the sequence number
    //
    bSeq = 1;
```

```
        //
        // set the communications to polled
        //
        fOrigPolled = TSMGetPollingEnabled( nGlobalComId );
        if ( !fOrigPolled )
           TSMEnablePolling( nGlobalComId );

        //
        // initialize the FSM state
        //
        nFSMState = EXPECT_INIT;

        //
        // start a timer
        //
        bPollTimer = SetTimer( hDlg, POLL_TIMER, 250, NULL );
        bDataTimer = SetTimer( hDlg, DATA_TIMER, 60000, NULL );
        nDataTimerCount = 0;

        //
        // read characters from the COM port
        //
        TSMReadComm( nGlobalComId, hDlg );
        break;

case WM_COMMAND:
        //
        // process based on the parameter
        //
        switch( wParam ) {
           case IDCANCEL:
              //
              // user press the CANCEL button
              //
              // set the result code, send a WM_CLOSE, and end
              // the dialog with a FALSE
              //
              szTemp1[0] = szTemp1[1] = cCAN;
              TSMWriteComm( nGlobalComId, 2, szTemp1 );
              nTransferResult = FT_LOCAL_CANCEL;
              SendMessage( hDlg, WM_CLOSE, 0, 0l );
              EndDialog( hDlg, FALSE );
```

continues

Listing 7.3. continued

```
                break;

            default:
                //
                // indicate that we didn't process this message
                //
                bProcessed = FALSE;
                break;
        }
        break;

    case WM_TIMER:
        //
        // process the timer tick based on the timer ID
        //
        switch ( wParam ) {
            case POLL_TIMER:
                //
                // read characters from the communications port
                //
                TSMReadComm( nGlobalComId, hDlg );
                break;

            case DATA_TIMER:
                //
                // timeout waiting for data
                //
                // check whether we are waiting for initiation
                // from the receiver
                //
                if ( nFSMState == EXPECT_INIT ) {
                    //
                    // we have timed out waiting for the receiver
                    //
                    nTransferResult = FT_TIMEOUT;
                    SendMessage( hDlg, WM_CLOSE, 0, 0l );
                    EndDialog( hDlg, FALSE );
                    break;
                }

                //
                // increment the timeout counter
                //
```

```
                    nDataTimerCount++;

                    //
                    // check for maximum CRC startup timeouts
                    //
                    if ( nDataTimerCount == 3 ) {

                        //
                        // we have timed out waiting for a ACK or NAK
                        // from receiver
                        //
                        szTemp1[0] = szTemp1[1] = cCAN;
                        TSMWriteComm( nGlobalComId, 2, szTemp1 );
                        nTransferResult = FT_TIMEOUT;
                        SendMessage( hDlg, WM_CLOSE, 0, 0l );
                        EndDialog( hDlg, FALSE );
                        break;
                    }

                    //
                    // rewrite the current block
                    //
                    if ( fCRC )
                        TSMWriteComm( nGlobalComId, 133, szXMData );
                    else
                        TSMWriteComm( nGlobalComId, 132, szXMData );
                    break;
            }
            break;

        case WM_CLOSE:
            //
            // this is a fake WM_CLOSE that just does our
            // termination things
            //
            // close the file we were receiving
            //
            _lclose( hTransmitFile );

            //
            // kill the timer
            //
            if ( bPollTimer )
```

continues

Listing 7.3. continued

```
            KillTimer( hDlg, POLL_TIMER );
        if ( bDataTimer )
            KillTimer( hDlg, DATA_TIMER );

        //
        // restore the original communications method
        //
        if ( !fOrigPolled )
            TSMEnableMessages( nGlobalComId, hWndTerm );
        break;

    case WM_COMM_CHARS:
        //
        // process the characters received from the modem
        //
        for ( i = 0, lpCurrChar = (LPSTR)lParam; i < wParam;
              i++, lpCurrChar++ ) {
            //
            // process based on the current FSM state
            //
            switch ( nFSMState ) {
                case EXPECT_INIT:
                    if ( *lpCurrChar == cNAK ) {
                        //
                        // startup in CHECKSUM mode
                        //
                        fCRC = FALSE;

                        //
                        // display the error method in the dialog
                        // box
                        //
                        SetDlgItemText( hDlg, T_ERROR_METHOD_TEXT,
                                                    "CHECKSUM" );

                        //
                        // transmit the first data block
                        //
                        TransmitDataBlock( hDlg );

                        //
                        // move to EXPECT_ACK state
                        //
```

```
        nFSMState = EXPECT_ACK;

        //
        // restart the data timer
        //
        RestartTransTimer( hDlg );
} else if ( *lpCurrChar == 'C' ) {
    //
    // start up in CRC mode
    //
    fCRC = TRUE;

    //
    // display the error method in the dialog
    // box
    //
    SetDlgItemText( hDlg, T_ERROR_METHOD_TEXT,
                    "CRC" );

    //
    // transmit the first data block
    //
    TransmitDataBlock( hDlg );

    //
    // move to EXPECT_ACK state
    //
    nFSMState = EXPECT_ACK;

    //
    // restart the data timer
    //
    RestartTransTimer( hDlg );

} else if ( *lpCurrChar == cCAN ) {
    //
    // the remote side has canceled the
    // transmission
    //
    nTransferResult = FT_REMOTE_CANCEL;
    SendMessage( hDlg, WM_CLOSE, 0, 0l );
    EndDialog( hDlg, FALSE );
}
break;
```

continues

Listing 7.3. continued

```
case EXPECT_ACK:
    if ( *lpCurrChar == cACK ) {
        //
        // increment the sequence number
        //
        bSeq++;

        //
        // transmit the next data block
        //
        TransmitDataBlock( hDlg );

        //
        // restart the data timer
        //
        RestartTransTimer( hDlg );
    } else if ( *lpCurrChar == cNAK ) {
        //
        // rewrite the current block
        //
        if ( fCRC )
            TSMWriteComm( nGlobalComId, 133,
                          szXMData );
        else
            TSMWriteComm( nGlobalComId, 132,
                          szXMData );

        //
        // restart the data timer
        //
        RestartTransTimer( hDlg );
    } else if ( *lpCurrChar == cCAN ) {
        //
        // the remote side has canceled the
        // transmission
        //
        nTransferResult = FT_REMOTE_CANCEL;
        SendMessage( hDlg, WM_CLOSE, 0, 0l );
        EndDialog( hDlg, FALSE );
    }
    break;

case EXPECT_FINAL_ACK:
```

```
                    if ( *lpCurrChar == cACK ) {
                        //
                        //
                        //
                        nTransferResult = FT_SUCCESS;
                        SendMessage( hDlg, WM_CLOSE, 0, 0l );
                        EndDialog( hDlg, FALSE );
                    } else if ( *lpCurrChar == cNAK ) {
                        //
                        // resend the EOT
                        //
                        TSMWriteComm( nGlobalComId, 1, &cEOT );

                        //
                        // restart the data timer
                        //
                        RestartTransTimer( hDlg );
                    } else if ( *lpCurrChar == cCAN ) {
                        //
                        // the remote side has canceled the
                        // transmission
                        //
                        nTransferResult = FT_REMOTE_CANCEL;
                        SendMessage( hDlg, WM_CLOSE, 0, 0l );
                        EndDialog( hDlg, FALSE );
                    }
                    break;
                }
            }
            break;

        default:
            //
            // indicate that we didn't process this message
            //
            bProcessed = FALSE;
            break;
    }

    //
    // return the result value
    //
    return( bProcessed );
```

continues

Listing 7.3. continued

```
}

//
// UpdateTransCounts
//
void  UpdateTransCounts( HWND hDlg )
{
   //
   // automatic variable
   //
   int    iPercent;

   //
   // display percentage
   //
   iPercent = (lByteCount * 100l) / lFileSize;
   wsprintf( szTemp1, "%d%%", iPercent );
   SetDlgItemText( hDlg, T_PERCENT_TEXT, szTemp1 );

   //
   // display the byte count
   //
   wsprintf( szTemp1, "%ld", lByteCount );
   SetDlgItemText( hDlg, T_BYTE_COUNT_TEXT, szTemp1 );

   //
   // display the block count
   //
   wsprintf( szTemp1, "%ld", lBlockCount );
   SetDlgItemText( hDlg, T_BLOCK_COUNT_TEXT, szTemp1 );

   //
   // display the error count
   //
   wsprintf( szTemp1, "%ld", lErrorCount );
   SetDlgItemText( hDlg, T_ERROR_COUNT_TEXT, szTemp1 );
}

//
// RestartTransTimer
//
void RestartTransTimer( HWND hDlg )
{
```

```
        //
        // kill the timer
        //
        KillTimer( hDlg, DATA_TIMER );

        //
        // reset the counter
        //
        nDataTimerCount = 0;

        //
        // start the timer
        //
        bDataTimer = SetTimer( hDlg, DATA_TIMER, 30000, NULL );
}

//
// TransmitDataBlock
//
void TransmitDataBlock( HWND hDlg )
{
    //
    // automatic variables
    //
    int   nTransSize;

    //
    // read the data from the file
    //
    nReadStatus = _lread( hTransmitFile, &szXMData[ DATA_OFFSET ],
                          128 );
    if ( nReadStatus == HFILE_ERROR ) {
        //
        // the file read failed, so cancel
        //
        szTemp1[0] = szTemp1[1] = cCAN;
        TSMWriteComm( nGlobalComId, 2, szTemp1 );
        nTransferResult = FT_DISK_ERROR;
        SendMessage( hDlg, WM_CLOSE, 0, 0l );
        EndDialog( hDlg, FALSE );
    }
    if ( !nReadStatus ) {
        TSMWriteComm( nGlobalComId, 1, &cEOT );
        nFSMState = EXPECT_FINAL_ACK;
```

continues

Listing 7.3. continued

```
        //
        // restart data timer
        //
        RestartTransTimer( hDlg );

        //
        // exit the write routine
        //
        return;
    }

    if (nReadStatus < 128)
        szXMData[ DATA_OFFSET + nReadStatus ] = '\x1a';

    //
    // update the counts
    //
    lByteCount += nReadStatus;
    lBlockCount++;

    //
    // fill in the SOH
    //
    szXMData[ SOH_OFFSET ] = cSOH;

    //
    // fill in the sequence number
    //
    szXMData[ SEQ_OFFSET ] = bSeq;

    //
    // calculate and fill in the ones complement sequence number
    //
    szXMData[ CSEQ_OFFSET ] = ( 255 & bSeq ) ^ 255;

    //
    // fill in the appropriate check value
    //
    if ( fCRC ) {
        uCRCValue = CalcCRC16( &szXMData[ DATA_OFFSET ] );
        szXMData[ CHECK_OFFSET ] = HIBYTE( uCRCValue );
        szXMData[ CHECK_OFFSET + 1 ] = LOBYTE( uCRCValue );
        nTransSize = 133;
    } else {
        bCheck = CheckSum( &szXMData[ DATA_OFFSET ] );
```

```
        szXMData[ CHECK_OFFSET ] = bCheck;
        nTransSize = 132;
    }

    //
    // transmit the block
    //
    TSMWriteComm( nGlobalComId, nTransSize, szXMData );

    //
    // display the new counts
    //
    UpdateTransCounts( hDlg );
}
```

The first message processed by TransmitDialogProc() is, of course, WM_INITDIALOG. It starts processing this message by using OpenFile() to open the file that is to be transmitted, saving the file handle in a global variable. If an error occurs, it sets the transmission result code to FT_DISK_ERROR and ends the dialog box. It displays the filename in the dialog box, determines the size of the file, and displays that size as well. It then initializes the global count variables for bytes and blocks transmitted and for the error count. Calling UpdateTransCounts() displays these values in the dialog box and calculates and displays the percent complete. TransmitDialogProc() then initializes the sequence number to 1, gets the current communications method, and changes that method to polling if necessary.

Next, the FSM is initialized to EXPECT_INIT, and two timers are set. The first is POLL_TIMER, which expires every 250 milliseconds and polls the communications port for data when it expires. The second, DATA_TIMER, is used for timeouts and is initially set to 60 seconds. Finally, the first characters from the communications port are read.

The next message processed by TransmitDialogProc() is WM_TIMER. It processes this message based on the timer ID—either POLL_TIMER or DATA_TIMER. If POLL_TIMER has expired, TransmitDialogProc() reads the characters from the received character queue. If DATA_TIMER has expired, the routine checks first whether the FSM is in the EXPECT_INIT state. If it is, TransmitDialogProc() aborts the transmission, sending itself a WM_CLOSE message, and returning an FT_TIMEOUT result. If the FSM isn't in the EXPECT_INIT state, the routine increments the timeout and error counters. If the limit of 10 timeouts has been reached, the transmission is aborted, a WM_CLOSE message is sent, and FT_TIMEOUT is the result. If the 10 timeout limit hasn't been reached, the routine retransmits the XMODEM packet.

When the user presses the Cancel button, the routine receives a WM_COMMAND message. It processes this message by sending two CAN characters to the receiver and a WM_CLOSE message to itself. It then ends the dialog with an FT_LOCAL_CANCEL return value.

The WM_CLOSE message does the termination housekeeping. TransmitDialogProc() starts by closing the file it transmitted and killing the active timers. Finally, TransmitDialogProc() restores the original communications method, either polled or message-based.

The last, but most important, message processed by TransmitDialogProc() is WM_COMM_CHARS, which processes the incoming characters based on the current state of the FSM. The routine loops through the characters received with the WM_COMM_CHARS message and processes each individually.

When TransmitDialogProc() processes a character in the EXPECT_INIT state, it ignores all characters except NAK, CAN, and C. When it receives an NAK character, it sets the error-detection mode to checksum and displays that fact in the dialog box. Then it transmits the next XMODEM packet by calling TransmitDataBlock().

TransmitDataBlock(), shown in Listing 7.3, starts by reading 128 bytes into the XMODEM packet. If an error occurs, it sends two CAN characters to the receiver and a WM_CLOSE message to TransmitDialogProc(). The dialog box ends with an FT_DISK_ERROR return code. If no error occurs but TransmitDataBlock() doesn't read in any characters because it is at the end of the file, TransmitDataBlock() sends an EOT to the receiver, enters EXPECT_FINAL_ACK mode, and returns. Next, the routine checks whether it read in an entire block of data. If it didn't, it appends a Ctrl+Z to the data in the XMODEM packet. This helps to avoid some of the problems caused when extra data is added to text files. Next, TransmitDataBlock() fills in the SOH, the sequence number, and the complemented sequence number bytes of the packet. It then fills in the appropriate error-detection value and sets the transmission size. The last tasks this routine performs are to transmit the packet and to update the counts in the dialog box.

The EXPECT_INIT processing continues by changing the FSM state to EXPECT_ACK and resetting the DATA_TIMER. If TransmitDialogProc() receives a C while in the EXPECT_INIT state, it sets the error-detection code to CRC and displays that in the dialog box. It then transmits the first packet using TransmitDataBlock(), sets the FSM to EXPECT_ACK, and resets the DATA_TIMER. Finally, if the routine receives a CAN, TransmitDialogProc() sends itself a WM_CLOSE and ends the dialog box with the FT_REMOTE_CANCEL return code.

Processing characters in the EXPECT_ACK state is straightforward. If the routine receives an ACK, it increments the sequence number, transmits the next XMODEM packet, and resets the DATA_TIMER. If it receives an NAK, it retransmits the last XMODEM packet and resets the DATA_TIMER. Finally, it processes a CAN by sending itself a WM_CLOSE message and ending the dialog box with FT_REMOTE_CANCEL.

Character processing for the EXPECT_FINAL_ACK state is similar to EXPECT_ACK, except that receiving an ACK character causes TransmitDialogProc() to send itself a WM_CLOSE message and end the dialog with an FT_SUCCESS return code. The other difference is that if the routine receives an NAK, it retransmits EOT instead of the XMODEM packet.

FT_Receive()

Receiving files using the XMODEM protocol is more complicated than transmitting files. As you can see in Table 7.3, the states in the FSM for FT_Receive() are more numerous than for FT_Transmit().

Table 7.3. XMODEM Receive() FSM states.

State	Description
EXPECT_SOH	Expect the SOH character.
EXPECT_SEQ	Expect the sequence number.
EXPECT_CSEQ	Expect the complemented sequence number.
RECEIVE_DATA	Receive the 128 bytes of data.
EXPECT_CHECK	Expect the error-detection value.

FT_Receive() starts by initializing the special communications characters used by XMODEM, as does FT_Transmit(), except that instead of opening the XMODEM Transmission dialog box, FT_Receive() starts the XMODEM Receive dialog box, shown in Figure 7.6. This dialog box displays the name of the file being received as well as the reception statistics. It also contains a CANCEL button, which enables the user to abort the transfer.

Figure 7.6.
XMODEM
Receive
dialog box.

> **XMODEM Receive**
>
> **XMODEM Recieve Of**
>
> **QWKTXT45.ZIP**
>
> Error Method: CRC
>
> Bytes Received: 3584
>
> Blocks Received: 28
>
> Error Count: 0
>
> [Cancel]

ReceiveDialogProc() processes five different messages for the XMODEM Receive dialog box. The first is WM_INITDIALOG, where the routine starts with OpenFile(), which opens the file to be received. If the file exists, it is truncated to 0 bytes. Should an error occur during the opening, the dialog ends with an FT_DISK_ERROR indication. The routine continues by displaying the filename in the dialog box using SetDlgItemText(). It initializes all the statistics to 0 and displays them. Then it sets the expected sequence number to 1 and saves the current communications method. If the current communications method is message-based, the routine sets it to polling. ReceiveDialogProc() then initializes the FSM to EXPECT_SOH and sets the error-detection method to CRC. It also sets a special flag that says it is attempting CRC start-up. Then ReceiveDialogProc() writes the C to the communications port. The routine then sets the two timers, POLL_TIMER and DATA_TIMER. These timers are used by ReceiveDialogProc() in much the same way they are used by TransmitDialogProc(). The routine then reads the initial characters from the received character queue.

The next message processed in ReceiveDialogProc() is the WM_TIMER message. If the expired timer is POLL_TIMER, the routine reads characters from the communications port. If DATA_TIMER is expired, the first task of the routine is to determine whether CRC is the active start-up mode. If it is, ReceiveDialogProc() increments the DATA_TIMER counter by 1 and checks whether it has reached 3. If it has, the routine sets the error-detection mode back to checksum, turns off the CRC start-up mode, writes an NAK to the communications port, resets the DATA_TIMER counter, and restarts DATA_TIMER itself. It also displays the string "CHECKSUM" in the dialog box. If the DATA_TIMER counter has not reached 3, the routine transmits another C.

If CRC isn't the active start-up mode, ReceiveDialogProc() sends an NAK and increments the DATA_TIMER count. If the count reaches 10, the routine terminates the transfer by sending two CAN characters to the receiver. It also sends a WM_CLOSE to do housekeeping and ends the dialog box with an FT_TIMEOUT indication.

The WM_COMMAND message is processed when the user presses the CANCEL button. The ReceiveDialogProc() routine processes this message by transmitting two CAN characters. It also sends a WM_CLOSE message to the dialog box and ends the dialog box with an FT_LOCAL_CANCEL return code.

The WM_CLOSE message is processed whenever the dialog box is about to terminate. This message is sent by ReceiveDialogProc() to itself. The processing starts by closing the file that the computer has been receiving. It then kills the active timers and finally restores the original communications method.

Most of the processing is done when ReceiveDialogProc() receives the WM_COMM_CHARS message. Processing this message implements the XMODEM reception FSM. Each character received is processed based on the current state of the FSM. The initial state of the FSM is EXPECT_SOH. When characters are processed in this state, the routine recognizes only SOH, CAN, or EOT. If ReceiveDialogProc() receives an SOH, it starts by checking whether CRC is still the start-up mode. If it is, the routine turns the start-up mode off and displays "CRC" in the dialog box. ReceiveDialogProc() continues by setting the state of the FSM to EXPECT_SEQ and by resetting the DATA_TIMER. If the character received is CAN, the routine cancels the transfer by sending itself a WM_CLOSE message and ends the dialog box with an FT_REMOTE_CANCEL indication. Finally, if the character received is EOT, ReceiveDialogProc() responds by transmitting an ACK and sending a WM_CLOSE message to itself. The dialog box is then terminated with an FT_SUCCESS return code. All other characters are ignored.

When processing a character in the EXPECT_SEQ state, ReceiveDialogProc() simply stores the byte in a global variable, resets the DATA_TIMER, and moves to the EXPECT_CSEQ state. When processing a character in the EXPECT_CSEQ state, the routine starts by saving the byte in a global variable and checking whether the sequence number and the complemented sequence number match. If they don't, ReceiveDialogProc() sends the transmitter an NAK and returns to the EXPECT_SOH state.

If the sequence number and complemented sequence number match, the routine checks whether this is the expected sequence number. If it isn't the expected sequence number, the routine checks whether this is the previous sequence number. If it is, the routine transmits an ACK and goes back to the EXPECT_SOH state.

If the sequence number received is neither the expected sequence number nor the previous sequence number, the routine declares a sequence number error and terminates the dialog with an FT_SEQUENCE_ERROR indication. If all the sequence numbers are correct, ReceiveDialogProc() moves to the RECEIVE_DATA state, initializes the received data count, and resets the DATA_TIMER.

When processing in the RECEIVE_DATA state, the routine stores the received byte in the data array until it has collected 128 data bytes. ReceiveDialogProc() then moves to the EXPECT_CHECK state.

Processing in the EXPECT_CHECK state depends on the error-detection method in use. If using CRC, the routine saves the first byte of the CRC value and waits to receive the second byte. When it receives the second byte, ReceiveDialogProc() calls CalcCRC16(), which calculates the CRC of the data received. The routine then checks whether the calculated CRC matches the received CRC. If the two match, the fCheckOK flag is set to TRUE; if not, fCheckOK is set to FALSE.

If you're using checksum error detection, ReceiveDialogProc() calls CheckSum() to calculate the checksum of the data received. ReceiveDialogProc() compares the calculated checksum with the received checksum and sets fCheckOK accordingly.

After fCheckOK is set, processing proceeds in the same manner for both types of error detection. If fCheckOK is TRUE, ReceiveDialogProc() has received a correct block of data. It writes the block of data to the disk, checking for and processing disk errors appropriately. It transmits an ACK to the transmitter and updates the last sequence number and the expected sequence number. It updates the statistics and displays them in the dialog box. Finally, the routine returns to EXPECT_SOH to receive the next packet. If an error is detected in the data, the ReceiveDialogProc() routine sends the transmitter an NAK and returns to the EXPECT_SOH state.

Listing 7.4 shows the ReceiveDialogProc() routine. The routines discussed here are used to transfer files using the XMODEM protocol. The next section addresses adding this capability to TSMTerm.

Listing 7.4. XMDMREC.C FT_Receive() routine.

```
//
// XMODEM File Transfer DLL
//
// xmdmrec.c
//
// receive a file via XMODEM
```

```
//
// int FAR PASCAL _export FT_Receive( int nComId, LPCSTR lpFile,
//                              LPCSTR lpFileTitle, HWND hWnd )
//
// parameters:
//    int      nComId       communications port to use for
//                          transfer
//    LPCSTR   lpFile       far pointer to a fully qualified
//                          filename
//    LPCSTR   lpFileTitle  far pointer to just the filename
//                          and extension
//    HWND     hWnd         window handle of the terminal
//                          window
//
// returns:
//    FT_SUCCESS           if the reception succeeds
//    FT_LOCAL_CANCEL      if the local user cancels the
//                         reception
//    FT_REMOTE_CANCEL     if the remote system cancels the
//                         reception
//    FT_TIMEOUT           if the reception is aborted due to
//                         timeouts
//    FT_DISK_ERROR        if the reception is aborted due to a
//                         disk error
//    FT_SEQUENCE_ERROR    if the reception is aborted due to a
//                         sequence error
//


//
// system include files
//
#include <windows.h>
#ifdef __BORLANDC__
#pragma hdrstop
#endif


//
// local include files
//
#include "..\tsmcomm\tsmcomm.h"
#include "xmodem.h"
#include "xmdmglob.h"
#include "xmdmstrg.h"
#include "xmdmrec.h"
```

continues

Listing 7.4. continued

```
#include "xmdmchar.h"

//
// local function prototypes
//
BOOL FAR PASCAL _export ReceiveDialogProc( HWND hDlg, UINT wMsg,
                                           WPARAM wParam, LPARAM lParam );
void                    UpdateCounts( HWND hDlg );
void                    RestartDataTimer( HWND hDlg );

//
// local 'global' variables
//
static LPCSTR    lpFullFileName;
static LPCSTR    lpDispFileName;
static HWND      hWndTerm;
static int       nTransferResult,
                 nGlobalComId,
                 nDataTimerCount,
                 nFSMState,
                 nDataCount,
                 nCRCdigit;
static LONG      lByteCount,
                 lBlockCount,
                 lErrorCount;
static OFSTRUCT  OFStruct;
static HFILE     hReceiveFile;
static char      cCAN,
                 cACK,
                 cNAK,
                 cSOH,
                 cEOT,
                 szData[128];
static BOOL      fOrigPolled,
                 bPollTimer,
                 bDataTimer,
                 fCRC,
                 fCRCStartup,
                 fCheckOK;
static BYTE      bSeq,
                 bOneSeq,
                 bExpectedSeq,
```

```
                bLastSeq,
                bCheck,
                bHOCRCByte,
                bLOCRCByte;
static UINT     uWriteStatus,
                uCRCValue;


//
// XModemReceive
//
int FAR PASCAL _export FT_Receive( int nComId, LPCSTR lpFile,
                                LPCSTR lpFileTitle, HWND hWnd )
{
   //
   // initialize the communications characters
   //
   cSOH = SOH;
   cACK = ACK;
   cNAK = NAK;
   cCAN = CAN;
   cEOT = EOT;

   //
   // point the display variables to the name and number
   //
   lpFullFileName = lpFile;
   lpDispFileName = lpFileTitle;

   //
   // store the window handle
   //
   hWndTerm = hWnd;

   //
   // store the port ID
   //
   nGlobalComId = nComId;

   //
   // start the dialing dialog box
   //
   LoadString( hLibInst, IDS_RECEIVE_DIALOG, szTemp1,
                                        sizeof( szTemp1 ) );
```

continues

Listing 7.4. continued

```
   DialogBox( hLibInst, szTemp1, hWnd, ReceiveDialogProc );

   //
   // return the result
   //
   return( nTransferResult );
}



//
// BOOL FAR PASCAL _export ReceiveDialogProc( HWND hDlg,
//                                    UINT wMsg, WPARAM wParam,
//                                    LPARAM lParam )
//
// parameters:
//    HWND     hDlg      handle to the dialog window
//    UINT     wMsg      window message being sent
//    WPARAM   wParam    word parameter of the message
//    LPARAM   lParam    long parameter of the message
//
// returns:
//    TRUE   if the message has been processed
//    FALSE  if the message is not processed
//
//
#ifdef _ _BORLANDC_ _
#pragma argsused
#endif
BOOL FAR PASCAL _export ReceiveDialogProc( HWND hDlg, UINT wMsg,
                                  WPARAM wParam, LPARAM lParam )

{
   //
   // automatic variables
   //
   BOOL  bProcessed = TRUE;
   int   i;
   LPSTR lpCurrChar;

   //
   // process based on the message
   //
   switch( wMsg ) {
      case WM_INITDIALOG:
```

```
//
// open the file that we are receiving
//
hReceiveFile = OpenFile( lpFullFileName, &OFStruct,
                         OF_CREATE ¦ OF_WRITE );
if ( hReceiveFile == HFILE_ERROR ) {
   //
   // the file can't be opened, so quit with an error
   //
   nTransferResult = FT_DISK_ERROR;
   EndDialog( hDlg, FALSE );
}

//
// display the filename
//
SetDlgItemText( hDlg, NAME_TEXT, lpDispFileName );

//
// initialize the counts
//
lByteCount = lBlockCount = lErrorCount = 0;

//
// update the counts in the window
//
UpdateCounts( hDlg );

//
// initialize the expected sequence number
//
bExpectedSeq = 1;

//
// set the communications to polled
//
fOrigPolled = TSMGetPollingEnabled( nGlobalComId );
if ( !fOrigPolled )
   TSMEnablePolling( nGlobalComId );

//
// initialize the FSM state
//
nFSMState = EXPECT_SOH;
```

continues

Listing 7.4. continued

```
        //
        // indicate that we are using CRC and are in the
        // initiate mode
        //
        fCRC = TRUE;
        fCRCStartup = TRUE;

        //
        // write the starting C to the port
        //
        TSMWriteComm( nGlobalComId, 1, "C" );

        //
        // start a timer
        //
        bPollTimer = SetTimer( hDlg, POLL_TIMER, 250, NULL );
        bDataTimer = SetTimer( hDlg, DATA_TIMER, 3000, NULL );
        nDataTimerCount = 0;

        //
        // read characters from the COM port
        //
        TSMReadComm( nGlobalComId, hDlg );
        break;

    case WM_COMMAND:
        //
        // process based on the parameter
        //
        switch( wParam ) {
            case IDCANCEL:
                //
                // user press the CANCEL button
                //
                // set the result code, send a WM_CLOSE, and end
                // the dialog with a FALSE
                //
                szTemp1[0] = szTemp1[1] = cCAN;
                TSMWriteComm( nGlobalComId, 2, szTemp1 );
                nTransferResult = FT_LOCAL_CANCEL;
                SendMessage( hDlg, WM_CLOSE, 0, 0l );
                EndDialog( hDlg, FALSE );
```

```
                break;

        default:
            //
            // indicate that routine didn't process this message
            //
            bProcessed = FALSE;
            break;
    }
    break;

case WM_TIMER:
    //
    // process the timer tick based on the timer ID
    //
    switch ( wParam ) {
        case POLL_TIMER:
            //
            // read characters from the communications port
            //
            TSMReadComm( nGlobalComId, hDlg );
            break;

        case DATA_TIMER:
            //
            // time out waiting for data
            //
            // determine whether we are in CRC startup mode
            //
            if ( fCRCStartup ) {
                //
                // increment the timeout counter
                //
                nDataTimerCount++;

                //
                // check for maximum CRC startup timeouts
                //
                if ( nDataTimerCount == 3 ) {
                    //
                    // send a NAK
                    //
                    TSMWriteComm( nGlobalComId, 1, &cNAK );
```

continues

339

Listing 7.4. continued

```
                    //
                    // turn of CRC mode and CRC startup mode
                    //
                    fCRC = fCRCStartup = FALSE;

                    //
                    // display the error method in the dialog
                    // box
                    //
                    SetDlgItemText( hDlg, ERROR_METHOD_TEXT,
                                    "Checksum" );

                    //
                    // restart the data timer
                    //
                    RestartDataTimer( hDlg );
                } else {
                    //
                    // send another C
                    //
                    TSMWriteComm( nGlobalComId, 1, "C" );
                }
            } else {
                //
                // in normal data mode, write a NAK to the port
                //
                TSMWriteComm( nGlobalComId, 1, &cNAK );

                //
                // increment the timeout count
                //
                nDataTimerCount++;

                //
                // if it is 10 then send 2 cancels and cancel
                // the transfer
                //
                if ( nDataTimerCount == 10 ) {
                    szTemp1[0] = szTemp1[1] = cCAN;
                    TSMWriteComm( nGlobalComId, 2, szTemp1 );
                    nTransferResult = FT_TIMEOUT;
                    SendMessage( hDlg, WM_CLOSE, 0, 0l );
```

```
                    EndDialog( hDlg, FALSE );
                }
            }
            break;
    }
    break;
case WM_CLOSE:
    //
    // this is a fake WM_CLOSE that just does
    // termination things
    //
    // close the file
    //
    _lclose( hReceiveFile );

    //
    // kill the timer
    //
    if ( bPollTimer )
        KillTimer( hDlg, POLL_TIMER );
    if ( bDataTimer )
        KillTimer( hDlg, DATA_TIMER );

    //
    // restore the original communications method
    //
    if ( !fOrigPolled )
        TSMEnableMessages( nGlobalComId, hWndTerm );
    break;

case WM_COMM_CHARS:
    //
    // process the characters received from the modem
    //
    for ( i = 0, lpCurrChar = (LPSTR)lParam; i < wParam;
                                    i++, lpCurrChar++ ) {
        //
        // process based on the current FSM state
        //
        switch ( nFSMState ) {
            case EXPECT_SOH:
                if ( *lpCurrChar == cSOH ) {
                    //
                    // if we are in CRC startup the set the
```

continues

Listing 7.4. continued

```
                       // flags and the dialog box text
                       //
                       if ( fCRCStartup ) {
                           //
                           // turn off CRC startup mode
                           //
                           fCRCStartup = FALSE;

                           //
                           // display the error method in the dialog
                           // box
                           //
                           SetDlgItemText( hDlg, ERROR_METHOD_TEXT,
                                           "CRC" );
                       }

                       //
                       // move to EXPECT_SEQ state
                       //
                       nFSMState = EXPECT_SEQ;

                       //
                       // restart the data timer
                       //
                       RestartDataTimer( hDlg );
                   } else if ( *lpCurrChar == cCAN ) {
                       //
                       // the remote side has cancelled the
                       // transmission
                       //
                       nTransferResult = FT_REMOTE_CANCEL;
                       SendMessage( hDlg, WM_CLOSE, 0, 0l );
                       EndDialog( hDlg, FALSE );
                   } else if ( *lpCurrChar == cEOT ) {
                       //
                       // done, so send an ACK and terminate
                       //
                       TSMWriteComm( nGlobalComId, 1, &cACK );
                       nTransferResult = FT_SUCCESS;
                       SendMessage( hDlg, WM_CLOSE, 0, 0l );
                       EndDialog( hDlg, TRUE );
                   }
```

```
        break;

case EXPECT_SEQ:
    //
    // save the sequence number and go to
    // EXPECT_CSEQ state
    //
    bSeq = *lpCurrChar;
    nFSMState = EXPECT_CSEQ;

    //
    // restart the data timer
    //
    RestartDataTimer( hDlg );
    break;

case EXPECT_CSEQ:
    //
    // save the ones complement sequence number
    //
    bOneSeq = *lpCurrChar;

    //
    // check whether the sequence numbers are the
    // same
    //
    if ( bSeq != ( ( 255 & bOneSeq ) ^ 255 ) ) {
        //
        // send a NAK to the transmitter and go back
        // to EXPECT_SOH state
        //
        TSMWriteComm( nGlobalComId, 1, &cNAK );
        nFSMState = EXPECT_SOH;

        //
        // restart the data timer
        //
        RestartDataTimer( hDlg );
        break;
    }

    //
    // check whether this is the expected
    // sequence number
    //
```

continues

Listing 7.4. continued

```
                          if ( bExpectedSeq != bSeq ) {
                             //
                             // see whether this is the last sequence number
                             //
                             if ( bLastSeq == bSeq ) {
                                //
                                // send an ACK
                                //
                                TSMWriteComm( nGlobalComId, 1, &cACK );
                                nFSMState = EXPECT_SOH;
                             } else {
                                //
                                // cancel the transmission
                                //
                                szTemp1[0] = szTemp1[1] = cCAN;
                                TSMWriteComm( nGlobalComId, 2, szTemp1 );
                                nTransferResult = FT_SEQUENCE_ERROR;
                                SendMessage( hDlg, WM_CLOSE, 0, 0l );
                                EndDialog( hDlg, FALSE );
                                break;
                             }
                          } else {
                             //
                             // change to RECEIVE_DATA state
                             //
                             nFSMState = RECEIVE_DATA;
                             nDataCount = 0;
                          }

                          //
                          // restart the data timer
                          //
                          RestartDataTimer( hDlg );
                          break;

                       case RECEIVE_DATA:
                          szData[ nDataCount ] = *lpCurrChar;
                          nDataCount++;
                          if ( nDataCount == 128 ) {
                             nFSMState = EXPECT_CHECK;
                          }
```

```
                //
                // restart the data timer
                //
                RestartDataTimer( hDlg );
                break;

            case EXPECT_CHECK:
                if ( fCRC ) {
                    //
                    // handle the CRC processing
                    //
                    if ( nCRCdigit == 0 ) {
                        //
                        // handle receiving the first byte of the
                        // CRC
                        //
                        bHOCRCByte = *lpCurrChar;
                        nCRCdigit++;
                        break;
                    } else if ( nCRCdigit == 1 ) {
                        //
                        // combine the digits for the CRC value
                        //
                        bLOCRCByte = *lpCurrChar;
                        uCRCValue = CalcCRC16( szData );
                        if ( (LOBYTE(uCRCValue) == bLOCRCByte) &&
                           ( HIBYTE( uCRCValue ) == bHOCRCByte ) )
                            fCheckOK = TRUE;
                        else
                            fCheckOK = FALSE;

                        //
                        // reset the digit value
                        //
                        nCRCdigit = 0;
                    }
                } else {
                    //
                    // handle checksum processing
                    //
                    bCheck = CheckSum( szData );
                    if ( (BYTE)*lpCurrChar == bCheck )
                        fCheckOK = TRUE;
                    else
```

continues

Listing 7.4. continued

```
                            fCheckOK = FALSE;
                }

                if ( fCheckOK ) {
                    //
                    // write the data to the file
                    //
                    uWriteStatus = _lwrite( hReceiveFile,
                                            szData, 128 );
                    if ( uWriteStatus == (UINT)HFILE_ERROR ) {
                        //
                        // a write error occurred, so terminate
                        // the transmission
                        //
                        szTemp1[0] = szTemp1[1] = cCAN;
                        TSMWriteComm( nGlobalComId, 2, szTemp1 );
                        nTransferResult = FT_DISK_ERROR;
                        SendMessage( hDlg, WM_CLOSE, 0, 0l );
                        EndDialog( hDlg, FALSE );
                        break;
                    }

                    //
                    // send an ACK
                    //
                    TSMWriteComm( nGlobalComId, 1, &cACK );

                    //
                    // update the packet numbers
                    //
                    bLastSeq = bExpectedSeq;
                    bExpectedSeq++;

                    //
                    // update the byte and packet counts
                    //
                    lByteCount += 128;
                    lBlockCount++;
                    UpdateCounts( hDlg );

                    //
                    // set the new FSM state
                    //
```

```
                    nFSMState = EXPECT_SOH;
                } else {
                    //
                    // send a NAK to the transmitter and go back
                    // to EXPECT_SOH state
                    //
                    TSMWriteComm( nGlobalComId, 1, &cNAK );
                    nFSMState = EXPECT_SOH;
                }

                //
                // restart the data timer
                //
                RestartDataTimer( hDlg );
                break;
            }
        }
        break;

    default:
        //
        // indicate that we didn't process this message
        //
        bProcessed = FALSE;
        break;
    }

    //
    // return the result value
    //
    return( bProcessed );
}


//
// UpdateCounts
//
void  UpdateCounts( HWND hDlg )
{
    //
    // display the byte count
    //
    wsprintf( szTemp1, "%ld", lByteCount );
    SetDlgItemText( hDlg, BYTE_COUNT_TEXT, szTemp1 );
```

continues

Listing 7.4. continued

```
    //
    // display the block count
    //
    wsprintf( szTemp1, "%ld", lBlockCount );
    SetDlgItemText( hDlg, BLOCK_COUNT_TEXT, szTemp1 );

    //
    // display the error count
    //
    wsprintf( szTemp1, "%ld", lErrorCount );
    SetDlgItemText( hDlg, ERROR_COUNT_TEXT, szTemp1 );
}
//
// RestartDataTimer
//
void RestartDataTimer( HWND hDlg )
{
    //
    // kill the timer
    //
    KillTimer( hDlg, DATA_TIMER );

    //
    // reset the counter
    //
    nDataTimerCount = 0;

    //
    // start the timer
    //
    bDataTimer = SetTimer( hDlg, DATA_TIMER, 10000, NULL );
}
```

Adding XMODEM to TSMTerm

Adding the XMODEM file transfer capability to TSMTerm is fairly simple. You start by adding a drop-down menu, File **T**ransfer, to the TSMTerm menu, shown in Figure 7.7. The File Transfer menu contains two items: XMODEM File Receive and XMODEM File Send. The processing for each of these menu items is discussed in the next sections.

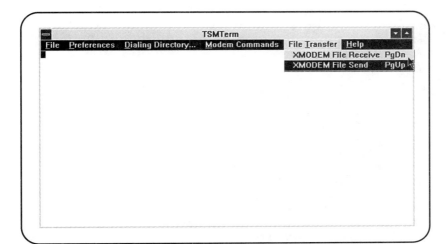

Figure 7.7. TSMTerm menu containing the File Transfer option.

XMODEM File Send

When you select XMODEM File Send from the File Transfer menu, `TSMTermWindowProc()` receives a `WM_COMMAND` message with a control ID of `IDM_FILE_TRANS_SEND`. The processing for this message is shown in the following code:

```
case IDM_FILE_TRANS_SEND:
   //
   // ask for the name of the file to send
   //
   // get and process the filter string
   //
   i = LoadString( hInst, IDS_FILE_TRANS_FILTER, szFilter,
                   sizeof( szFilter ) );
   cReplace = szFilter[ i - 1 ];
   for ( i = 0; szFilter[i]; i++ ) {
      if ( szFilter[i] == cReplace )
         szFilter[i] = '\0';
   }

   //
   // clear the entire OPENFILENAME structure
```

```
//
memset( &ofn, 0, sizeof(OPENFILENAME) );

//
// clear the filename and title fields
//
szFile[0] = '\0';
szFileTitle[0] = '\0';
//
// initialize OPENFILE fields
//
ofn.lStructSize = sizeof( OPENFILENAME );
ofn.hwndOwner = hWnd;
ofn.lpstrFilter = szFilter;
ofn.lpstrFile = szFile;
ofn.nMaxFile = sizeof( szFile );
ofn.lpstrFileTitle = szFileTitle;
ofn.nMaxFileTitle = sizeof( szFileTitle );
ofn.lpstrTitle = "XMODEM Send File";
ofn.Flags = OFN_HIDEREADONLY | OFN_FILEMUSTEXIST |
            OFN_PATHMUSTEXIST;

//
// run the common Open File dialog box
//
if ( !GetOpenFileName( &ofn ) ) {
   //
   // the dialog box failed, so just quit processing
   //
   break;
}

//
// load the terminal emulation library
//
uOldError = SetErrorMode( SEM_NOOPENFILEERRORBOX );
hInstFT = LoadLibrary( "XMODEM.DLL" );
SetErrorMode( uOldError );
if ( hInstFT > HINSTANCE_ERROR ) {
   //
   // the library was loaded, so get the address of the
   // file transmit routine
   //
   if ( !(lpfnFT_Transmit = GetProcAddress( hInstFT,
                                 "FT_Transmit" ) ) ) {
```

```
    //
    // display an error message
    //
    MessageBox( hWnd,
                "Error getting XMODEM Receive address",
                szTSMTerm, MB_ICONSTOP ¦ MB_OK );
} else {
    //
    // call the transmit
    //
    nFTResult = lpfnFT_Transmit( nComId, szFile,
                                 szFileTitle, hWnd );


    //
    // display a result message
    //
    switch ( nFTResult ) {
        case FT_SUCCESS:
            lstrcpy( szTemp1, "File Transfer Succeeded" );
            break;

        case FT_LOCAL_CANCEL:
            lstrcpy( szTemp1,
                     "File Transfer Canceled Locally" );
            break;
        case FT_REMOTE_CANCEL:
            lstrcpy( szTemp1,
                 "File Transfer Canceled by Remote System" );
            break;

        case FT_TIMEOUT:
            lstrcpy( szTemp1, "File Transfer Timed Out" );
            break;

        case FT_DISK_ERROR:
            lstrcpy( szTemp1,
                     "File Transfer Caused a Disk Error" );
            break;

        default:
            lstrcpy( szTemp1,
                     "UNKNOWN File Transfer Result" );
            break;
    }
    MessageBox( hWnd, szTemp1, szTSMTerm,
```

```
                   MB_ICONINFORMATION ¦ MB_OK );
    }
} else {
   //
   // error loading the library so display an
   // error message
   //
   MessageBox( hWnd, "Error loading XMODEM routines",
             szTSMTerm, MB_ICONSTOP ¦ MB_OK );
}

//
// free the library if we have one
//
if ( hInstFT > HINSTANCE_ERROR )
   FreeLibrary( hInstFT );
break;
```

Using the common Open File dialog box included with Windows 3.1, TSMTermWindowProc() asks the user which file to transmit. It then processes the filter string to fill the List Files of Type combo box and clears an OPENFILENAME structure by using memset(). It clears the filename and file title character arrays and, as necessary, initializes the OPENFILENAME structure fields. In this example, the title of the dialog box is XMODEM Send File. The XMODEM Send File dialog box, shown in Figure 7.8, is displayed when the routine calls GetOpenFileName().

Figure 7.8.
XMODEM
Send File
dialog box.

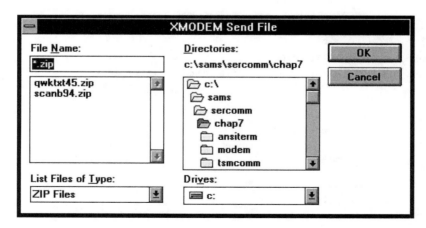

If the user selects a legal file in the XMODEM Send dialog box, the routine continues by using LoadLibrary() to load the dynamic link library, XMODEM.DLL. If failure occurs at this point, an error message is displayed; if not, the process continues. TSMTermWindowProc() gets a pointer to the file transfer transmit routine, using GetProcAddress(). This method ensures that files can be transferred even if a library other than XMODEM.DLL is loaded. If the address of the transmit routine is successfully retrieved, TSMTermWindowProc() calls FT_Transmit() to transfer the file. When the transfer is complete, the routine displays a message indicating the result of the transfer.

XMODEM File Receive

Selecting the XMODEM File Receive menu item causes a WM_COMMAND message to be sent with an IDM_FILE_TRANS_RECEIVE control ID. This message is processed in much the same way as the IDM_FILE_TRANS_SEND message with two exceptions. The IDM_FILE_TRANS_RECEIVE message uses the common File Save As dialog box and gets the FT_Receive() procedure address.

Summary

This chapter examined in detail the XMODEM file transfer protocol. Using this protocol, you learned to develop XMODEM.DLL, which enables you to transmit and receive files using XMODEM. You learned to complete the TSMTerm program by adding these file transfer capabilities to TSMTerm.

Microsoft Windows presents many challenges for the communications program. This book has taught you the basics of communications programming for Windows. With this knowledge, you can now write communications programs you can be proud of and overcome easily the challenges that remain.

Windows Serial Communications API Reference

One of the problems that Windows communications programmers have is that the documentation for the API routines and structures is spread across several manuals. This appendix will

☐ document each of the Windows communications routines

☐ document the structures used in Windows communications programming

Functions

BuildCommDCB()

Syntax: `int WINAPI BuildCommDCB( LPCSTR lpszDef, DCB FAR *lpDcb)`

What it does: Translates a device control string into a device control block (DCB).

Parameters: `lpszDef`: Pointer to a null-terminated string that specifies device control information. This string must have the same format as the parameters used in the DOS MODE command.

     `lpDcb`: Pointer to a structure that receives the translated settings for the serial communications device.

What it returns: A value of 0 indicates success. A value of less than 0 indicates an error.

Example:

```
//
// open and set for 9600 baud, 8-N-1 and RTS/CTS flow

// control
ComId = OpenComm( "COM1", 4096, 1024 );
if (ComId < 0)
   return( 0 );

//
```

```
// use BuildCommDCB to specify baud, parity, data and stop
//
err = BuildCommDCB( "COM1:9600,n,8,1", &dcb );
if (err < 0)
   return( 0 );

//
// save conio in DCB
//
dcb.ID = ComId

//
// call SetCommState() to make settings active
//
err = SetCommState( &dcb );
if (err < 0)
   return( 0 );
```

Things to watch for: Only a few settings can be specified with **BuildCommDCB()** (baud rate, parity, data bits, and stop bits). If your program needs to override any other default settings in the DCB, like flow control, it is more efficient to use **GetCommDCB()** and **SetCommDCB()** instead of **BuildCommDCB()** and **SetCommDCB()**.

See also: **SetCommState()**, **GetCommState()**

ClearCommBreak()

Syntax: `int WINAPI ClearCommBreak( int ComIdDev )`

What it does: Stops transmitting a break signal, and resumes character transmission if there are characters remaining in the transmit queue.

Parameters: ComIdDev: Handle to the serial device, returned by **OpenComm()**.

What it returns: A value of 0 indicates success. A value of less than 0 indicates an error.

Example: See **SetCommBreak()** for an example of a timed break using both **SetCommBreak()** and **ClearCommBreak()**.

See also: **SetCommBreak()**

CloseComm()

Syntax: `int WINAPI CloseComm( int ComIdDev )`

What it does: Closes the specified communications device and frees any memory allocated for the device's transmit and receive queues.

Parameters: `ComIdDev`: Handle to the serial device, returned by `OpenComm()`.

What it returns: A value of 0 indicates success. A value of less than 0 indicates an error.

Example:
```
//
// open the serial port
//
ComId = OpenComm( "COM1", 4096, 1024 )
if ( ComId < 0 )
    ProcessError();

//
// close the serial port
//
Close Comm ( ComId );
```

Things to watch for: Your application must call this function when the program is finished with a port. If an application exits without closing an opened port, no other application can use the port.

The standard communications driver in Windows 3.0 and Windows 3.1 waits for as much as 30 seconds in the `CloseComm()` function if there is data in the transmit queue and transmission has been stopped by flow control.

See also: `OpenComm()`

EnableCommNotification()

Syntax: `int WINAPI EnableCommNotification( int ComIdDev, HWND hwnd,`
`                   int cbWriteNotify, int cbOutQueue )`

What it does: Enables or disables posting of the `WM_COMMNOTIFY` message to the given window.

357

Parameters: `ComIdDev`: Handle to the serial device, returned by **OpenComm()**.

`hwnd`: Handle to the window to receive `WM_COMMNOTIFY` messages; or, if NULL, posting `WM_COMMNOTIFY` messages is disabled for the current window.

`cbWriteNotify`: Number of bytes the communications driver stores in its input queue before posting a `WM_COMMNOTIFY` message. The message signals the application to read data from the receive queue.

`cbOutQueue`: Minimum number of bytes in the output queue. When the number of bytes in the output queue falls below this number, the communications driver posts a `WM_COMMNOTIFY` message to the application, signaling the application to write data to the output queue.

What it returns: A value of nonzero indicates success. A value of 0 indicates an error—an invalid communications port handle, a port that is not open, or a function that is not supported by the communications driver.

Example:

```
//
// use EnableCommNotification to get WM_COMMNOTIFY
// messages for incoming data and changes in CD
//
switch (wmsg)
{
   case WM_USER_CONNECT:
       ComId = OpenComm( "COM1", 4096, 1024 );
       SetCommEventMask( ComId, EV_RXCHAR | EV_RLSD );
       EnableCommNotification( ComId, hwnd, 10, -1 );
       bCarrierDetect = 0;

   case WM_COMMNOTIFY:

       // clear the event in order to receive more notifies
       //
       uEvt = GetCommEventMask( ComId, EV_RXCHAR | EV_RLSD );
       nNotifyStatus = LOWORD( wParam );
       if (nNotifyStatus == CN_RECEIVE)
          //
          // at least 10 bytes in the receive queue. Call a
          // local function, which should call ReadComm.
          //
          ReadIncomingData( ComId );
```

```
                    if (uEvt & EV_RLSD)
                    {
                      // carrier detect signal has changed state
                      // determine new state and process it
                      //
                      bCarrierDetect = !(bCarrierDetect);
                      ProcessCDChange( bCarrierDetect );
                    }
                  }
```

Things to
watch for: `EnableCommNotification()` is a new function for Windows
3.1 and is unavailable in Windows 3.0. If a 3.0 communications driver, which doesn't support this function, is used,
EnableCommNotification() returns an error.

The `WM_COMMNOTIFY` message that is sent indicates the reason
for the message by combining the three indicators: `CN_EVENT`,
`CN_TRANSIT`, and `CN_RECEIVE`.

If `cbOutQueue` has been initiated, you will not receive `CN_TRANSMIT`
messages unless the number of bytes in the transmit queue
exceeds `cbOutQueue`.

The `CN_RECEIVE` message will be sent when `cbWriteNotify` characters are in the input queue. It will also be sent if a timeout
occurs before `cbWriteNotify` characters are received. This
time is fixed at 100 milliseconds. Once a `CN_RECEIVE` message
is sent, another message will not be sent until the input queue
falls below `cbWriteNotify` bytes.

See also: `GetCommError()`

EscapeCommFunction()

Syntax: `long WINAPI EscapeCommFunction( int ComIdDev, int nFunction )`

What it does: Directs the communications device to perform the given
function.

Parameters: `ComIdDev`: Handle to the serial device, returned by `OpenComm()`.

`nFunction`: Function code, which can be one of the following:

`GETMAXCOM` returns the maximum COM port identifier for the
system. This value ranges from 0x00 to 0x7F, such that 0x00
corresponds to COM1, 0x01 to COM2, and so on.

GETMAXLPT returns the maximum LPT port identifier for the system. This value ranges from 0x80 to 0xFF, such that 0x80 corresponds to LPT1, 0x81 to LPT2, and so on.

RESETDEV resets the printer device if ComIdDev is an LPT port. No action results if ComIdDev is a COM port.

CLRDTR clears (lowers) the DTR signal.

CLRRTS clears (lowers) the RTS signal.

SETDTR sets (raises) the DTR signal.

SETRTS sets (raises) the RTS signal.

SETXOFF causes transmission to behave as if an XOFF character has been received.

SETXON causes transmission to behave as if an XON character has been received.

What it returns: A value of 0 indicates success. A value of less than 0 indicates an error.

Example:
```
//
// toggle the DTR signal on COM1
// ComId = OpenComm( "COM1", 4096, 1024 );
if (ComId)
{
    EscapeCommFunction( ComId, SETDTR );
    EscapeCommFunction( ComId, CLRDTR );
    CloseComm( ComId );
}
```

Things to watch for: RESETDEV has no effect on serial devices. It does not reset a modem.

 GETMAXCOM is new for Windows 3.1. This function returns only the maximum port number supported by the driver. It does not tell you which ports are valid in a given system. For example, the standard communications driver provided with Windows supports COM1–COM4, so GETMAXCOM always returns 4.

 GETMAXLPT is new for Windows 3.1. This function returns only the maximum port number supported by the driver. It does not tell you which ports are valid in a given system. For example, the standard communications driver provided with Windows supports LPT1–LPT3, so GETMAXLPT always returns 3.

FlushComm()

Syntax: `int WINAPI FlushComm( int ComIdDev, int fnQueue )`

What it does: Flushes all characters from the device's transmit or receive queue.

Parameters: `ComIdDev`: Handle to the serial device, which is returned by **OpenComm()**.

`fnQueue`: Queue to be flushed. If the queue is 0, the transmit queue is flushed. If it's 1, the receiving queue is flushed.

What it returns: A value of 0 indicates success. A value of less than 0 indicates `ComIdDev` is not a valid device or `fnQueue` is not a valid queue. A value of greater than zero indicates an error for the specified device—see **GetCommError()**.

Example:
```
//
// open the port
//
nComId = OpenComm( "COM1", 4096, 1024 );
if( nComId < 0 )
    Process Error();

//
// flush any stray characters we have received
//
FlushComm( nComId, 1 );
```

Things to watch for: This function has no effect if `ComIdDev` specifies a parallel device, because parallel devices have no queues.

A return of greater than 0 doesn't indicate an error in the flush operation itself. It indicates that there was already an outstanding error condition on the port at the time of the flush.

See also: **GetCommError()**, **OpenComm()**

GetCommError()

Syntax: `int WINAPI GetCommError( int ComIdDev, COMSTAT FAR * lpStat )`

What it does: Retrieves the most recent error value and the current status for a serial or parallel device.

Parameters: `ComIdDev`: Handle to the serial device, returned by `OpenComm()`.

`lpStat`: Pointer to the `COMSTAT` structure to receive the device status or NULL to return only the error value. See the `COMSTAT` description for detailed information about the `COMSTAT` structure.

What it returns: Most recent error value, which can be a combination of the following values:

`CE_CTSTO` CTS timeout: While you were transmitting a character, CTS was low for the duration specified by the `fCtsHold` member of the DCB structure.

`CE_DSRTO` DSR timeout: While you were transmitting a character, DSR was low for the duration specified by the `fDsrHold` member of the DCB structure.

`CE_RLSDTO` RLSD timeout: While you were transmitting a character, RLSD was low for the duration specified by the `fRlsdHold` member of the DCB structure.

`CE_FRAME`: Hardware detected a framing error on a received character.

`CE_RXPARITY`: Hardware detected a parity error on a received character.

`CE_BREAK`: Hardware detected a break condition.

`CE_OVERRUN`: Hardware detected an overrun error. A character was lost.

`CE_RXOVER`: Receive queue overflowed. Either a character was received when the input queue was full, or a character was received after the end-of-file character was received.

`CE_TXFULL`: Transmit queue was full at time of last `WriteComm()`.

`CE_MODE`: Requested mode not supported, or the `ComIdDev` parameter is invalid. If set, this is the only valid error.

CE_DNS: Parallel device was not selected.

CE_IOE: I/O error occurred while you were communicating with a parallel device.

CE_OOP: Parallel device signaled that it is out of paper.

CE_PTO: Timeout occurred while you were communicating with a parallel device.

Example:
```
//
// call GetCommError for error conditions, transmit
// status, and both the transmit and receive queues
//
ComId = OpenComm( "COM1", RX_BUF_SIZE, TX_BUF_SIZE );
err = GetCommError( ComId, &Stat );
if (err)
    ReportCommError( err );
if (Stat.status)
    ReportCommStatus( Stat.status );
if (Stat.cbInQue)
    //
    // receive data available; go retrieve it
    //
    ReadIncomingData( ComIdDev );
if (Stat.cbOutQue < TX_BUF_SIZE)
    //
    // room in transmit queue if we want to transmit
    //
    SendData( ComIdDev );
```

Things to watch for: In addition to reporting error conditions, `GetCommError()` also reports the number of bytes in both the transmit and receive queues. If there are bytes in the receive queue, `ReadComm()` should be called to retrieve the bytes.

The cbOutQue member of the COMSTAT structure returns the number of characters in the transmit queue. To determine the amount of space available in the queue for new characters, you subtract cbOutQue from the total size of the transmit queue, specified in the OpenComm() call.

See also: COMSTAT

363

GetCommEventMask()

Syntax:	`UINT WINAPI GetCommEventMask( int ComIdDev, int fnEvtClear )`
What it does:	Retrieves, then clears, the event word for the given communication device.
Parameters:	`ComIdDev`: Handle to the serial device, returned by `OpenComm()`.
	`fnEvtClear`: Events to be cleared. For a complete list, see the **`SetCommEventMask()`** description.
What it returns:	Current event word. Each bit corresponds to an event: each bit is set to 1 if the corresponding event occurred since the last time `GetCommEventMask()` was called.

Example:

```
//
// code outside of message loop to open port, and so on
//
bCarrierDetect = 0;
ComId = OpenComm( ComId, 4096, 1024 );
pEvt = SetCommEventMask( ComId, EV_RLSD );
if (*pEvt & EV_RLSD)

    // CD has changed since OpenComm.

    bCarrierDetect = !bCarrierDetect;

//
// window proc code to monitor changes in carrier detect
//
switch( wMsg )
{
    case WM_TIMER:
        //
        // check for change in CD; clear
        // only events that are processed here
        evt = GetCommEventMask( ComId, EV_RLSD );
        if (evt & EV_RLSD)
        {
            // if CD was off, it is now on
            // if CD was on, it is now off
            bCarrierDetect = !bCarrierDetect;
            ProcessCDChange( bCarrierDetect );
        }
        break;
```

```
//
// other message processing here...
// }
```

Things to watch for: `GetCommEventMask()` doesn't clear all events, just those specified by the `fnEvtClear` parameter. All other events remain set until a subsequent call to `GetCommEventMask()` explicitly clears them.

See also: `GetCommError()`, `SetCommEventMask()`

GetCommState()

Syntax: `int WINAPI GetCommState( int ComIdDev, DCB FAR *lpDcb )`

What it does: Retrieves the device control block for the communication device.

Parameters: `ComIdDev`: Handle to the serial device, returned by `OpenComm()`.

`lpDcb`: Pointer to the structure to receive the device control block, which defines the control settings for the device. For details, see the `DCB` structure description.

What it returns: A value of 0 indicates success. A value of less than 0 indicates an error.

Example:
```
//
// open and set for 9600 baud, 8-N-1 and RTS/CTS flow
// control
ComId = OpenComm( "COM1", 4096, 1024 );
if (ComId < 0)
    return( 0 );

//
// get current DCB
//
err = GetCommState( ComId, &dcb );
if (err < 0)
    return( 0 );

//
// modify the RTS/CTS flow control members in the DCB
//
dcb.fOutX = dcb.fInX = 0;
dcb.fOutxCtsFlow = dcb.fOutxRtsFlow = 1;

//
```

```
                    // call SetCommState to make RTS/CTS take effect
                    //
                    err = SetCommState( &dcb );
                    if (err < 0)
                       return( 0 );
```

See also: **SetCommState()**

OpenComm()

Syntax:
```
int WINAPI OpenComm(LPCSTR lpszDevControl, UINT cbInQueue,
                    UINT cbOutQueue)
```

What it does: Opens a communications device, allocating memory for the receive and transmit queues.

Parameters: lpszDevControl: Pointer to a null-terminated string that identifies the device, in the form COMn or LPTn, where n is the device number.

cbInQueue: Size, in bytes, of the receive queue.

cbOutQueue: Size, in bytes, of the transmit queue.

What it returns: A value of 0 or above indicates success. A value of less than 0 indicates an error, which can be one of the following values:

IE_BADID: The device identifier is invalid or unsupported.

IE_BAUDRATE: The baud rate is unsupported.

IE_BYTESIZE: The byte size is unsupported.

IE_DEFAULT: Error in the default parameters.

IE_HARDWARE: The hardware is not available.

IE_MEMORY: Failed to allocate memory for the queues.

IE_NOPEN: The device is not open.

IE_OPEN: The device is already open.

Example:
```
//
// build abPorts, an array of BOOLEANS indexed by port
// number
// set value to TRUE if port exists and FALSE otherwise
//
BOOLEAN abPortExists[ 9 ];
strcpy( szComN, "COM?" );
```

```
for (i=0; i < 9; i++)
{
    szComN[ 3 ] = '0' + i;
    ComId = OpenComm( szComN, 16, 16 );
    if ( (ComId == IE_BADID) ||
         (ComId == IE_HARDWARE) ||
         (ComId == IE_MEMORY) )
        //
        // these error codes mean port doesn't exist
        //
        abPortExists[ i ] = FALSE;
    else
        //
        // no error because port opened OK, or
        // an error occurred but port does exist
        //
        abPortsExists[ i ] = TRUE;

    //
    // close port only if open was successful
    //
    if (ComId)
        CloseComm( ComId );
}
```

Things to The cbInQueue and cbOutQueue parameters are ignored for a
watch for: parallel device, and no queues are allocated.

Windows itself allows COM1 through COM9 and LPT1
through LPT3. If the port is in this range, Windows passes the
request on to the communications driver. If the driver
doesn't support a specific port or the hardware isn't present
for a specific port, **OpenComm()** returns with an IE_BADID error
code.

OpenComm() initializes the device to a default configuration,
specified by the default values of the DCB structure. Use
SetCommState() to set the device to a different set of values.

An error return of IE_BADID means the device is not supported
by the driver. For example, the standard Microsoft communications driver returns IE_BADID if your program attempts to
open COM5, because the driver only supports COM1–COM4.
An error return of IE_HARDWARE means the device doesn't exist
on this system. For example, the driver returns IE_HARDWARE if
you try to open COM2 and there is no COM2 present.

See also: **CloseComm(), SetCommState()**

367

ReadComm()

Syntax: int WINAPI ReadComm(int ComIdDev, void FAR *lpBuf, int cbRead)

What it does: Reads up to a specified number of bytes from the communications device.

Parameters: ComIdDev: Handle to the serial device, returned by **OpenComm()**.

     lpBuf: Pointer to the pointer to the buffer for the read bytes.

     cbRead: Number of bytes to read.

What it returns: Greater than 0 indicates success, and the return value is the number of bytes read. Less than 0 indicates an error, and the absolute value of the return value indicates the number of bytes read. (**GetCommError()** should be called to determine the error.) For parallel devices, the return value is always 0.

Example:

```
while (TRUE)
{
    if (PeekMessage( &msg, NULL, 0, 0, PM_REMOVE ))
    {
        if (WM_QUIT == msg.message)
            break;
        else
        {
            if (!TranslateAccelerator( hwnd, hAccel, &msg ))
            {
                TranslateMessage( &msg ) ;
                DispatchMessage( &msg ) ;
            }
        }
    }
    else
    {

        //
        // check for receive data
        //
        err = GetCommError( ComId, &Stat );
        if (Stat.cbInQue)
            cbBytesRead = ReadComm( ComId, aBuf, min(
                                    sizeof( aBuf ),
                                    Stat.cbInQue ) );
    }
}
```

Things to watch for: If `ReadComm()` returns an error (less than 0), all subsequent calls to `ReadComm()` also return an error until a call to `GetCommError()` clears the error condition.

`ReadComm()` does not wait for incoming data; it copies only data that has already been received by the port and stored in the port's receive queue.

If you don't use `EnableCommNotification()` to receive a message when incoming data is received, you must ensure that `ReadComm()` is called often enough to prevent the receive queue from overflowing. Use `PeekMessage()` in your message loop instead of `GetMessage()`, because `GetMessage()` doesn't return control to your program until a message is available. If you do use `EnableCommNotification()`, call `ReadComm()` only in response to the WM_COMMNOTIFY message. In this case, you don't need `PeekMessage()`.

See also: `GetCommError()`, `WriteComm()`

SetCommBreak()

Syntax: `int WINAPI SetCommBreak( int ComIdDev )`

What it does: Suspends transmission and begins transmitting a break signal.

Parameters: `ComIdDev`: Handle to the serial device, returned by `OpenComm()`.

What it returns: A value of 0 indicates success. A value of less than 0 indicates an error.

Example:
```
//
// window proc code to demonstrate sending a timed break
//
switch(  wMsg )
{
   case WM_USER_START_BREAK:
      //
      // on receipt of "start break" message,
      // call communications
      // function to start break and also start
      // a 500-ms timer.
      // In the call to SetTimer, hWnd is handle to the
      // window associated with this window proc.
      //
```

```
                    SetCommBreak( ComId );
                    idBreakTimer = SetTimer( hWnd, 0, 500, NULL );
                    break;

                case WM_TIMER:
                    //
                    // on receipt of a WM_TIMER message,
                    // call communications
                    // function to stop break and also kill timer
                    //
                    ClearCommBreak( ComId );
                    KillTimer( idBreakTimer );
                    break;

            //
            // other message processing here...
            }
```

See also: **ClearCommBreak()**

SetCommEventMask()

Syntax: UINT * WINAPI SetCommEventMask(int ComIdDev, int fuEventMask)

What it does: Enables events in the event word of the specified communications device.

Parameters: ComIdDev: Handle to the serial device, which is returned by **OpenComm()**.

fuEventMask: Events to be enabled, which can be any combination of the following values:

EV_DSR: Set when the DSR signal changes state.

EV_CTS: Set when the CTS signal changes state.

EV_CTSS: Set to indicate the current state of CTS.

EV_RLSD: Set when the RLSD (CD) signal changes state.

EV_RLSDS: Set to indicate the current state of RLSD (CD).

EV_BREAK: Set when a break is received.

EV_ERR: Set when a line status error (CE_FRAME, CE_OVERRUN, or CE_PARITY) occurs.

EV_PERR: Set when a printer error (CE_DNS, CE_IOE, CE_LOOP, or CE_PTR) occurs on a parallel device.

EV_RING: Set to indicate the state of the ring indicator during the last modem interrupt.

EV_RXCHAR: Set when any character is received and placed in the receive queue.

EV_RXFLAG: Set when the event character is received and placed in the receive queue. The event character is specified in the EvtChar member of the device's DCB.

EV_TXEMPTY: Set when the last character in the transmit queue is sent.

What it returns: The return value points to the integer event mask. Each bit of the mask specifies whether an event has occurred. Each bit is 1 if the corresponding event has occurred.

Example: See GetCommEventMask() description for an example using both SetCommEventMask() and GetCommEventMask().

See also: GetCommEventMask()

SetCommState()

Syntax: `int WINAPI SetCommState( FAR *DCB lpDcb )`

What it does: Sets a communications device to the state specified by a device control block.

Parameters: lpDcb: Pointer to a DCB structure that contains the desired communications settings for the device. The Id member of the DCB structure must identify the device.

What it returns: A value of 0 indicates success. A value of less than 0 indicates an error.

Example: See descriptions of **BuildCommDCB()** and **GetCommState()** for sample code using **SetCommState()**.

Things to watch for: SetCommState doesn't take a ComIdDev parameter. Instead, the Id member of the DCB structure identifies the device associated with the DCB.

See also: BuildCommDCB(), **GetCommState()**

TransmitCommChar()

Syntax: `int WINAPI TransmitCommChar( int ComIdDev, char chTransmit )`

What it does: Places the specified character at the head of the device's transmit queue.

Parameters: ComIdDev: Handle to the serial device, returned by **OpenComm()**.

chTransmit: Character to be transmitted.

What it returns: A value of 0 indicates success. A value of less than 0 indicates an error.

Example:
```
//
// window proc code to demonstrate TransmitCommChar
//
switch(  wMsg )
{
    case WM_USER_ABORT_TRANSFER:
        // abort a file transfer by sending an ESC character.
        // Don't want to wait until the transmit buffer is
        // empty to send the ESC, so use TransmitCommChar.
        //
        TransmitCommChar( ComId, 0x27 );
        break;

    //
    // other message processing here...
    }
```

Things to watch for: **TransmitCommChar()** returns an error if the character in the previous call to **TransmitCommChar()** hasn't been transmitted yet, usually because the transmission has been halted due to flow control.

See also: **WriteComm()**

UngetCommChar()

Syntax: `int WINAPI UngetCommChar( int ComIdDev, char chUnget )`

What it does: Places the specified character in the device's receive queue so that the next **ReadComm()** processes this character first.

Parameters: `ComIdDev`: Handle to the serial device, returned by **OpenComm()**.

`chUnget`: Character to be placed in the receive queue.

What it returns: A value of 0 indicates success. A value of less than 0 indicates an error.

Example:
```
BOOLEAN CheckForEsacape()
{
   ReadComm( ComId, &cSingle, 1 );
   if (cSingle == 0x27)
   {
      ProcessEscape();
      return( TRUE );
   }
   else
   {
      UngetCommChar( ComId, cSingle );
      return( FALSE );
   }
}

if (!CheckForEscape())
{
   ReadComm( ComId, aMyBuf, sizeof( MyBuf ) );
}
```

Things to watch for: `ReadComm()` has a bug in Windows 3.1 that makes `UngetCommChar()` unusable with the Windows 3.1 COMM.DRV.

Windows 3.1

See also: **ReadComm()**

WriteComm()

Syntax: `int WINAPI WriteComm( int ComIdDev, const void FAR *lpvBuf,`
`                int cbWrite )`

What it does: Writes to the communications (serial or parallel) device.

Parameters: ComIdDev: Handle to the serial device, returned by **OpenComm()**.

lpvBuf: Pointer to the buffer containing the bytes to be written.

cbWrite: Number of bytes to be written.

What it returns: Greater than 0 indicates success, and the return value is the number of bytes written. A value of less than 0 indicates an error, and the absolute value of the return value indicates the number of bytes written. (**GetCommError()** should be called to determine the error.)

Example:
```
//
// transmit 1K bytes from aBuf
//
cbTotalWritten = 0;
cbRequest = 1024;
while (cbWritten < 1024)
{
    cbWritten = WriteComm( ComIdDev, aBuf, cbRequest );
    if (cbWritten < 0)
    GetCommError();
        //
        // negative return value from WriteComm
        // absolute value is number of bytes written
        //
        cbWritten = -(cbWritten);
    cbTotalWritten += cbWritten;

    //
    // write fewer bytes in next call to WriteComm
    //
    cbRequest -= cbWritten;
}
```

Things to watch for: **WriteComm()** returns as soon as the bytes are copied to the driver's transmit queue, which does not mean that the bytes have been transmitted.

See also: `GetCommError()`, `TransmitCommChar()`

Message

WM_COMMNOTIFY

When it is used: Posted by a communications device driver whenever a COM port event occurs. The message indicates the status of the driver's input or output queue.

Parameters: `idDevice` (`wParam`): Handle to the communications device posting the message.

`nNotifyStatus` (`LOWORD lParam`): Can be one or more of the following:

`CN_EVENT` indicates an event has occurred. This event was enabled by a call to the `SetCommEventMask()` function. The application should call `GetCommEventMask()` to determine which event occurred and to clear the event.

`CN_RECEIVE` indicates at least `cbWriteNotify` bytes are in the input queue. `cbWriteNotify` is a parameter of the `EnableCommNotification()` function.

`CN_TRANSMIT` indicates that less than `cbOutQueue` bytes are in the transmit queue waiting to be transmitted. `cbOutQueue` is a parameter of the `EnableCommNotification()` function.

Return value: An application should return 0 if it processes the message.

See also: `EnableCommNotification()`

APPENDIX

A

Structures

COMSTAT

```
typedef structure tagCOMSTAT {
  BYTE status;
  UINT cbInQueue;
  UINT cbOutQueue;
} COMSTAT;
```

Members: status: Transmission status. This member can be set to one or more of the following flags:

CSTF_CTSHOLD: Set if the transmitter is waiting for the CTS signal to be asserted.

CSTF_DSRHOLD: Set if the transmitter is waiting for the DSR signal to be asserted.

CSTF_RLSDHOLD: Set if the transmitter is waiting for the RLSD (CD) signal to be asserted.

CSTF_XOFFHOLD: Set if the transmitter is waiting as a result of the XOFF character being received.

CSTF_XOFFSENT: Set if the transmitter is waiting as a result of the XOFF character being transmitted. Transmission halts when the XOFF character is transmitted and used by the systems that take the next character as XON, regardless of the actual character.

CSTF_EOF: Set if the end-of-file character has been received.

CSTF_TXIM: Set if a character is in the transmit queue, waiting to be transmitted.

cbInQue: Number of bytes currently in receive queue.

cbOutQue: Number of bytes currently in transmit queue.

See also: GetCommError()

DCB

```
typedef struct tagDCB {
  BYTE Id;
  UINT BaudRate;
  BYTE ByteSize;
  BYTE Parity;
  BYTE StopBits;
  UINT RlsTimeout;
  UINT CtsTimeout;
  UINT DsrTimeout;

  UINT fBinary:1;
  UINT fRtsDisable:1;
  UINT fParity:1;
  UINT fOutxCtsFlow:1;
  UINT fOutxDsrFlow:1;
  UINT fDummy:1;
  UINT fDtrDisable:1;

  UINT fOutX:1;
  UINT fInX:1;
  UINT fPeChar:1;
  UINT fNull:1;
  UINT fChEvt:1;
  UINT fDtrFlow:1;
  UINT fRtsFlow:1;
  UINT fDummy2:1;

  char XonChar;
  char XoffChar;
  UINT XonLim;
  UINT XoffLim;
  char PeChar;
  char EofChar;
  char EvtChar;
  UINT TxDelay;
} DCB;
```

Members: Id: Value identifying the communications device. This is the same value as is retrieved by OpenComm(). It must be set by the programmer.

BaudRate: Number representing the actual baud rate if the high-order byte is not 0xFF. If the high-order byte is 0xFF, the low-order byte specifies a baud-rate index, which can be one of the following values:

```
CBR_110
CBR_300
CBR_600
CBR_1200
CBR_2400
CBR_4800
CBR_9600
CBR_14400
CBR_19200
CBR_38400
CBR_56000
CBR_128000
CBR_256000
```

ByteSize: Number of data bits in the characters transmitted and received. This member can be any number from 4 to 8.

Parity: Parity scheme to be used in transmitting and receiving characters. This member can be any one of the following values:

```
EVENPARITY
MARKPARITY
NOPARITY
ODDPARITY
```

StopBits: Number of stop bits in the received and transmitted characters. This member can be any one of the following values:

```
ONESTOPBIT
ONE5STOPBITS
TWOSTOPBITS
```

RlsTimeout: Maximum amount of time, in milliseconds, that the device should wait for the RLSD (CD) signal to be asserted before transmitting.

CtsTimeout: Maximum amount of time, in milliseconds, that the device should wait for the CTS signal to be asserted before transmitting.

DsrTimeout: Maximum amount of time, in milliseconds, that the device should wait for the DSR signal to be asserted before transmitting.

fBinary: Binary mode if set, or nonbinary mode if clear. In nonbinary mode, the EofChar character is recognized on input and treated as the end of the data. In binary mode, the EofChar character receives no special treatment.

fRtsDisable: If set, RTS is not used by the driver. If clear, RTS is set when the device is opened and cleared when the device is closed.

fParity: If set, parity checking is performed and parity errors are reported. If clear, parity errors are not reported.

fOutxCtsFlow: If set, CTS signal is to be used for output flow control, so that transmission is suspended while CTS is low.

fOutxDsrFlow: If set, DSR signal is to be used for output flow control, so that transmission is suspended while DSR is low.

fDummy: Reserved.

fDtrDisable: If set, DTR is not used by the driver. If clear, DTR is set when the device is opened and cleared when the device is closed.

fOutX: If set, XON/XOFF flow control is used during transmission. Transmission stops when the XoffChar is received and resumes when the XonChar is received.

fInX: If set, XON/XOFF flow control is used during reception. XonChar is sent when the receiving queue is within XoffLim characters of being full, and the XonChar is sent when the receiving queue is within XonLim characters of being empty.

fPeChar: If set, characters received with parity errors are replaced with characters specified by the PeChar member.

fNull: If set, specifies that received Null characters are to be discarded.

fChEvt: If set, an EV_RXFLAG event is recorded when this character is received.

fDtrFlow: If set, the DTR signal is used for receive flow control: DTR is dropped when the receive queue is within XoffLim characters of being full, and RTS is raised again when the receive queue is within XonLim characters of being empty.

fRtsFlow: If set, the RTS signal is used for receive flow control: RTS is dropped when the receive queue is within XoffLim characters of being full, and RTS is raised again when the receive queue is within XonLim characters of being empty.

fDummy2: Reserved.

XonChar: Used as the XON character when either transmit flow control (fOutx) or receive flow control (fInX) is set.

XoffChar: Used as the XOFF character when either transmit flow control (fOutx) or receive flow control (fInX) is set.

XonLim: Minimum number of bytes in the receive queue before any of the following: XON is sent (if fInX is set), RTS is raised (if fRtsFlow is set), or DTR is raised (if fDtrFlow is set).

XoffLim: Maximum number of bytes in receive queue before any of the following: XOFF is sent (if fOutX is set), RTS is dropped (if fRtsFlow is set), or DTR is dropped (if fDtrFlow is set).

PeChar: Character used to replace characters received with a parity error, when fPeChar is also set.

EofChar: Character used to signal end of data, when fBinary is set.

EvtChar: Character used as event character, when fEvtChar is set.

TxDelay: Not used in either Windows 3.0 or Windows 3.1.

See also: **BuildCommDCB(), SetCommState(), GetCommState()**

B

TSM Communications API Reference

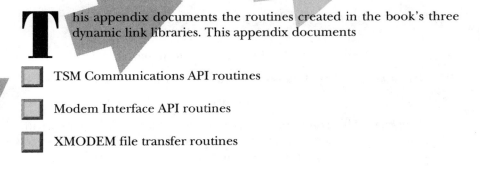

This appendix documents the routines created in the book's three dynamic link libraries. This appendix documents

TSM Communications API routines

Modem Interface API routines

XMODEM file transfer routines

TSM Communications Routines

This section documents the functions available from TSMCOMM.DLL.

TSMCloseComm( )

Syntax:	`int FAR PASCAL _export TSMCloseComm( int ComId )`
What it does:	Closes a communications port that was opened with `TSMOpenComm()`.
Parameters:	`ComId` ID of the COM port to close.
What it returns:	`0` if the close was successful.
	`<0` if an error occurred.
Things to watch for:	The port that you are attempting to close must have been opened using `TSMOpenComm()`. If it wasn't, this function returns an error.
See also:	`TSMOpenComm()`

TSMEnableMessages( )

Syntax:	`int TSMEnableMessages( int nComId,` `HWND hWnd )`

What it does:	Sets message-based communications as the communications method.
Parameters:	nComId port ID on which you want to use message-based communications.
	hWnd window handle of the terminal window.
What it returns:	0 if message-based communications were enabled.
	<0 if an error occurred.
Things to watch for:	The communications port must have been opened with TSMOpenComm(). The window procedure for hWnd should expect to receive the WM_COMMNOTIFY messages.
See also:	TSMEnablePolling(), TSMGetPollingEnabled(), TSMOpenComm(), TSMProcessCommNotify()

TSMEnablePolling( )

Syntax:	`int FAR PASCAL _export TSMEnablePolling( int nComId )`
What it does:	Enable polling as the current method of communications for the nComId communications port.
Parameters:	nComId ID of port to enable polling for.
What it returns:	0 if polling was enabled as the current communications method.
	<0 if an error occurred.
Things to watch for:	The port, nComId, must have been opened with TSMOpenComm(). If message-based polling is active when this routine is called, the terminal window must be active when you make this call.
See also:	TSMEnableMessages(), TSMGetPollingEnabled(), TSMOpenComm()

TSMGetBaudRate( )

Syntax:	`int TSMGetBaudRate( int nComId )`
What it does:	Returns the current baud rate of the communications port.
Parameters:	nComId port ID.

What it returns: baud rate if successful:

```
CBR_110
CBR_300
CBR_600
CBR_1200
CBR_2400
CBR_4800
CBR_9600
CBR_14400
CBR_19200
CBR_38400
CBR_56000
CBR_128000
CBR_256000
```

-1 to -12 if an error occurs.

What to watch for: The port must have been opened with TSMOpenComm().

See also: TSMOpenComm(), TSMSetBaudRate()

TSMGetDataBits()

Syntax: `int TSMGetDataBits( int nComId )`

What it does: Returns the current data bit setting of the communications port.

Parameters: nComId   port ID.

What it returns: >0   number of data bits:

```
FOURDATABITS
FIVEDATABITS
SIXDATABITS
SEVENDATABITS
EIGHTDATABITS
```

<0   if error occurred

What to watch for: The port must have been opened with TSMOpenComm().

See also: TSMOpenComm(), TSMSetDataBits()

TSMGetErrorCount()

Syntax:	`int FAR PASCAL _export TSMGetErrorCount( int nComId,`
	`                                        LPCOMMERRORCOUNT`
	`                                        lpCommErrorCount )`

What it does:	Fills the LPCOMMERRORCOUNT structure with the current error counts.
Parameters:	`nComId` port ID.
	`LPCOMMERRORCOUNT lpCommErrorCount` pointer to the error count structure.
What it returns:	`0` if successful.
	`<0` if an error occurred.
What to watch for:	The port must be opened with `TSMOpenComm()`. The error counts are returned in the LPCOMMERRORCOUNT structure. This structure includes fields as defined in Table B.1.

Table B.1. LPCOMMERRORCOUNT structure.

Field	Description
nCEMode	Number of mode errors that have occurred
nCEBreak	Number of BREAKs that have been detected
nCECtsTO	Number of CTS timeouts that have occurred
nCEDsrTO	Number of DSR timeouts that have occurred
Field	Description
nCEFrame	Number of frame errors that have occurred
nCEOverrun	Number of hardware overrun errors that have occurred
nCERlsdTO	Number of RLSD (CD) timeouts that have occurred
nCERXOver	Number of receive-queue overrun errors that have occurred
nCERXParity	Number of parity errors that have occurred
nCETXFull	Number of transmit queue full errors that have occurred

See also:	`TSMOpenComm()`, `TSMSetErrorProcessing()`

TSMGetErrorProcessing()

Syntax: `int FAR PASCAL _export TSMGetErrorProcessing( int nComId )`

What it does: Returns the current error processing setting of the communications port.

Parameters: `nComId`   port ID.

What it returns: `>0`   error processing setting if successful.

        `ERROR_COUNT`
        `ERROR_DISPLAY`

        `<0`   if an error occurred.

What to watch for: The port must be opened with `TSMOpenComm()`.

See also: `TSMGetErrorCount()`, `TSMOpenComm()`, `TSMSetErrorProcessing()`

TSMGetParity()

Syntax: `WORD FAR PASCAL _export TSMGetParity( int nComId )`

What it does: Returns the current parity setting of the communications port.

Parameters: `nComId`   port ID.

What it returns: `>0`   parity setting if successful.

        `NOPARITY`
        `ODDPARITY`
        `EVENPARITY`
        `MARKPARITY`
        `SPACEPARITY`

        `<0`   if an error occurred.

What to watch for: The port must be opened with `TSMOpenComm()`.

See also: `TSMOpenComm()`, `TSMSetParity()`

TSMGetPollingEnabled()

Syntax:	`BOOL FAR PASCAL _export TSMGetPollingEnabled( int nComId )`
What it does:	Returns a flag indicating whether the program is currently using polled communications.
Parameters:	`nComId` port ID.
What it returns:	`TRUE` if you're using polled communications.
	`FALSE` if you're using message-based communications.
Things to watch for:	The communications port must have been opened with `TSMOpenComm()`.
See also:	`TSMEnableMessages()`, `TSMEnablePolling()`, `TSMOpenComm()`

TSMGetStopBits()

Syntax:	`WORD FAR PASCAL _export TSMGetStopBits( int nComId )`
What it does:	Returns the current stop bit setting of the communications port.
Parameters:	`nComId` port ID.
What it returns:	`>0` stop bit setting if successful.
	`ONESTOPBIT`
	`ONE5STOPBITS`
	`TWOSTOPBITS`
	`<0` if an error occurred.
What to watch for:	The port must be opened with `TSMOpenComm()`.
See also:	`TSMOpenComm()`, `TSMSetStopBits()`

TSMOpenComm()

Syntax:	`int FAR PASCAL _export TSMOpenComm( LPCSTR lpDevice,`
	`                                    WORD wBaudRate,`
	`                                    WORD wParity,`

```
                          WORD wDataBits,
                          WORD wStopBits,
                          UINT uInQueue,
                          UINT uOutQueue )
```

What it does: Opens a communications port and sets the port's initial communications parameters.

Parameters: lpDevice   zero-terminated string containing the port's name.

wBaudRate   initial baud rate.

wParity   initial parity.

wDataBits   initial number of data bits.

wStopBits   initial number of stop bits.

uInQueue   size of the port's receive queue.

uOutQueue   size of the port's transmit queue.

What it returns: ComId >= 0   if the function was successful.

error code < 0   if not successful.

Things to watch for: The port is originally opened in polled communications mode. The port must be closed using TSMCloseComm() before you exit the program that opened the port.

See also: TSMCloseComm()

TSMPollEvents()

Syntax:
```
int FAR PASCAL _export TSMPollEvents( int nComId,
                                      HWND hWnd )
```

What it does: Polls the event mask and sends WM_COMM_EVENT messages to the specified window.

Parameters: nComId   port ID.

hWnd   window handle to receive the WM_COMM_EVENT messages.

What it returns: 0   if successful.

<0   if an error occurred.

389

What to watch for: The communications port must have been opened with TSMOpenComm(). The window, hWnd, must process the WM_COMM_EVENT messages if the application is going to process events.

See also: TSMOpenComm(), TSMSetEvents()

TSMProcessCommNotify()

Syntax:
```
int  FAR PASCAL _export TSMProcessCommNotify( int nComId,
                                 int nNotification,
                                 HWND hWnd )
```

What it does: Performs the necessary functions to process the WM_COMMNOTIFY message.

Parameters:

nComId   port ID.

hNotification   notification flag received with the WM_COMMNOTIFY message.

hWnd   window handle of the window that received the WM_COMMNOTIFY message.

What it returns:

0   if successful.

<0   if an error occurred.

Things to watch for: The port must have been opened with TSMOpenComm(). The window associated with hWnd, receives all messages generated by this call.

See also: TSMEnableMessages(), TSMOpenComm()

TSMReadComm()

Syntax:
```
int FAR PASCAL _export TSMReadComm( int nComId,
                              HWND hWndComm )
```

What it does: Sends any characters in the received-character queue for nComId to hWndComm in a WM_COMM_CHARS message.

Parameters:

nComId   port ID.

hWndComm   window to which to send the WM_COMM_CHARS message.

What it returns: 0   if successful.

                     <0   if an error occurred.

Things to watch for: The communications port must have been opened with `TSMOpenComm()`. The window proceedure for `hWndComm` must process the `WM_COMM_CHARS` message for the window to receive any characters.

See also: `TSMOpenComm()`

TSMReadCommChar()

Syntax: `int FAR PASCAL _export TSMReadCommChar( int nComId )`

What it does: Reads a single character from the communications port.

Parameters: `nComId`   port ID.

What it returns: the single character read from the port.

                     <0   if an error occurred.

                     0   if no characters were available.

Things to watch for: The port must have been opened with `TSMOpenComm()`. This routine assumes that you will never receive a NULL character.

See also: `TSMOpenComm()`, `TSMReadComm()`

TSMSetBaudRate()

Syntax: `int TSMSetBaudRate( int nComId, WORD wBaudRate )`

What it does: Sets the baud rate of the serial port.

Parameters: `nComId`   port ID.

            `wBaudRate`   new baud rate setting.

What it returns: 0   if successful.

                     <0   if an error occurred.

Things to watch for: The port must have been opened with `TSMOpenComm()`. The new baud rate can be one of the following:

```
CBR_110
CBR_300
CBR_600
CBR_1200
CBR_2400
CBR_4800
CBR_9600
CBR_14400
CBR_19200
CBR_38400
CBR_56000
CBR_128000
CBR_256000
```

See also: TSMGetBaudRate( ), TSMOpenComm( )

TSMSetDataBits( )

Syntax: `int TSMSetDataBits( int nComId, WORD wDataBits )`

What it does: Sets the number of data bits processed by the serial port.

Parameters: nComId   port ID.

             wDataBits   new data bit setting.

What it returns: 0   if successful.

             <0   if an error occurred.

Things to   The port, nComId, must have been opened with TSMOpenComm( ).
watch for: The new data bit value must be one of the following values:

```
FIVEDATABITS
SIXDATABITS
SEVENDATABITS
EIGHTDATABITS
```

See also: TSMGetDataBits( ), TSMOpenComm( )

TSMSetErrorProcessing( )

Syntax: `int FAR PASCAL _export TSMSetErrorProcessing( int nComId,`
                                                           `int nErrorType )`

What it does: Sets the type of error processing performed by the communications port.

Parameters: nComId   port ID.

                       nErrorType   new error processing setting.

What it returns: 0   if successful.

                       <0   if an error occurred.

What to
watch for: The port must be opened with TSMOpenComm(). The new error processing value must be one of the following values:

                       ERROR_COUNT
                       ERROR_DISPLAY

See also: TSMGetErrorCount(), TSMGetErrorProcessing(), TSMOpenComm()

TSMSetEvents()

Syntax: int FAR PASCAL _export TSMSetEvents(int nComId,
                                        UINT uEvents)

What it does: Enables users to set which events they are interested in receiving notification about.

Parameters: nComId   port ID.

                       uEvents   mask of events.

What it returns: 0   if the event mask was successfully updated.

                       <0   if an error occurred.

What to
watch for: The communications port must have been opened with TSMOpenComm(). The uEvents parameter is a combination of the following events:

           EV_BREAK
           EV_CTS
           EV_CTSS
           EV_DSR
           EV_ERR
           EV_RING
           EV_RLSD
           EV_RLSDS
           EV_RXCHAR

EV_RXFLAG
EV_TXEMPTY

See also: TSMOpenComm(), TSMPollEvents()

TSMSetFCLimits()

Syntax:
```
int FAR PASCAL _export TSMSetFCLimits( int nComId,
                                       WORD wBottom,
                                       WORD wTop )
```

What it does: Sets the type of error processing performed by the communications port.

Parameters:

nComId   port ID.

wBottom   number of bytes remaining in the queue when flow control is turned off.

wTop   number of bytes in the queue when flow control is started.

What it returns:

0   if successful.

<0   if an error occurred.

What to watch for: The port must be opened with TSMOpenComm().

See also: TSMOpenComm(), TSMSetFlowControl()

TSMSetFlowControl()

Syntax:
```
int FAR PASCAL _export TSMSetFlowControl( int nComId,
                                          WORD wDirection,
                                          WORD wFlowControl )
```

What it does: Returns the current parity setting of the communications port.

Parameters:

nComId   port ID.

wDirection   transmit/receive indicator.

wFlowControl   new flow control setting.

What it returns: >0   if successful.

                   <0   if an error occurred.

What to   The port must be opened with TSMOpenComm(). The wDirection
watch for: parameter must be one of the following values:

         FLOW_INCOMING
         FLOW_OUTGOING

         The wFlowControl parameter must be one of these values:

         FLOW_NONE
         FLOW_HARDWARE
         FLOW_XONXOFF

See also: TSMOpenComm(), TSMSetFCLimits()

TSMSetParity()

Syntax: int FAR PASCAL _export TSMSetParity(int nComId,
                                         WORD wParity)

What it does: Sets the parity used by the communications port.

Parameters: nComId   port ID.

         wParity new parity setting.

What it returns: 0   if successful.

                   <0   if an error occurred.

What to   The port must be opened with TSMOpenComm(). The new parity
watch for: setting must be one of the following values.

         NOPARITY
         ODDPARITY
         EVENPARITY
         MARKPARITY
         SPACEPARITY

See also: TSMOpenComm(), TSMGetParity()

TSMSetStopBits()

Syntax: `int FAR PASCAL _export TSMSetStopBits( int nComId,`
`WORD wStopBits )`

What it does: Sets the number of stop bits used by the communications port.

Parameters: nComId   port ID.

wStopBits   new stop bit setting.

What it returns: >0   if successful.

<0   if an error occurred.

Things to watch for: The port must be opened with TSMOpenComm(). The new stop bit value must be one of the following values:

```
ONESTOPBIT
ONE5STOPBITS
TWOSTOPBITS
```

See also: TSMGetStopBits(), TSMOpenComm()

TSMWriteComm()

Syntax: `int FAR PASCAL _export TSMWriteComm( int nComId, int nCount,`
`CSTR lpOutChars )`

What it does: Writes nCount characters, starting at lpOutChars, to the communications port identified by nComId.

Parameters: nComId   port ID.

nCount   number of characters to write.

lpOutChars   far pointer to the characters to be written.

What it returns: 0   if the write was successful.

<0   if an error occurred.

Things to watch for: The port must have been opened with TSMOpenComm().

See also: TSMOpenComm()

Modem Routines

The following sections document the functions available from MODEM.DLL.

ModemDial()

Syntax:
```
int FAR PASCAL _export ModemDial( int nComId,
                                  LPCSTR szName,
                                  LPCSTR szNumber,
                                  HWND hWnd )
```

What it does: Sends a dial command to the modem connected to nComId. This command dials the number pointed to by szNumber.

Parameters:

nComId   port to which the modem is connected.

szName   far pointer to the name of the system being dialed.

szNumber   far pointer to the telephone number.

hWnd   window handle of the terminal window.

What it returns:

DIAL_CONNECT   if dial was successful.

DIAL_FAIL   if one of the fail codes was recognized.

DIAL_CANCEL   if user presses the CANCEL button.

DIAL_TIMEOUT   if 45 seconds pass without recognizing a connect or fail code.

Things to watch for: The modem must have been initialized using ModemInitialize(). Also, the modem might be set to wait less than 45 seconds for a call.

See also: ModemHangup(), ModemInitialize()

ModemHangup()

Syntax:
```
int FAR PASCAL _export ModemHangup( int nComId,
                                    BOOL bSoftware,
                                    HWND hWnd )
```

What it does: Disconnects the active call on the modem.

Parameters:	nComId	port to which the modem is connected.
	bSoftware	TRUE if software hang-up, FALSE if hardware hang-up.
	hWnd	window handle of terminal window.

What it returns:	0	if hang-up was successful.
	<0	if hang-up failed.

Things to watch for: The modem on nComId must have been initialized using ModemInitialize(). Also, not all modems support hanging up by dropping DTR.

See also: ModemDial(), ModemInitialize()

ModemInitialize()

Syntax:
```
int FAR PASCAL _export ModemInitialize( int nComId,
                                        LPCSTR szINIFile )
```

What it does: Initializes the global MODEM.DLL variables for the modem connected to nComId.

Parameters:	nComId	port to which the modem is connected.
	szINIFile	far pointer to a zero-terminated .INI filename.

What it returns:	0	if initialization was successful.
	<0	if initialization failed.

Things to watch for: The current implementation only allows one modem to be active at a time.

See also: ModemTerminate()

ModemSendInitString()

Syntax:
```
int FAR PASCAL _export ModemSendInitString( int nComId,
                                            HWND hWnd )
```

What it does: Sends the modem initialization string from the Settings dialog to the modem.

Parameters:	nComId	port to which the modem is connected.
	hWnd	window handle of the terminal window.
What it returns:	0	if the modem initialization was successful.
	<0	if initialization failed.
	1	if the initialization string caused the modem to return ERROR.

Things to watch for: The modem must have been initialized with ModemInitialize(). The modem initialization command comes from the .INI file specified in the ModemInitialize() call.

See also: ModemInitialize()

ModemSettings()

Syntax: `int FAR PASCAL _export ModemSettings( int nComId )`

What it does: Displays a dialog box that enables the user to enter the following commands: modem initialization command, dialing prefix, dialing suffix, and modem hang-up command. It also enables four connect result strings and four fail result strings.

Parameters: nComId   port to which the modem is connected.

What it returns: 0   if the dialog box was successful.

<0   if an error occurred.

Things to watch for: The commands and result strings entered into the dialog box fields are stored in the .INI file passed to ModemInitialize(). The commands can include ^M, which is sent as a carriage return.

See also: ModemInitialize()

ModemTerminate()

Syntax: `int FAR PASCAL _export ModemTerminate( int nComId )`

What it does: Releases the MODEM.DLL for use by another program.

Parameters: nComId   port to which the modem is connected.

What it returns:	0	if the termination succeeded.
	<0	if the termination failed.

Things to watch for: The modem on port nComId must have been initialized with ModemInitialize() for this function to succeed.

See also: ModemInitialize()

XMODEM Routines

This section documents the functions available from XMODEM.DLL.

FT_Receive()

Syntax:
```
int FAR PASCAL _export FT_Receive( int nComId,
                                   LPCSTR lpFile,
                                   LPCSTR lpFileTitle,
                                   HWND hWnd )
```

What it does: Receives a file from a remote computer using the XMODEM file transfer protocol.

Parameters:

nComId	communications port to use for transfer.
lpFile	far pointer to a fully qualified filename.
lpFileTitle	far pointer to just the filename and extension.
hWnd	window handle of the terminal window.

What it returns:

FT_SUCCESS	if the reception succeeds.
FT_LOCAL_CANCEL	if the local user cancels the reception.
FT_REMOTE_CANCEL	if the remote system cancels the reception.
FT_TIMEOUT	if the reception is aborted due to time outs.
FT_DISK_ERROR	if the reception is aborted due to a disk error.
FT_SEQUENCE_ERROR	if the reception is aborted due to a sequence error.

Things to
watch for: The file pointed to by lpFile is overwritten if it exists. Also, if the transfer is not successful, a partial file remains on the disk.

See also: FT_Transmit()

FT_Transmit()

Syntax:
```
int FAR PASCAL _export FT_Transmit( int nComId,
                                    LPCSTR lpFile,
                                    LPCSTR lpFileTitle,
                                    HWND hWnd )
```

What it does: Sends a file to a remote system using the XMODEM file transfer protocol.

Parameters:

nComId	communications port to use for transfer.
lpFile	far pointer to a fully qualified filename.
lpFileTitle	far pointer to the filename and extension.
hWnd	window handle of the terminal window.

What it returns:

FT_SUCCESS	if the transmission succeeds.
FT_LOCAL_CANCEL	if the local user cancels the transmission.
FT_REMOTE_CANCEL	if the remote system cancels the transmission.
FT_TIMEOUT	if the transmission is aborted due to timeouts.
FT_DISK_ERROR	if the transmission is aborted due to a disk error.

See also: FT_Receive()

ASCII
Character
Reference

This appendix documents the ASCII character set. For the most part, you shouldn't be concerned with what data bytes are being transferred during serial communications. However, both the sender and receiver of the transmission must agree what the data bytes mean. The American Standard Code for Information Interchange (ASCII) is defined by ANSI as a standard way to interpret a data byte. This appendix

■ Gives a short description of the ASCII code

■ Documents the ASCII character set

ASCII Basics

ASCII is a 7-bit code defined as 0–127 (00h–7Fh). The eighth bit of the byte is not defined in the ASCII code, leaving 128–255 (80h–FFh) unused. IBM defined an *Extended ASCII code* for the PC, an 8-bit code that uses the full 0–255 range. The characters in the upper half of the range are referred to as *extended characters*. Table C.1 defines the standard ASCII code and Table C.2 defines the extended characters. The first 32 standard characters are known as *control characters*. Some of these characters have significance in communications and are described in the Description column of Table C.1.

Table C.1. ASCII characters.

Decimal	Hex	Display	Description
0	00		NUL—the null character.
1	01	☺	SOH—start of header, which indicates the beginning of header information. Used in the XMODEM protocol.
2	02	●	STX—start of text, which indicates the start of the data block.
3	03	♥	ETX—end of text, which indicates the end of the data block.

continues

Table C.1. continued

Decimal	Hex	Display	Description
4	04	◆	EOT—end of transmission, which terminates the data flow. Used in the XMODEM protocol.
5	05	♣	ENQ—inquiry, which requests identification from the other system.
6	06	♠	ACK—acknowledge, which accepts a packet received from the remote system. Used in the XMODEM protocol.
7	07	•	BEL—bell, which beeps the terminal.
8	08	◘	BS—backspace.
9	09	○	HT—tab.
10	0A	◙	LF—line feed.
11	0B	♂	VT—vertical tab.
12	0C	♀	FF—form feed.
13	0D	♪	CR—carriage return.
14	0E	♫	SO—shift out, which shifts to a new character set.
15	0F	¤	SI—shift in, which shifts back to the original character set.
16	10	▶	DLE—data link escape.
17	11	◀	DC1—Device Control 1.
18	12	↕	DC2—Device Control 2.
19	13	‼	DC3—Device Control 3.
20	14	¶	DC4—Device Control 4.
21	15	§	NAK—negative acknowledge, which rejects a packet received from a remote system. Used in the XMODEM protocol.
22	16	▬	SYN—synchronous idle, which establishes and maintains synchronization on a synchronous connection.
23	17	↨	ETB—end of transmission block, which marks the end of a data block.
24	18	↑	CAN—cancel.

Decimal	Hex	Display	Description
25	19	↓	EM—end of medium.
26	1A	→	SUB—substitute.
27	1B	←	ESC—escape.
28	1C	∟	FS—file separator.
29	1D	↔	GS—group separator.
30	1E	▲	RS—record separator.
31	1F	▼	US—unit separator.
32	20		Space.
33	21	!	
34	22	"	
35	23	#	
36	24	$	
37	25	%	
38	26	&	
39	27	'	Quote.
40	28	(	
41	29	)	
42	2A	*	
43	2B	+	
44	2C	,	Comma.
45	2D	–	Dash.
46	2E	.	Period.
47	2F	/	Slash.
48	30	0	
49	31	1	
50	32	2	
51	33	3	
52	34	4	

continues

Table C.1. continued

Decimal	Hex	Display	Description
53	35	5	
54	36	6	
55	37	7	
56	38	8	
57	39	9	
58	3A	:	
59	3B	;	
60	3C	<	
61	3D	=	
62	3E	>	
63	3F	?	
64	40	@	
65	41	A	
66	42	B	
67	43	C	
68	44	D	
69	45	E	
70	46	F	
71	47	G	
72	48	H	
73	49	I	
74	4A	J	
75	4B	K	
76	4C	L	
77	4D	M	
78	4E	N	
79	4F	O	

Decimal	Hex	Display	Description
80	50	P	
81	51	Q	
82	52	R	
83	53	S	
84	54	T	
85	55	U	
86	56	V	
87	57	W	
88	58	X	
89	59	Y	
90	5A	Z	
91	5B	[	
92	5C	\	Backslash.
93	5D	]	
94	5E	^	Caret.
95	5F	_	Underscore.
96	60	`	Accent.
97	61	a	
98	62	b	
99	63	c	
100	64	d	
101	65	e	
102	66	f	
103	67	g	
104	68	h	
105	69	i	
106	6A	j	
107	6B	k	

continues

Table C.1. continued

Decimal	Hex	Display	Description
108	6C	l	
109	6D	m	
110	6E	n	
111	6F	o	
112	70	p	
113	71	q	
114	72	r	
115	73	s	
116	74	t	
117	75	u	
118	76	v	
119	77	w	
120	78	x	
121	79	y	
122	7A	z	
123	7B	{	
124	7C	¦	
125	7D	}	
126	7E	~	
127	7F	⌂	DEL.

Table C.2. Extended ASCII characters.

Decimal	Hex	Display
128	80	Ç
129	81	ü
130	82	é

Decimal	Hex	Display
131	83	â
132	84	ä
133	85	à
134	86	å
135	87	ç
136	88	ê
137	89	ë
138	8A	è
139	8B	ï
140	8C	î
141	8D	ì
142	8E	Ä
143	8F	Å
144	90	É
145	91	æ
146	92	Æ
147	93	ô
148	94	ö
149	95	ò
150	96	û
151	97	ù
152	98	ÿ
153	99	Ö
154	9A	Ü
155	9B	¢
156	9C	£
157	9D	¥
158	9E	P_t

continues

Table C.2. continued

Decimal	Hex	Display
159	9F	ƒ
160	A0	á
161	A1	í
162	A2	ó
163	A3	ú
164	A4	ñ
165	A5	Ñ
166	A6	ª
167	A7	º
168	A8	¿
169	A9	⌐
170	AA	¬
171	AB	½
172	AC	¼
173	AD	¡
174	AE	«
175	AF	»
176	B0	░
177	B1	▒
178	B2	▓
179	B3	│
180	B4	┤
181	B5	╡
182	B6	╢
183	B7	╖
184	B8	╕
185	B9	╣

Decimal	Hex	Display
186	BA	‖
187	BB	╗
188	BC	╝
189	BD	╜
190	BE	╛
191	BF	┐
192	C0	└
193	C1	┴
194	C2	┬
195	C3	├
196	C4	─
197	C5	+
198	C6	╞
199	C7	╟
200	C8	╚
201	C9	╔
202	CA	╩
203	CB	╦
204	CC	╠
205	CD	=
206	CE	╬
207	CF	╧
208	D0	╨
209	D1	╤
210	D2	╥
211	D3	╙
212	D4	╘
213	D5	╒

continues

Table C.2. continued

Decimal	Hex	Display
214	D6	π
215	D7	$\#$
216	D8	$\frac{\perp}{\top}$
217	D9	⌟
218	DA	⌐
219	DB	▮
220	DC	▬
221	DD	▌
222	DE	▐
223	DF	▀
224	E0	α
225	E1	β
226	E2	Γ
227	E3	π
228	E4	Σ
229	E5	σ
230	E6	μ
231	E7	γ
232	E8	Φ
233	E9	θ
234	EA	Ω
235	EB	δ
236	EC	∞
237	ED	$\varnothing$
238	EE	ε
239	EF	η
240	F0	$\equiv$

Decimal	Hex	Display
241	F1	±
242	F2	≥
243	F3	≤
244	F4	⌠
245	F5	⌡
246	F6	÷
247	F7	≈
248	F8	°
249	F9	■
250	FA	■
251	FB	√
252	FC	n
253	FD	2
254	FE	▮
255	FF	a

Index

G

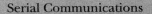

What's on the Disk

The disk enclosed in the back cover of this book contains the following items:

- Source code for each code listing in the book, including

  TSMTerm, the author's exclusive terminal emulation program.

  Modem functions that dial, communicate with, and disconnect from other computers.

  File transfer routines to maximize communication efficiency.

- Borland project files.
- Makefiles for each program.
- A README.TXT file

The most important file on the disk is the README.TXT file. This file contains a complete description of the files on the disk and the directory structure.

Installation Instructions

The files on the diskette are included in two self-extracting files. The instructions that follow will help you install these files. The extracted files take up approximately 3.2 megabytes of hard disk space.

1. Create a directory named WPGSERCM on your hard disk.

   ```
   md \wpgsercm
   ```

2. Change to the directory you just created.

   ```
   cd \wpgsercm
   ```

3. Insert the diskette in your floppy drive. The following instructions assume it is the A drive.

4. Extract the files to your hard drive by executing these two commands:

   ```
   a:wpg-sc1
   a:wpg-sc2
   ```

(See the file README.TXT on the disk for more information.)